Juan Mayorga

Juan Mayorga: Six Plays is the first collection of Spanish dramatist Juan Mayorga's plays in English, offering a compelling insight into the extraordinary range and quality of one of the Spanish-speaking world's most distinctive voices.

The six plays are presented in translations that are both readable and eminently performable. Each is accompanied by a translator's note that discusses the strategies and decisions used in making the play performable in English as well as the play's key themes. The book also features an introduction to Mayorga's life and work, emphasising his commitment to plays whose range of forms and innovative theatre-making practice re-imagines the nature of theatre and performance each time anew. The plays themselves are brilliant treatises on our times, inspiring conversation about and critical examination of our troubled world.

These scripts will be of interest to professional practitioners but are no less suited to both university and amateur settings, making this the definitive collection of Mayorga's work in English for theatremakers, students, and scholars.

Jerelyn Johnson is Professor of Spanish in the Department of Modern Languages and Literatures at Fairfield University, Fairfield, Connecticut, USA.

David Johnston is an award-winning translator and scholar, who is currently Professor of Translation and Interpreting at Queen's University, Belfast, Northern Ireland.

Juan Mayorga is Spain's most renowned living dramatist, best known in English-speaking countries for his 2004 play *Way to Heaven* (*Himmelweg*).

Juan Mayorga
Six Plays

Edited and translated by
Jerelyn Johnson and David Johnston

Routledge
Taylor & Francis Group

LONDON AND NEW YORK

Designed cover image: © Photograph by Laura Raposo for the Teatro de la Abadía

First published 2024
by Routledge
4 Park Square, Milton Park, Abingdon, Oxon OX14 4RN

and by Routledge
605 Third Avenue, New York, NY 10158

Routledge is an imprint of the Taylor & Francis Group, an informa business

British Library Cataloguing-in-Publication Data
A catalogue record for this book is available from the British Library

ISBN: 978-1-032-13245-7 (hbk)
ISBN: 978-1-032-13244-0 (pbk)
ISBN: 978-1-003-22830-1 (ebk)

DOI: 10.4324/9781003228301

Typeset in Galliard
by codeMantra

Contents

Contents

Preface

When Juan Mayorga was elected to the Royal Spanish Academy in 2019 as the then youngest member of that august body, his accession speech was simply entitled *Silencio* – "Silence." Of course, silence is anything but simple. As part of a stage language, it can be a very concrete thing – a moment of escape, a pause to reflect, a truce, an instant when language is overwhelmed by emotion or contemplation, its capacity for meaningful response stripped away. Silence disturbs, unsettles, creates unpredictability, suggests confusion, or brings to a dead end a situation that is growing increasingly untenable. Of course, it can also be a command, and in the mouth of the tyrannical Bernarda Alba it is the closing word of Lorca's final play, *The House of Bernarda Alba*, written in 1936 just as the Spanish Civil War was about to flare, prefiguring a silence that in many ways was to last throughout the long Francoist dictatorship, those nearly four recent decades that linger still painfully in memory. Chekhovian, Beckettian, Pinteresque, the theatre world of Juan Mayorga stages a constant battle against the unsaid, against evasion, against the fear of communication that locks us into privacy. The hovering presence of silence in his work is always there, a tangible and audible reminder of what happens when language fails.

In his speech Mayorga refers to himself as "suffering (*enfermo*) from theatre, my life hanging on what people do with words and what words do with people." In many ways, again like Chekhov, Beckett and Pinter, Mayorga lifts much of his drama from the apparently mundane. He finds in everyday banality (the banality that Hannah Arendt saw could mask even the most appalling evil) both the visible traces of repressed pathos, tension, anxiety, violence and desire, and the roots of the great philosophical questions, now translated into the dilemmas and predicaments of ordinary lives that become, in their living, less than ordinary. His is a theatre that weaves together the words of everyday life into mathematical patterns (he refers frequently to the figure of the ellipse) and around philosophical echoes. This is language as both a shaped and lived phenomenon. Mayorga continues in the same speech:

> I don't study language. I'm a pickpocket, a rag and bone man, a cobbler together. Always on the lookout for words, words overheard on the street or on the metro, that perhaps, stitched together with other words, might deserve one night to find themselves on stage.

In that way, in this obsessive concern with the language and situations of everyday life, Mayorga has created a theatre that translates, although perhaps it is more accurate to say that it is open to being translated. Not in the sense of any spurious universality, because that is a category to which very few things indeed may aspire – all acts of translation are based on securing the bilateral, two-way relationships between one language and another, one moment in time and space with another. But to say that his is a body of work especially open to translation is to highlight his storytelling, the way in which, to use his phrase (in translation), he cobbles together patterns of words that bring dramatic structure to the very recognisable human dramas playing themselves out behind those words. For that reason, time and time again, we read that he is one of the most translated of Spanish writers, and this book, in the translations of six of his plays that it offers, is nothing but timely. It is certainly not that his theatre is unknown in English, and there have been professional productions of his plays throughout the English-speaking world. But this book is geared towards the next step, which is to bring a broader selection of his extraordinary plays to the attention of the Anglophone theatre world.

We use the wider descriptor Anglophone rather than British/Irish or American, because this book is transatlantic, its editor-translators American and Irish respectively. The perceptive reader will notice tiny differences of language use, which we have chosen to maintain as an indication of our distaste for the homogenised. Juan Mayorga's work is receiving increasing attention on both sides of the Atlantic, and the book also seeks to address practitioners and scholars right across the English-speaking world. Inevitably, its ultimate aim is to prompt new productions of plays published together here for the first time, and on the basis that translation and performance alike are ephemeral manifestations of a written source text (usually), always in transition towards a notionally better or more complete re-creation, the detail of these translations should not be considered as being metaphorically written in stone.

Translation and performance are always conditioned and shaped by interpretive choice. So too is editorial choice, and some justification of the specific plays included in this volume is called for. It is idle to say that they are plays chosen for their stageworthiness, and of course each translation is offered as being equally stageworthy. But, in the broadest of terms, these six plays reflect a cross section of the diversity of Juan Mayorga's theatre, capturing something of the radical and innovative vision of his theatre-making that they embody. Subjectivity is no less embodied in choice on the part of editors, and we do not claim that these are, objectively speaking, Mayorga's greatest plays. But they are certainly among them. In the final analysis, they are only part of and reflect a body of work that is characterised by its commitment to making and re-making performance. Moreover, a number of the other plays that are included in that body of work are discussed at various points in these pages.

The plays themselves are the stars of this volume. But context is also important; they are preceded by a general introduction to the work of Juan Mayorga, with detailed reference to the six chosen plays themselves, so that the reader might situate them in his wider writing practice. This scene-setting is followed by a thematic essay that looks at his theatre from the perspective both of its performance dynamics, and of its concerns with language and the great philosophical questions that he sees as insinuating themselves inextricably into the predicaments and impasses of our everyday being. Finally, each of the individual plays is prefaced in turn by a Translator Note that sets out the interpretive understanding of the translated play that the translator has been working to, as well as discussing some of the decisions at work within the translation itself.

In conclusion, a note of profound thanks to a number of people who have contributed in different ways to this book; first, and above all else, to Juan Mayorga himself for making his plays available to us as translators, and for the warmth and unfailing loyalty that he brings to all of his relationships; second, to the directors and actors, too numerous to mention by name, whose work has helped us shape our understanding of what these plays are and what they can be; and third to so many colleagues, students and theatregoers, with whom we have discussed and debated the impact of these plays on stage.

Jerelyn Johnson
David Johnston

Action, Emotion, Poetry, and Thought

An Introduction to Juan Mayorga and his Work

Jerelyn Johnson

I Juan Mayorga

Action, emotion, poetry, and thought: four words that characterize the theater Spanish playwright Juan Mayorga (b. Madrid, 1965) aspires to write, attend, and promote. He is a theater director, philosopher, mathematician, academic, artistic director, and perhaps the most lauded Spanish playwright working today. He is also the contemporary Spanish playwright with the broadest international exposure, with his work having been performed in 43 countries and translated into 32 different languages.[1] Despite this, few English speakers will be familiar with his work. While a few English translations of his plays have been published in different venues, this volume represents the first attempt to publish a collection of his works in English.

To illustrate Mayorga's stature in Spain, here is a look at the 2021–22 theater season in Madrid: In October 2021, his play *Voltaire* was produced at the Teatro Galileo, directed by Ernesto Caballero; in November, a revival of *La lengua en pedazos* in the Teatro del Barrio, directed by Mayorga himself; in January 2022, *Silencio*, in the Teatro Español, directed by Mayorga and starring the renowned actor Blanca Portillo; in February, a new play *El Golem*, in the Teatro María Guerrero of the Centro Dramático Nacional, directed by Alfredo Sanzol; and in April, his adaptation of the seventeenth-century novel *El diablo cojuelo* at the Teatro de la Comedia (which had premiered in Valencia the January prior). In the 2022–23 season, two other plays were produced: *Amistad*, and the new play *María Luisa*, which he directed. And, he directed *La colección* in March of 2024. This is not including the dozens of productions scheduled across Spain and the globe.

So, what is Mayorga's appeal? Why do so many want to produce Mayorga's work, both within Spain and abroad? Mayorga himself explained the public receptivity to his work in this way: "I have been loyal to certain questions … basically one, the same already proposed by the Greeks: the fragility of human beings, and, at the same time, their right to freedom, dignity, and beauty, which violence and injustice continue to oppose" (Ojeda).[2] That is, regardless of the setting and characters of the individual plays, what remains constant in his work is the examination of the vulnerability of these human rights when

DOI: 10.4324/9781003228301-1

presented with violence and injustice. His plays are also contained in a limited theatrical space, small in scale, easily adaptable to most stage circumstances, and take an original and nuanced approach to the critique and examination of current societal concerns. His plays provoke the audience to reflect on our shared, difficult history, and they do not offer easy answers.

To date, he has written 35 original full-length plays and 44 one-act plays. He is also the author of dozens of essays about theater and society. He revisits and revises these plays continually (which is a source of perpetual anxiety for his translators). But he does not stop there: he has written adaptations of 16 classic and canonical works ranging from Euripides to Dürrenmatt. This is a writer who is constantly working. He revisits his plays; writes new ones; responds to current events through essays or a new work; directs his own plays; writes adaptations of classic Spanish and world theater; serves on the Real Academia Española de la Lengua (Spanish Royal Academy of the Language); directs the master's program in Theatrical Creation at the Carlos III University in Madrid; directs the Teatro Abadía Foundation; and continues to give his time generously to those who study his work. It is remarkable that such an internationally acclaimed playwright does not have more attention paid to him by scholars and theater practitioners in the US and in the UK.

Mayorga, born and raised in Madrid, where he continues to reside, received his BA in Philosophy from the National University for Distance Education (UNED), and Mathematics at the Autonomous University of Madrid (UAM), both in 1988. He continued his philosophy studies in Münster, Paris, and Berlin, and received his Doctorate in Philosophy in 1997 from UNED, writing on Walter Benjamin's philosophy of history under the direction of Reyes Mate, a renowned Spanish intellectual whose focus is on the place of philosophy in a post-Holocaust world. His dissertation and subsequent first book are both titled *Conservative Revolution and Revolutionary Conservation: Politics and Memory in Walter Benjamin*. He later taught playwriting and history of thought at Madrid's Royal Academy of Dramatic Art (RESAD), and directed the seminar "Memory and Thought in Contemporary Theatre" at the Spanish National Research Council (CSIC). His many awards include the 2022 Princess of Asturias Award for Literature; the European Prize for Theatrical Realities (2016); the National Prize for Dramatic Literature (2013), among many others. His play *El chico de la última fila* (*Boy at the Back*), included in this volume, was adapted by François Ozon for the film *Dans la maison*, which won the Concha de Oro prize for Best Film and the Special Jury Prize for best screenplay at the San Sebastian Film Festival in 2012.

Fascinated by the theater since a class trip to see Federico García Lorca's *Doña Rosita the Spinster* at age 16, Juan Mayorga has dedicated his life to the theater. He started attending playwrighting workshops at the suggestion of a friend, and from there, he and other playwrights he met at these workshops formed the theater group El Astillero. From the beginning, his work has been based on collaboration with other intellectuals and particularly other theater practitioners. In an interview with the Spanish daily newspaper *El País* on the occasion of being awarded the 2022 Princess of Asturias Prize in Literature, Mayorga responded with his usual collaborative focus, saying that the recognition of his work

> signals the relevance of dramatic literature … and with that, the theater, because dramatic literature cannot exist without the theater. For that reason, I consider a part of this prize is for the actors, directors, set designers, costume designers, and all the artists and technicians that have accompanied me on my trajectory. And of course, the audience.
>
> (Vidales)

As this quotation reveals, Mayorga considers his work to be, fundamentally, a partnership with everyone involved in producing a stage production.

Mayorga is aware, as an author and also as a director, that there is a dynamic and creative interplay between the written text and the process of interpreting, directing, and staging a live performance of the text. He is known to alter his plays for the benefit of the stage, and then, as a director – and even as a spectator of another director's version of his plays – he continues to learn about his own plays, as he so often says, and then will subsequently edit and revise his plays based on his own evolving understanding of the work. He understands that

> the text will come into conflict with its staging. It will have no more authority over it than that which it earns. It will be subject to rewrites as corresponds to the nature of an art that is made in a particular time […] A text knows things that its author does not.
>
> ("Razón" 72)

Accordingly, the performance is not simply an enactment of his literary text but might be said to be the framework on which the "form" of a play can be built around. As he has said:

> The form of a play is irreducible to the structure of the literary text. The type of word constitutes form. Space, light, and sound constitute form. The type of acting, the actors' relationship with the spectators, and their position on the stage constitute form. The performance space constitutes form.
>
> ("Razón" 71)

The respect he has for theater practitioners, and the subsequent freedom he gives them to stage his plays makes this a collection of intriguing possibilities for any theater company. As a playwright and director, he recognizes that there are multiple stages of creativity that must be respected between the intent of the writer and the moment of aesthetic engagement with an audience in performance:

> When you write you are the reader's representative and, when you direct, the spectator's [...] A play isn't made based on a text, but in conflict with it. A clash between the two of them is inevitable [...] This produces a permanent agitation, which later will lead one to ask themselves which text to finally turn in to the publisher. You don't know up to what point the discoveries that surfaced during the staging should remain in the final version, or to the contrary, could close off new interpretations by other directors.
>
> (Ojeda)

His plays give directors the latitude to express their vision. For instance, Mayorga has a light touch when it comes to stage directions, so much so that many of Mayorga's plays are best understood only after they have been interpreted by a director and realized by the actors, rather than when first read – the shape, the intent, the pace, and the tone often need to be discovered in production. The plays in this collection have a varying number of characters in each, ranging from three to twelve, demand little in terms of set design, and can be easily adapted to any performance space. Because Mayorga's work is imaginatively engaged with the social, cultural, and political questions of our time, any staging will encourage discussion, in the theater itself, over a post-show dinner, or in seminar.

Mayorga's work has a broad interdisciplinary application for many academic settings as well as public intellectual discussions, including, but not limited to, courses, seminars, or festivals, in theater, Hispanic studies, and Judaic studies; and could also be valuable resources for any event or course organized around themes of politics, art history, education, and history. He is an astute and prolific critic of his own theater, and of theater in general. He has published several articles in which he analyzes his own works and that of others. A literary critic as well as a philosopher, Mayorga himself provides a theoretical prism for the study of the role and power of the theater, and these ideas are then put in to practice in his plays.

Mayorga would argue that it is difficult to find a vehicle more efficient than the theater for providing us with the tools and perspective needed for critical, cultural, self-examination, and that in our current age, we need the theater as much as we ever have, holding before us the spectacle of the subjugation of human dignity, perpetually rationalized by the discourses of political necessity or expediency. By highlighting historical moments – the Holocaust, the "war on terror," and so on – Mayorga reminds us that history is not an ineluctable, dialectical trending towards a better world but is instead a continual recurrence of human inclination toward the application of power to achieve dominion over others, with the siren call of revanchism always in the air. The gravity of past ills – easily forgotten and unexamined – are always at work beneath the surface, struggling to be rediscovered and re-integrated into the present.

So, for Mayorga, the theater is clearly not principally about entertainment or diversion, but has a deeper, more ritualistic potential, as a desirable element in a healthily functioning society that needs to be engaged in the ongoing work of self-examination. He deems the theater to be inherently political because it brings the polis together in a community setting to challenge the community's unexamined assumptions. It is the community talking to itself about itself, even speaking of things that it might prefer not to know about itself:

> Some citizens, actors, convening people in order to represent certain possibilities of human life: that is the theater. It is born from listening to the city, but it cannot settle for simply returning its noise. It must deliver a poetic experience. It's not a carbon copy of reality, it is a map. That poetic experience is inevitably political because it is made before an assembly.
>
> ("Teatro y cartografía" 86)

Mayorga's plays create a theatrical space in which the polis is confronted by a map of its own lost history, repressed memories, and forbidden landscapes. He treats historical and socio-political themes while eschewing a naturalistic presentation. His plays are difficult to watch, engrossing, and a challenge to the spectator:

> Within the conflicts that the theater can offer, there is none more important than that which is not on the stage, but between the stage and the audience. The theater convenes the city to challenge it; to present a map of what the city doesn't see because it is unable or reluctant to see.
>
> ("Teatro y cartografía" 87)

His work relies on the spectator to imbue the meaning in to the work, and depends upon theater practitioners, like himself, to accompany the spectator on that journey.

II   The Plays in this Volume

While all six plays in this volume are representative of his work as a whole, and are richly philosophical and morally substantive, they can be thought of as falling into three thematic clusters to which Mayorga returns: those concerned with general issues arising from political structures (*Perpetual Peace* and *Reykjavik*); those stemming from the contemplation of historical trauma (*Way to Heaven*, *The Mapmaker*); and those concerned with cultural values and personal relationships (*Boy at the Back* and *The Collection*). The political plays examine issues surrounding dehumanizing covert and explicit governmental and institutional policies, including the use of state-sanctioned torture in the so-called war on terror (*Perpetual Peace*), and state activities during the Cold War (*Reykjavik*). *Perpetual Peace* depicts three dogs as characters in competition for a top security position within the state apparatus, ultimately probing their willingness to use violence in dealing with a suspected terrorist, if that violence might prevent a terrorist attack. *Reykjavik* uses the World Chess Championship match of 1972 in Reykjavik, Iceland, between Bobby Fischer and Boris Spassky as a compelling metaphor of the Cold War.

Of particular note are the two plays included in this collection set during the Holocaust: *Way to Heaven* (*Himmelweg*), loosely based on the sham, Potemkin-style Jewish village set up in the Theresienstadt (Terezin) concentration camp; the other, *The Mapmaker*, in the Warsaw Ghetto. These two works reflect Mayorga's interest in developing theater about the Holocaust as a way to both memorialize and recognize what happened, and to keep us vigilant with regards to similar injustices and barbaric behavior today. In an oft-cited article "La representación teatral del Holocausto" ("Theatrical Representation of the Holocaust"), that has been reprinted in several venues, Mayorga addresses the challenges faced when trying to represent the Holocaust. He asks "how can we represent something that seems to have an intractable opacity? How can we communicate that which seems incomprehensible? How can we recover that which should be unrepeatable?" (170). He justifies his work on the Holocaust as necessary and urgent because "[t]he memory of the Shoah is our best weapon in the resistance against old and new forms of humiliation of one person by another, and the theater cannot stay on the margin of this battle" (170–71). He adds that a theater that addresses the Holocaust will make the audience more critical and more compassionate, more vigilant, and more courageous in resisting these new and present ways that humans subjugate each other (172). Mayorga works toward this awareness in his spectators not by simply attempting to replicate a carbon copy of history, but by using the plays as if they were a map, leading us from waypoint to waypoint to our own discoveries: we are not watching a facsimile of the past, but are continually moved to connect lines, points and traces of that past, and in doing so, see how they may be alive and functioning in our present. Utilizing fractured narratives of time, space, and memory, these plays require the performers and the audience to use their imaginations to develop a personal, interiorized picture of the whole canvas that cannot help but draw on our own cultural familiarities and personal experiences of disorientation, erasure, and injustice, and can be used as a point of departure for conversations about the mechanics of political oppression and injustice.

Lastly, two plays in the volume reflect and investigate a world of more domestic, small-scale moral compromise and exploitation, this time through the relationship between a teacher and his student; and one between an older couple looking to bequeath their renowned art collection. In *Boy at the Back*, a writing teacher becomes fascinated by and ultimately drawn into the life and fantasies of a pupil. Ultimately, the desire to observe and imagine the lives of others – to become the other, just like the characters in *Reykjavik* – drifts into voyeurism and appropriation. The play questions the moral ambivalence that lies at the heart of our current construction of culture and how this too can lead to a dehumanization of the other. In *The Collection*, we meet an elderly, childless, married couple who are looking for an appropriate heir for their significant art collection. Could we consider this potential heir as yet another acquisition for the couple's collection? Through this frame, the playwright explores marriage, inheritance, nostalgia, desire, and power. It is also a play about the passing of time, and about the mysterious relationship between people and their objects.

All six plays are, in this way, concerned with power relations on an historical and personal scale, while simultaneously engaging the audience in a self-examination of their own personal and political complicity in the dynamics represented on stage. These are plays that present compelling indictments of moral failure while at the same time recognizing that we rarely have access to all the facts or the benefit of complete understanding. They are plays that never let the audience settle back into the role of the mere spectator, or allow us to disengage from history as though time has made us exceptions to the mechanisms of power that have created our world, from which we have both benefited and suffered. And a world for which we nevertheless remain morally responsible, regardless of our wish to believe that the passage of time, or our circumstances, or cleverness or good intentions, have insulated us.

Way to Heaven (Himmelweg) (2002)

Way to Heaven (*Himmelweg*) is regarded by many as one of the most powerful Spanish plays of the last fifty years as it addresses the vulnerability of historical memory to revision and manipulation. This is explored through an imagining of the creation and the theatrical presentation of a sham Jewish village, much like the model village the Germans constructed in the Theresienstadt/Terezin concentration camp, which was presented to the International Committee of the Red Cross (ICRC) as a means to disguise the camp's true purpose. We witness a tormented Red Cross observer tell his story of how he visited the camp and, duly fooled, proceeded to write a positive review of conditions at the camp having seen nothing amiss. We are then presented with the Commandant of the camp as he constructs and directs his particularly misleading piece of theatre, directing several prisoners in various scenes – two boys playing with a top, a young couple having a lovers' spat on a park bench, a little girl teaching her doll to swim in a river, and so on – preparing their performances for the pending visit. Through a non-linear structure and dislocation of time and space, Mayorga implies that the historical injustices of the past are always in danger of being forgotten, misrepresented, written out of the narrative, and subject to distortion while being packaged for palatable consumption in the present.

Boy at the Back (2006)

In *Boy at the Back*, a bored and disillusioned secondary-school literature teacher receives a series of compelling written accounts of daily life in the wealthy household of one of his pupils. The accounts are written by another pupil – Claudio – a boy who normally sits at the back of the class and who, as an apparent confidant of the rich boy, has schemed and lied his way into his classmate's home. The teacher's wife, the owner of an art gallery – which is becoming increasingly economically unviable – warns him that Claudio's duplicity is incompatible with art, especially within an educational context; but the teacher is increasingly caught up in the rhythm and darkly suggestive implications of the young intruder's accounts of the lives of others. The teacher believes the boy has talent as a writer, and isn't it the responsibility of the teacher to nurture this talent? Claudio, it emerges, seems determined to save his classmate's mother from an existence he views as loveless. Very quickly, the boundaries between life and art, teacher and pupil, observer and observed, begin to blur and the lives of others, as imagined in these snooping accounts, maliciously seep into the teacher's sheltered and comfortable world.

Perpetual Peace (2007)

Perpetual Peace examines the question of what is permissible in the interests of national security, and the extent to which we are willing to sacrifice human rights in order to guarantee that security. In the play we see three dogs, Odin (Rottweiler), Immanuel (German Shepherd), and John-John (Mixed Breed), competing for a single, coveted position with an elite security organization. The dogs pass through a series of tests overseen by human masters to see which one is worthy of the white-collar. One of the tests, the final one, presents them with the dilemma of whether it is against their moral code to torture a human being in order to acquire information that could potentially save thousands, perhaps millions of others. The play poses questions such as: just how far would we go to protect the state in the name of security? When is state-sponsored violence morally acceptable, if ever? If we succumb to these security needs, how will the world remember us? The use of animals as characters instead of humans ingeniously allows the audience to better sympathize with the dilemma – these are only dogs after all, facing impossible moral choices that must be made in a split second, with limited knowledge and faculties, driven as much by affection and instinct as by high moral reasoning, much as are we.

The Mapmaker (Warsaw 1:400,000) (2010)

In *The Mapmaker (Warsaw 1:400,000)*, Mayorga explores the resonances and echoes of undigested historical and personal trauma. Set in Warsaw, both in the present day and in 1943, *The Mapmaker* centers around Blanca, the wife of a Spanish diplomat who has recently been transferred to the city. Walking the city's streets, Blanca stumbles upon an exhibition of photos from the Warsaw Ghetto in an old synagogue, and there she hears the legend of a mapmaker of the ghetto, who, along with his granddaughter, is said to have created a map meant to preserve the memory of Jewish life in the days and weeks prior to its liquidation. Intrigued, Blanca investigates further – seeking confirmation of the existence of the map, the mapmaker, and his granddaughter. In the process she finds herself beginning to map her own, personal trauma, the source of which the audience will eventually become aware of. In a separate narrative strand, presented concurrently, but set during the period of the Warsaw Ghetto Uprising, we also meet an elderly mapmaker and his granddaughter as they struggle to finish a map of the ghetto. The play overlays these two narratives, a woman trying to uncover a map of a past that has been erased partly out of a need to map her own loss and grief, while we simultaneously watch a map being created of a world that will ultimately be erased, only to survive in our imagining. Similar to *Way to Heaven*, where the non-linear structure supports the metaphor of a type of dislocated map as an optimal way to construct and represent an otherwise unrepresentable historical event, *The Mapmaker*'s structure – a series of scenes alternating between different pasts and the present but moving forward through time – comments on the indissoluble if fractured relationship between the past and the present.

Reykjavik (2014)

Reykjavik centers around the meeting of the Russian chess player Boris Spassky and his American opponent, Bobby Fischer, in the World Chess Championship in Reykjavik, Iceland, 1972. It is an attempt to understand the men behind the match of the century, their idiosyncrasies, and the political pressure they faced. Like chess, this play is about memory and imagination, a re-imagining of the quintessential duel of the Cold War, a meeting of two pawns in a larger game of confrontation and strategy. Just as the United States and the Soviet Union lived the Cold War through these two men, Waterloo and Baylen, the two characters we meet in a nondescript park, live their present through the lives of Bobby, Boris, and countless others who are wrapped up in the Fischer–Spassky duel. These two characters, along with a third who serves as spectator and eventual participant, will act out several characters in the play. With only the dialogue to signal changes, Mayorga complicates the representation of time and space, of character and performance through the presentation of multiple historical figures, settings, and moments in time.

The Collection (2024)

The Collection is a masterpiece of construction and tension. A childless couple, who have devoted their lives to amassing works of art for what is rumored to be the finest private collection in the world (we only ever see it through the eyes of others), have invited a young woman to their house (which may or may not be part of the collection) to assess her suitability as a possible heir. Also in the house is a young man, ostensibly the assistant to the couple, but possibly another competitor to inherit the collection, or even part of the collection himself. Through the self-contained and relentlessly self-obsessed atmosphere of a house where the only thing that ostensibly matters is art, the play sets out a fascinating debate between the value of the life of art, perceived as eternal, and the quality of lives lived with a sense of responsibility to others. The young woman is herself a collector in her own right and has to balance the demands placed on her by the couple's increasingly inquisitive assessment, and an opportunity to buy a letter that she has been stalking for some time. But when it finally comes, the letter as a work of art opens up new perspectives on what our responsibility to each other might actually entail. (*The Collection* will be staged in Madrid in March 2024, and the text will be published around the same time).

This Edition

As noted in the preface, this collection of translations of six of Juan Mayorga's most significant plays is a transatlantic collaboration between David Johnston of Queens University, Belfast, Northern Ireland, and Jerelyn Johnson of Fairfield University, Fairfield, Connecticut, United States. Due to this unique collaboration, we have decided to avoid a standardization of our use of English. That is, David Johnston's three translations will be written in British English, while Jerelyn Johnson's three will be in American English, with any specific usage explained in the translator's notes to each play. We believe this distinction adds to the richness of the collection and speaks to the broad universal appeal of Juan Mayorga's work.

The plays are presented here in chronological order, as above in this introduction. They represent the most recent version of the plays as of this writing, but readers and practitioners should be aware of Mayorga's propensity to revise and republish multiple versions of his plays.

Notes

1 For a list of all Juan Mayorga's works and prizes, please see the Appendix.
2 All translations of Mayorga's critical essays and interviews are mine, unless otherwise noted.

Theatre, Translation, Philosophy

David Johnston

I

Translation is at the heart of this book – in part, of course, in terms of how it is conventionally thought of, as a transaction between languages and cultures, the prime mover of cultural transmission that drives the key shaping processes of world literature. In that regard, put simply, Juan Mayorga is the most translated Spanish-language playwright since Federico García Lorca. But no process of translation can or should be reduced to a simple "of course," and accordingly each play in this volume is prefaced by a translational foreword that discusses how it has been translated, the strategies and decisions employed in the balancing act of making the play performable in English while ensuring that it remains recognisably itself. The concern with translation that underpins the theatre of Juan Mayorga, on the other hand, takes much more the form of a profound and sustained meditation on language in all of its slipperiness, on its deceptive synchronicities, and its capacity to manipulate while suggesting just the opposite.

The practices of translation and theatre alike inevitably query the ethics of language as a tool of representation, prompting a constant and restless interrogation that, in turn, lies at the heart of Mayorga's intellectual anxieties. In that way, his theatre makes an extraordinary contribution to an ethics of recognition, hostile to the fictions that, consciously and unconsciously, animate the individual and collective unfreedoms of our times. The result is a body of work that powerfully examines the hidden folds of each individual life through a different lens each time, as every play emerges from and embodies a new way of making theatre, a new way of exploding the self-serving pieties and peddled commodifications of quietism. In that way, the individual play itself is an act of translation, confronting and attempting to respond to complex ethical questions about how we represent the lives of others, questions that in Mayorga's case are embedded in a distrust of the surface slickness of the performative and representational, and driven by a commitment to seeing and understanding the confused entanglements of human relatedness. Theatre and translation, as practices concerned more with representation than communication, are disabled, stripped of their capacity for meaning, when they refuse to explode

DOI: 10.4324/9781003228301-2

quietist complacencies and to expose the manipulations inherent in the most persuasive and apparently self-assured of our speech acts – the use of the term "speech act" is deliberate here, reminding us of the way in which language creates whole worlds that envelope us in the force of their ostensible truths.

Towards the end of *Hamelin*, Mayorga's multi-award winning play of 2005, the child psychologist Raquel pigeonholes Josemari, a ten-year-old victim of sexual abuse, as the subject of a clinical case study in order to initiate the due legal process that sequesters him into a care home. The play's Commentator turns to the audience:

> "Life project". She's talking about a ten-year-old boy. "Life project". The words should ring out in the theatre. Words: "Care Home". "Child Protection Agency". "Human Rights". This is a play about language. About how language forms and how it deforms. Raquel is still talking at the other side of the table. She doesn't say "family", she says "family unit". She doesn't say "Josemari", she says "patient". Raquel talks and Montero looks through the window. Some boys are playing football outside. Montero watches one who isn't joining in. Montero would love to break the window to see out, to be able to breathe.
> (Johnston, unpublished translation, performed in London 2014)

There is already a translational issue here in that the Spanish name of the Commentator is *Acotador*, a term whose range of meanings falls somewhere between scene-setter (in the sense of stage directions) and qualifier (in the sense of enabling, making qualified). In that way, the given translation of Commentator is open to debate, as all translation should be. What matters is that the character in performance never functions as a Brechtian narrator, ideologically certain, but rather, as the range of Spanish meanings suggests, one who both contextualises the action and complicates things, particularly language and its powers of representation. This is a character designed both to require and enable the audience to engage intellectually and emotionally with the lives of the characters of this highly charged world, while at the same time reminding them that so-called facts are constructions of language and that knowledge is inevitably riddled with the epistemological gaps arising from what John Berger calls the "the relationship between what we see and what we know [that] is never settled" (*Ways of Seeing*).

II

"Never settled" but always to be examined, the uncertainties that bedevil thought and understanding, but which cannot be allowed to define human life. It is around this challenge, this paradox, of epistemological deficit and ethical responsibility, that Juan Mayorga's theatre coalesces as philosophical enquiry, Cartesian in its scepticism, Socratic in its determination to uncover the truths of our condition. Returning to *Hamelin*, Montero is the investigating judge who, in the Spanish system, is charged with assessing whether or not the wealthy and publicly significant accused has a case to answer. His "I'm looking for the truth. The origin of the evil, that's what I'm looking for," broadens judicial response to the extreme criminality of paedophilia into a timeless enquiry into moral darkness, so that Montero the judge comes to represent the conscience of the spectator on a black-box stage on which the interrogation of the great epistemological paradox inevitably merges with the theatre act itself. Montero and the Commentator, taken together, are respectively the moral compass of a striving to know and the agent of distanciation, not in the Brechtian sense of alienation from the affective, but instead, nudging the spectator towards the realisation that the acts of representation performed by others are often smokescreens; that, ultimately, to strive to know is a parlous task. In the end, in order to fill in the gaps of our understanding, between the so-called facts that we currently purport to know and what is important to know beyond those facts (the accused is certainly guilty, but what drives such evil?) Montero finally resorts to the sort of complex understanding that is enshrined in myth rather than deduced history, from the metaphoricity of narrative shape rather than the reductionism of identifiable fact. The "Pied Piper of Hamelin", Robert Browning's narrative poem of 1842 that retells, via Goethe and the Brothers Grimm, the notorious events of thirteenth-century Hamelin, becomes the only meaningful way he can find to meditate on the seemingly indissoluble unity of opposites in human life – lure and threat, generosity and greed, hope and despair, good and evil.

Mayorga's plays engage audiences through the ragged edges of unexpected – simply fascinating – juxtapositions of character and situation. It is through these improbable concurrences that fiction enacts the complex lie through which easy truths are most meaningfully dismantled. David Hare, in his essay "The Play is in the Air" (24–37), reminds us that theatre happens somewhere between stage and auditorium, that from the play as truthful fiction emanates an energy that seeks to advance understanding in the minds or imaginations of those spectators who care enough to pay attention. It is a telling phrase. "Being in the air," Hare's version of Bob Dylan's "Blowin' in the Wind," is an assertion that whatever the play might be about, the energies it generates are directed towards the as yet unrealised, that any hope that it raises is not transcendent, but rather immanent in the potentials and willingness of spectators to think and feel. The sharp distinction which Hare draws in the same essay, between the truth seeking of playmaking and the commodified truths of bad journalism, takes us into the heart of the pragmatics of communication, how language can be pressganged into as many uses as there are intentions and agendas. At the heart of this contrast, indeed schism, between language as the bulwark of the invariant, and language as, in the words of anti-Francoist Spanish poet Gabriel Celaya in his poem of 1955, "a weapon loaded with future" (*Cantos Iberos*), stands the great collective challenge of our history. Of what Gayatri Chakravorty Spivak has termed keeping "the door open to the 'to come'" (6).

"We are all called to be philosophers" is, accordingly, Mayorga's defining statement of his sense of the relationship between theatre and audience ("Todos estamos llamados a ser filósofos"). The fact that many of his plays draw upon and frequently cite a range of philosophers, including Aristotle, Pascal, Kant and Hegel, as well as Walter Benjamin (of whom, more later), suggests stodgy thesis theatre, worthily cerebral rather than vividly dramatic. Nothing could be further from the truth. Mayorga is an extraordinary storyteller. Anyone who has ever been in his effervescent company knows how he continually leaps to his feet in order to transform his ideas into a gestural language that, in turn, translates meaning into situation and action. All theatre happens through acts of physical imagination, and Mayorga's theatre, as the plays included in this volume eloquently attest, restlessly offers different frames of performance and angles of scrutiny to explore how our experience, the dilemmas and machinations of everyday life, remain anchored to the great ideas of the past, fully intelligible only within this temporally extended context. In that way, this is a theatre that physicalises philosophy as a metacommentary on human life, so that if the spectator is called to be a philosopher, it is in the guise of someone who wrestles to understand what is actually happening under the canopy of those ideas.

III

Past ideas contour future actions. In order to keep the door open, in Spivak's sense, between how the past has shaped us and what future might emerge from that shaping, the theatre of Juan Mayorga returns obsessively to how we use and abuse language, how language measures up to the pressures of the contexts it has to address. And how so frequently it obfuscates any real understanding of those contexts. Like Harold Pinter, Mayorga creates a theatre that is resolutely and comprehensively existential in its refusal of commodified symmetries and clichéd resolutions, Pinteresque, too, in his creation of a stage language that is deceptively direct, structured around internal loops and repetitions, and punctuated by carefully orchestrated pauses and silences. It is language that, through its poetic interplays of verbal recurrences and silences, exerts a magnetic force in the way it draws spectators into the heart of the situation; but at the same time refuses to allow them to reduce the human dilemmas playing out within that situation to ready categories of understanding. This is why Montero, echoing Hare, is suspicious too of journalistic shorthand and as the case develops, dismisses press reports as "irresponsible. I can just see the journalist rubbing their hands: 'the story of the year'. They've got the story of the year so they write cheap literature instead of sticking to the truth." The facts. The truth. Theatre, of course, has no direct access to either. But it does constitute a process – cognitive, affective and hermeneutic – through which the spectator is prompted towards understanding, towards Mayorga's radically liberal concern not for the abstract discourse of rights or justice, but for what Vaclav Havel called "responsibility to an order of being" (19). In Havel's case,

in the post-Communist Czech Republic, that order is individual freedom, politically conceived and resistant to the homogenising discourses of nationalist
identity, while in Mayorga it lies in what we might think of as a call to consciousness. To be aware is the great responsibility of our times.

In that way, his theatre stages its own philosophical enquiry, in the final
analysis no less political than that of Hare or Havel, but always focussed on
the moral, on the ethical duty to search out what is silent and what is hidden.
Theatre in that way, as Mayorga puts it, is a dialogue, a "marginal interlinear
space" (*Elipses* 14) between actor and spectator, between what is seen and not
seen, between what is said and not said, so that the spectator is always witness-
ing a story that moves in and out of visibility and invisibility, weaving itself
between conditions of narrative presence and absence. Mayorga is the most
economical of storytellers, not only in terms of narrative rhythm, but also in
these suggestive interplays of what is said and seen and what is left open only
to meaningful conjecture. Or to use the more technical term, to hermeneutic
scrutiny. In that way, his theatre responds to the same interplay of presence
and absence that Berger, probably the most connected English cultural theo-
rist of the last six or so decades, detects in the form of the photograph:

> The true content of a photograph is invisible, for it derives from a play not
> with form but with time. One might argue that photography is as close
> to music as to painting. I have said that a photograph bears witness to a
> human choice being exercised. This choice is not between photograph-
> ing x and y: but between photographing at x moment or at y moment.
> The objects recorded in any photograph (from the most effective to the
> most commonplace) carry approximately the same weight, the same con-
> viction. What varies is the intensity with which we are made aware of the
> poles of absence and presence. Between these two poles photography
> finds its proper meaning. The most popular use of the photograph is as a
> memento of the absent. ("Understanding a Photograph" 2)

What happens on stage is, of course, an illusion, a contrivance. The real is
invoked but rarely present, as the Commandant in *Way to Heaven* suggests
when he says, "When an actor is hammering a nail, he is doing two things:
he is hammering a nail, and he is doing absolutely nothing." But this absence
of the real on stage does not invalidate theatre as a referent of the real. The
whole purpose of the Camp Commandant in his theatrical montage of Hitler's
model village is to dupe and silence the only spectator who matters in this case,
the Red Cross Delegate who, both historically and in this extraordinary play,
has come to bear witness to the truth of the Holocaust. The play, in that way,
captures most completely the century-old tradition of disquiet at the treachery
of images, from Magritte through Foucault to Berger, treachery – *trahison* in
Magritte's original – residing in the deceptive synchronicities referred to earlier in this essay that come into play when slickness of representation lulls the
viewer into dulling certainty.

This is certainly one of the reasons why Juan Mayorga's theatre constantly makes and unmakes its own forms, continuously experimenting with the conduits of relatedness that happen in the air between stage and auditorium. Not only this; he is also constantly rewriting and retouching notionally finished plays (often to the chagrin of his translators) so that his whole body of work, in terms of its forms and language, presents itself in a state of flux, always provisional, embodying the search of the philosophical mindset for, in Berger's words, the never settled, for the invisible set outside the immediate field of knowing. Seamus Heaney, writing about W.B. Yeats, notes similarly that any sense of completion, in the act of writing and in the processes of knowing and understanding alike, is ultimately a lurch into complacency:

> He reminds you that revision and slog-work are what you may have to undergo if you seek the satisfaction of finish; he bothers you with the suggestion that if you have managed to do one kind of poem in your own way, you should cast off that way and face into another area of your experience until you have learned a new voice to say that area properly. (110)

In the same way, the theatre that Mayorga both imagines and writes captures in its forms and impacts the functioning of the life of the restless mind. Life, of course, does not happen wholly in the mind; but theatre provides that special place where an audience reflects both on what it sees and what is hidden from it, piecing together stories from the evidence available (which, in the case of Mayorga's plays, tends to be distanced and fragmented behind silences, hidden agendas, and situations that outstrip the expressive capacity of language itself). We know the actor is not really hammering a nail, but that suspension of disbelief should not stop us from examining the truthfulness inherent in the world of the stage. And it is the spectator, like Montero, who is called upon to understand the story in terms of the complex moral and philosophically rich hinterland in which Mayorga invariably sets it.

IV

It is precisely in this interplay between absence and presence that Mayorga's theatre connects most completely with translation as both writing practice and cognitive method. In the most direct sense, of course, any text in translation stands in a metaphorical relationship to the absent original, negotiating patterns of sameness and difference with another text that, for the vast majority of readers or spectators, will invariably remain invisible to them. So, for example, the word Commentator emerges from the original *Acotador* necessarily carrying with it the translational paradox of hermeneutic surplus and semantic deficit, recognisable but also inevitably different in terms of nuance. For that reason, in view of the fact that the semantic and pragmatic contours of words do not map accurately from one language culture to another so that the translator is called upon to make choices that derive from hermeneutics rather than any linguistic transaction or invariant substitution, we can say that translation traffics as much in conditions of difference as patterns of sameness.

To translate, in that sense, is to interpret, just as to interpret is to translate. Translation, like the acts of interpretation that configure it, abuts on ultimate untranslatability, ultimate unknowability, rooting out but never able to definitively affix the meanings beyond words that are hidden in the inexpressible and the unexpressed. The task of the literary translator here goes beyond words, to re-imagine the missing human dimension, to piece together the irreducible human being now, at least partially, obscured behind the mismatched contours of one language to another. In other words, when Mayorga describes theatre as "a marginal interlinear space," he is not only thinking that language as a tool of communication is inevitably flawed, that its communicative capacities are readily outstripped by complexities of experience, but also pointing to the way in which his plays map words against corresponding silences, notional meaning against the inexpressible as well as the unexpressed, so that words are undermined, echoed by silence, even as they are articulated.

In that way, the spectator becomes the translator of a stage world filled in turn with metareferences to translation both as an act of transformation and as a process of understanding. One of his earlier plays, *The Translator of Blumemberg* (2001), offers linguistic collages between the original Spanish, French and German in order to explore the fascinating subjective space between Blumemberg, who is almost but not quite the celebrated German philosopher Hans Blumenberg, and his translator. Beyond this, Mayorga's theatre also develops key metaphors for translation, especially mapmaking – including the masterly *Mapmaker* in this volume. Because, as Polish philosopher Alfred Korzybski famously noted, "a map is not the territory it represents" (58) any more than the translation is the original, a fundamental questioning once again of any representation of so -called reality. Put simply, reality duplicated is not real, because reality has to be subjectively and, at best, partially interpreted, translated through the complex system of signs that configure it.

This deconstruction of mapping as an act of verifiably accurate representation is at the centre of an extraordinary piece of theatrical montage. *Voltaire*, staged to great acclaim in Madrid in 2021, presents, as the reference in its title to the French writer suggests, a profound meditation on embedded intolerance and the fragility of philosophical liberalism. It takes the form of three short plays from Mayorga's collection of *Theatre in Minutes* (unpublished in English), a set of miniature pieces whose dramatic quirkiness, extraordinary concision, and intellectual shape-shifting are irresistibly reminiscent of the short stories of Jorge Luis Borges. Each of these three short pieces presents a different series of forms and signs that the spectator has to conflate into some sort of holistic understanding – that he or she is willing to do so attests to the extent to which each short play inescapably, magnetically, draws the spectator into its world, so that at the end of the show the spectator is inevitably confronted with the central question of theatre, of philosophy, and of translation:

"what might all of this, taken together, mean?" Voltaire, Borges, Mayorga, a line of writers who explore the secretive folds of human experience, and whose work constantly impels the reader or spectator towards committing to the philosophical search at hand.

The second of the three plays in particular, the fulcrum piece of the production, echoes Borges' single-paragraph story "On Exactitude in Science," which satirises the creation of a "Cartography so perfect" that the Map of the Empire "is the same size as the Empire and coincides with it point by point." As future generations rapidly come to see, this Map is useless and it is quickly discarded, ironically, as unrealistic. The story ends with the Map being shredded: "In the deserts of the West there are still to be found fragments of the Map, sheltering Animals and Beggars; in the Country as a whole there are no other relics of the Discipline of Geography" (90). The use of capitals in these quotations from Borges' 1946 story reflect those of the original, proposing in their own way another conundrum, another hermeneutic trail, for the reader. In the case of Mayorga's short play, however, the mapmaker is an artisan producer who creates different readings of Madrid in each map of the city he creates. The lighting design of the play itself almost imperceptibly insinuates the recognisable outline of Madrid on the floor so that, as the mapmaker describes each reading of the city – a mapping of the streets where judges live, a mapping of those bars that permit their customers to shout out political insults etc. – another interlinear space appears, this time between the standard mapping of the city and its hidden versions, the inward-turning secret spaces that make of any city an unknowable palimpsest that different citizens inhabit and translate in different ways. The city and its shredded maps. The map, after all, is not the terrain, but the representation of a way of seeing.

V

As a product of the Enlightenment, Voltaire believed fervently in the power of reason and of rational action to solve any problem. Mayorga, however, while sharing Voltaire's radical liberalism and moral determination to make sense of the past so as to better grasp the future, is shaped by a very different climate of ideas. The tone and moral timbre of that climate derives from a whole variety of thinkers, because Mayorga, to judge by the range of resonances and echoes in his plays, is nothing if not richly eclectic in his sources of inspiration. A major figure in the constellation of thinkers whose work is woven through the fabric of his theatre, configuring the philosophical terrain against which the compelling stories he tells are set, is Walter Benjamin.

Mayorga completed his doctoral thesis in 1997, "The Philosophy of History in Walter Benjamin," which characteristically includes an eclectic account of a series of thinkers – including Carl Schmitt, the controversial jurist philosopher whose radical defence of the state of exception is explored by Mayorga in a number of works, such as *Way to Heaven* and *Nocturnal Animals*. This latter play, performed as *Nocturnal* at London's Gate Theatre in 2009, explores and denounces how the current state of exception surrounding the movement of peoples in Western societies – the location of the play is left undefined – reduces the lives of refugees, asylum seekers and migrants to what Giorgio Agamben, in his recent critique of Schmitt's justification of the denial of human rights, refers to as "bare life" (*Homo Sacer: Sovereign Power and Bare Life*, 1995). This doctoral thesis was published in Spanish in revised book form in 2003 as *Conservative Revolution and Revolutionary Conservation: Politics and Memory in Walter Benjamin*, a book that significantly hones our understanding of one of Europe's most seminal thinkers whose work responds intimately, and at times undeniably haphazardly, to the intellectual ferment and subsequent political collapse of the Europe of the first four decades of the twentieth century. As we consider why Benjamin has become one of Mayorga's most significant elective affinities, among an extraordinary range of possible candidates, we begin by recognising that Benjamin, like Mayorga himself, cannot be reduced to a single school of thought, that his work is at least as poetically multifaceted as it is philosophically consistent.

That said, it is probably in his concept of history that Benjamin is most present in Juan Mayorga's theatre. An understanding of history for the German philosopher begins with a disavowal of complete immersion in the present, a sort of emotional and intellectual uprooting that enables what he thought of as the necessary pre-condition for establishing virtually random and enriching connections with different human lives across time and space. Of course, in that sense, the theatre itself, in Mayorga's conception, offers the same sort of fluid space where the spectator's initial act of surrender opens the door, paraphrasing Spivak again, into new possibilities of engagement. In terms of their settings, his plays range across a Europe that is both real and imaginary, never bogged down in naïve realism but always committed to the search for the philosophical underpinnings of the individual life. In *Hamelin*, the Commentator introduces Scene Nine in a markedly Benjaminian way:

> Hamelin. Scene Nine. Time has passed. Time is the most difficult thing of all in theatre. It's not enough to say: "Ten days later". Or "The card has been lying on the table for an hour". Only the spectator can create time in theatre. If that's what the spectator wants, then the card has been lying on the table for an hour, beside the phone.

This is a brief introduction to what Benjamin called the "infinite task" ("On the Programme of the Coming Philosophy" 100) – that of apprehending the bases for a new reality by more fully understanding our subjective experience of the interstices of time and space – now re-created as theatre practice. The task element is to re-connect with the human dimensions of a past that is not linear, nor accessible through the retrospective gaze of historicism, but that rather constitutes itself in terms of a subjective interlinearity with the present through images of recognisable similarity. History is created by the observer, just like time in Mayorga's theatre. We create our understanding of the present – or the present of the stage world – through images that prefigure it in the past. This is another version of the interlinear dialogue that constitutes the point at which Mayorga's intellectual method and theatre practice most completely coincide. The past and present exist in a constellation of interstices, of simultaneities, and it is the "task" of the observer, playwright or spectator, to identify them and through that to establish meaningful connections with a past that is ongoing in the present. A powerful example of such a connection occurs in *Way to Heaven*, where the station clock in the camp-ghetto of what was then known as Theresienstadt, cynically reported by the Nazis to the Red Cross as a spa-town and model re-settlement, is proudly identified as the work of a master clockmaker of Nuremberg dating back to 1502, but whose central mechanism could be traced back to Toledo in 1492 and which was still work-ing in 1914 – thereby reviving for the contemporary audience images of the trials of 1945–46, the widespread expulsions and oppression that followed in the wake of the unification of Spain under the Catholic Monarchs in 1492, and the horrors of the First and Second World Wars. In that way, the spectator is confronted with a series of historical images that have nothing to do with progress, but rather represent what we might think of as a disease or distortion of the human spirit, hiding as a continuum in plain sight.

But why is the task "infinite?" Put simply, it is because the past is always with us; it is never completed nor is it ever fully gone. This is one of the main reasons why Benjamin was so hostile to any historicist concept of the past based on a sense of linear process. Process promulgates the fiction of progress. Like Mayorga, Benjamin had an extraordinary talent for translating the un-derpinnings of philosophy into meaningful concrete situation, into what we might think of as story as parable. He describes process as a walk through the mountains, glimpsing peaks on a far-flung horizon, that, as the traveller pro-gresses, never seem to get any closer, but which remain distant as new vistas of hidden valleys and other hitherto unseen elevations emerge to the view (108). In that way, the task of reaching the mountains cannot be determined in ad-vance, any more than the future can be predicted. It is possible only within the individual experience of the traveller, in the same way that the potential for understanding is entirely immanent in the experience of the spectator in Mayorga's theatre. Nothing that the play can achieve, nor the full meaning of any situation it represents, may exist outside the collaboration of an audi-ence and its notional willingness to search between the lines of language and silence, past and present, here and there. In his essay "The Storyteller" Benja-min reflected on how the urgencies of modern life (in particular, the processes of mechanical reproduction and capitalist industrialisation in the wake of the First World War) had undermined both a sense of community and the pos-sibility of shared reflective understanding. The art of storytelling, in particu-lar, he argued, has lost its aura in an age given over wholly to commodified production and self-interested representation. With extraordinary insight, he complained that language has become information-bearing rather than car-rying within it the imprint of real speech (echoing the complaints of David

Hare and Montero in *Hamelin* regarding the limitations of journalism) with the result that knowing is constrained behind structures of information rather than ignited by hermeneutic engagement.

VI

Mayorga's theatre-making offers a conscious antidote to Benjamin's depiction of the impact of this particular form of what might be considered a modern secularisation, with its onslaught on the vitality of the human spirit. In their verbal loops and repetitions, punctuated by pauses and silences, his plays offer a stage language that is both real – again Pinter comes to mind – but that also has a contemplative stillness at its core, couched in and generated by the hypnotic verbal echoes and compelling silences that are the dominant stylistic markers of his characters' speech patterns. Benjamin's disavowal of the self-contained present moment becomes in Mayorga an invitation to his audience metaphorically to stand still, to take time out in order to be alert to the interstices between other times and spaces and theirs, to pay attention to the interlinear spaces within language and history. There is an echo here, in Benjamin and Mayorga alike, of Kierkegaard's observation in his journals to the effect that life can only be understood backwards, although it has to be lived forwards (Bachmetjevas, 470–83), an insistence on the acts of concentrated attention in the midst of stillness that underpin awareness. Acts of attention, geared to the identification of the pools and patterns of sameness that give us the clearest awareness of the ongoing legacy of the past, acts of attention concerned to translate history itself.

There is, once again, a working sense of translation at the heart of this. Benjamin's famous and much misunderstood description of translation as providing the afterlife of the text has to be considered, he argued, with a completely unmetaphorical objectivity. In other words, the new text must necessarily exist within some sort of definable interlinear relationship with the original, in the same way as some moments of history echo others – the reason why Benjamin argues for a literalising interlinear translation practice. The life and afterlife of works of art, for Benjamin, exist in the same axes of perceived confluence as those of history. His "Translation passes through continua of transformation, not abstract ideas of identity and similarity" (62) is really a foundation statement of much of his thought, about history and translation alike. The paradox of these "continua of transformation" is a potent one, echoing of course the phases of Marxist dialectical materialism, but also reminding us of the lines of negotiated contact through which acts of translation support the impetus of global cultural transmission. But it goes further than this: it places these acts of translation at the centre of the way in which we might understand the flows and forces of the history we have inherited and that lives on around us. The diasporic repression post-1492 and the savagery of the Holocaust is such a continuum, taking place in very different loci of time and space, but deep down, really the same phenomenon. Which is why in the play itself the Camp

Commandant addresses the audience as though they were tourists visiting the camp – which, in one way, of course they are: "Take photographs of the flowers, if you want. We want you to take photographs. And, especially, look and see, and tell the world what you've seen. The world has to know. You are the eyes of the world."

"You are the eyes of the world." If translation is a way of "seeing" across the barriers of language, allowing us to recognise those continua of transformation that both connect and differentiate between cultures, theatre is a way of "seeing," this time keeping open Spivak's "door to the 'to come'," for better and for worse. Chillingly, in *Way to Heaven* it is precisely the Red Cross Delegate's refusal to open a door that perpetuates the lie and the cruelty of the camp. In that way, his acceptance of the propaganda, that a gas chamber is a hospital, demonstrates the persuasive powers of the fictions and duplicitous representations from which human lives derive their untested securities.

VII

Can theatre actually do anything to change this? If we think about theatre, translation and philosophy as three great manifestations of humanist thought, it is not only because they deal in the prime currencies of interpretation and representation, but also because they are animated by hope against hope, the tragic determination that final oblivion, ultimate silence, should be an injustice rather than logical consequence. There are no certainties in any areas of Mayorga's thought, other than the certainty that words have an impact and that theatre is a medium through which that impact is intensified.

As a thinker, Benjamin, as we have seen, always had his eye on the infinite. As a mathematician, Mayorga knows that the infinite is always with us, even as an imaginary. In the period of enforced lockdown during the COVID-19 pandemic, he posted a short video online, "I want to swarm," a poem of desires that brings together Borges and Benjamin in its intense series of yearning images for impossible things: "I want to be an imaginary number / the square root of minus 1 / if it hasn't already been taken" ("Quiero ser enjambre"). Like Benjamin's mountains, seemingly unattainable but always in sight, Mayorga's thought is similarly caught between radical uncertainty – who is really courageous enough to open the door into the gas chamber? – and the conviction that there is no meaningful alternative to resisting and challenging that uncertainty. The upshot of this could possibly signal a retreat into the irrational, as was the case with thinkers like Søren Kierkegaard and Miguel de Unamuno (interestingly, one of Mayorga's impossible yearnings in "I want to swarm" is "I want to dance the tango with Kierkegaard," an image perhaps of the order of life as a dance, collaborative but absurdly aestheticised. So what might embracing this condition of apparent absurdity mean in Mayorga's theatre? In one way, it is evident in the sudden code-switches of his plays, the juxtapositions of the improbable, the patterns of verbal and phonetic repetition, flashes of disruptive humour and destabilising revelations. But perhaps above all else it is present in what we might think of as a phenomenological spirituality. This is an echo of Benjamin's interest in the mystical tradition of the Kabbalah and how it might be applied to his own particular brand of Marxism in his urgent search for redemptive potentials at a time when faith in rationality was at its lowest ebb. The same mystical quest for redemption is echoed by Montero when he talks about his search for the origins of evil itself, or recurs nightly in the dreams of the Red Cross Delegate when, again and again, he finds himself standing outside the chillingly cold metal door of the gas chamber.

One of Mayorga's most philosophically challenging plays *Golem* – premiered in Madrid's prestigious María Guerrero Theatre in 2022 and as yet unpublished in English – brings Benjamin's spiritual search into the acutely observed portrayal of a society lurching into disturbingly predictable breakdown. Phenomenological spirituality by another name. The figure of the golem, of course, originates in the teachings of the Kabbalah, and illustrates the story of how shapeless inanimate matter, the root meaning of the name, can be brought to life through exposure to the incantatory force of numinous language. Like all myths, its metaphorical sweep lends itself to a range of interpretative narratives. In the case of this play, the central concern is essentially theatrical, with how the unthinking detached "I" might become the committed and self-aware "we" of action. The play poses – but significantly does not pretend to resolve – the question of what language, carefully engineered in an equally carefully contrived space, might actually achieve in terms of its influence on its interlocutors.

Theatre, of course, is one version of such a carefully contrived space, and the experience of theatricality remains the ultimate referent of the play. In many ways *Golem* is the work of a writer at the height of his creative powers reflecting on his own chosen medium. The play itself is set in a hospital left deliberately undefined, made enigmatic through the acts of imagination and fantasy of its residents – does the patient, Ismael, actually exist or not? – that undermine the notional physicality of the environment. The immersive depiction of the world of the central character, Felicia, is reminiscent of Antonio Buero Vallejo's acknowledged masterpiece of 1974, *The Foundation*. But while Buero's artistic foundation of intellectual freedom is finally unmasked as the gaol of the ongoing legacy of anti-Francoist resistance, Mayorga's hospital is set within a collapsing and increasingly callous political structure which threatens the very existence of the hospital as a site of care and medical ministration. Daily government proclamations listing diseases and conditions that will no longer be eligible for treatment seem to bring a note of science fiction to the play, but as one character declares darkly, "nothing grows old as quickly as the future." Mayorga, like Buero's generation before him, is signalling the fragility of the values of civilised life, a continuum itself in the face of the continuum of officially sponsored barbarism.

Felicia is married to Ismael. When we first meet her she is drinking beer from a plastic cup, living rough near the hospital. She is a young woman of little ambition and perhaps, as she acknowledges herself, of little awareness beyond her concern that Ismael, whose medical condition is never made clear, should not be ejected from the hospital by an increasingly brutal government. The range of meanings implicit in the hospital is further enriched when Salinas, who works there, proposes a radical treatment – if Felicia memorises a word from someone else every day, Ismael will be cured. Felicia does not hesitate: "If it's only words, it can't be very dangerous." Salinas' reply – "If it's words, it can be very dangerous" – not only echoes the Commentator's warnings about language that strips human beings to bare life, but now, in the context of the golem, raises hopes of redemption. It is the classical Mayorga juxtaposition, risk and redemption. That this path to salvation of some sort might originate in the illuminating power of language – the words of the Other – is further emphasised when Salinas, whom we initially take to be a doctor, declares herself to be a translator:

> I'm only a translator, Felicia. Nothing less than a translator. I translate a poet one day, a boxer the next: I'm no one. It's been my only passion. A task with no future because very soon it will be done by machines. That will be terrible: the extinction of translators. Because there's something that machines can never hear: something that isn't in the word, but somewhere between the word and the person that speaks it […] We're all translators of each other, and of ourselves, but we hardly ever translate well. Hearing is difficult, and translating is hearing. No one knows you like your translator, if your translator knows how to hear. You are exposed to your translator, and they can observe you like no one else can. They see your word and its shadow. They are your shadow.

The word is slippery, deceitful; but it also matters, it can cleanse, to move from Spivak to William Blake, the doors of perception to the infinite. Translation in that regard remains a necessarily imperfect process in terms of language transfer, but it also translates words into their potential. As Felicia is transformed by her ritualistic exposure to the meaning-laden words of the Other, she is overtaken by a new consciousness of revolt as a continuum, a new awareness of collectivity. At the end of the play she addresses the audience directly:

> Our wisdom is that of the cell; our knowledge is the knowledge of danger. We look at the world with sadness because our look carries the memory of the pain of those who have gone before us. We look at the world with joy because today we can redeem them. We look at the world with pride, because tyrants have no more power over us. They will order us to be silent but we will keep on asking questions.

VIII

This is theatre that insists on posing these same core questions, again and again. About who we are and how we think of ourselves. About how we speak to each other and how we relate to others. About how we live in the world and how we might understand it better. They are questions that are posed in powerful theatrical forms that act in tandem with the vivid human situations and dilemmas that bring questions to life, that flesh out the predicaments and complexities of our being. Questions that offer some sort of redemption. In her final address to the audience, possessed of her new awareness, Felicia speaks in words that she might have heard from Juan Mayorga or Walter Benjamin.

> I am not a prophet; I am here only to say what I have seen. What I have seen is anger and hope. I am not a prophet but I know that our first task will be to bear the vision of what is going to happen.

Seeing, hearing, knowing. These are the key qualities of awareness, the driving force of the phenomenological spirituality that keeps the doors of perception open, that encourages identification of the continua of transformation along which our lives are set and that act as ligatures between past and future.

Without the knowledge of those ligatures, Mayorga senses drift. People lost in a moment characterised by detachment from the increasingly hidden sources of what really matters.

1   *Way to Heaven* (*Himmelweg*)

Translated by David Johnston

Translator's Note

As the audience filed into the Royal Court's Theatre Upstairs for the 2005 English-language premiere of Juan Mayorga's *Way to Heaven*, each person was given a book, a work of classical European literature, to carry with them into the space. The civilised heart of Europe, enshrined in the writing of authors like Calderón, Dante, Goethe, Shakespeare, and Voltaire, was rendered coeval with the act of twentieth-century barbarism being played out on the stage, a witness to atrocity. Like the spectators themselves.

Set in what the German *Schutzstaffel* (SS) renamed as Theresienstadt (Terezin, in the Czech Republic), *Way to Heaven* is regarded by many as one of the most powerful plays written in Spanish in the last fifty years. It was in Theresienstadt, a concentration camp that had been established, ostensibly, as a Jewish ghetto by the SS in 1941, that the Nazi authorities attempted to mask the real business of the Final Solution when, in the summer of 1944, they invited Danish and International Red Cross representatives to attest to the relatively comfortable lives of internees who had been carefully rehearsed in order to evoke a sense of normality in an environment specially embellished for that purpose. It was already late in the war when the Red Cross eventually managed to secure permission to visit the civilian camps, and it was here that the Nazis took them first. But only after they had incinerated the sickly and emaciated prisoners whose suffering could not be disguised, and thrown their ashes into the river. They then scripted, rehearsed and produced both a film – *The Fuhrer Gives the Jews a City* (1944) – and devised an extended *in situ* performance to ensure that the Red Cross delegates were able to verify a contented people living in a model settlement. Not long after the delegates departed, many of those who had acted in the film and in the charade were, in turn, either gassed or moved on to other death camps.

These, simply stated, are the facts that we have.

In 2001, W.G. Sebald published his powerful novel *Austerlitz,* telling of these same ghosts forced to play out that cruellest of charades, the illusion of normality on the inescapable pathway to extinction. Like Sebald's extraordinary novel, *Way to Heaven* refuses to abandon the memory of people silently

DOI: 10.4324/9781003228301-3

condemned by this outrage in the heart of Europe, determined to expose the pact of forgetting and the spreading complacency that lingers dangerously in European identity today. But it is not a documentary. Mayorga maintains his and our distance from the physical horrors of extermination – as Sebald warns, "I don't think you can focus on the horror of the Holocaust. It's like the head of the Medusa: you carry it with you in a sack, but if you looked at it you'd be petrified."[1] The play weaves this world together instead through two sets of skilfully paired incongruencies – the contrivances of performance and aestheticism set against the inescapable realities of horror, and the brutality of the "final solution" offset by the almost trivial bureaucracy that supports it.

Way to Heaven is, put simply, a powerful account of devastation. Put simply again, the translator must serve this, finding the language and discourse in English that gives voice to these savagely paired incongruencies which reflect and refract this world. For it is through these conjoined processes of reflection and refraction that the audience is edged uncomfortably beyond the quiet pieties of remembrance and into the realisation that, in different ways, the horror is still with us. In that way, *Way to Heaven* draws the spectator into a realm of unnervingly heightened perception, immersing them there almost hypnotically through actions and language that loop and echo and run together until there is a final sense of enclosure, of no escape. In that way, this is the real task of the translator of this play: to avoid the temptation of the synonyms that speak in the main merely of verbal dexterity, and to allow the rhythms of recurrence to weave themselves together into the fabric of hopeless repetition in which the lives of characters and spectators alike, although in radically different times and spaces, are contained.

Finally, a note on the play's title. The play was originally called *Camino del cielo*, literally, *Way to Heaven*, but soon after Mayorga changed the title to *Himmelweg*. But it was as *Way to Heaven* that the play was first considered and programmed by the Royal Court. Shortly after that decision was taken, and when production processes were in their initial stages, the British media was replete with images of Prince Harry prancing disgracefully in a Nazi party costume. The resulting outrage from public and commentators alike may well have been a factor in the Royal Court's marketing department refusal to allow us to change the name of the play to the German word. Beyond this, of course, they had a point. There is a qualitative difference between a foreign-language title for the original play, and a foreign-language title for a play in translation. The former invites potential spectators to move outside their experience into a different representation of the European, whereas the latter, for potential spectators aware that this is a play in translation, sparks a confusing interplay is between the now invisible Spanish language and the foregrounded German.

For those reasons, more or less, the play was first performed in English as *Way to Heaven*. In dress rehearsals, I became immediately aware of a problem. With everyone sitting in the round, when the Red Cross Delegate suddenly stands up from among the audience to pronounce and explain the word "Himmelweg," the audience lacks any prior frame of reference. Moreover, in the Royal Court production, where the Delegate was played by Jeff Rawle, spectator attention was initially distracted by the sudden recognition of this very well-known television actor. Director Ramin Gray refused my request to insert a holding line right at the start – something along the lines of "I'll tell you about this place" – to settle spectator attention. He was indeed entitled to do this. But since then I have been convinced that the play in performance, in terms of posters, programmes etc, needs to straddle the worlds of the Holocaust and contemporary spectator. So, *Way to Heaven (Himmelweg)*.

Mayorga's thoughts about theatre and his own plays are always in a state of flux. And any translation is always a piece of writing in transition. There is a statement of principle in here for any would-be producer of this or any other of the plays contained in this volume.

Way to Heaven (Himmelweg) first premiered at the Alameda Theatre in Malaga on 17 October 2003, under the direction of Jorge Rivera. It was first published in the Spanish theatre magazine *Primer Acto* (First Act) in 2004. It won the Enrique Llovet Prize in Spain in 2003.

Note

1   See Maya Jaggi, "Recovered Memories," *The Guardian*, 22 September 2001.

Characters (in order of appearance)

Red Cross Representative
Boy 1
Boy 2
She 1
He
Girl
Boy 3
Boy 4
She 2
Commandant
Gershom Gottfried

I

The Clockmaker of Nuremberg

RED CROSS REPRESENTATIVE: You say "him-mel-veck." It sounds like one word, but it's two. "Himmel" means "heaven." "Weg" means "way." "Himmelweg:" way to heaven. This is where I heard it for the first time, in this very place, during the war.

I'd come to Germany as a Red Cross representative. I've always cared about people. That's why I wanted to work for the Red Cross. The biggest disappointment of my life was when I applied for a job, and they rejected me. But I tried again, not long after, and got in without any trouble. Times had changed, and the fact that I could speak German made me more useful. Nobody wanted to go to Germany then. But I said yes, straightaway.

I've always cared about people. When I was asked to go to Berlin as a Red Cross representative, I thought that I could do some good. It was my job to visit prisoner of war camps and make sure they were complying with all the international conventions. I felt useful ... inspecting hygienic conditions, accommodation, diet ... Whenever I could save a man's life, I would. I could point to an English pilot who'd been ordered to be shot and I could say to the Germans: "If you execute this man, there's a German pilot who's being held prisoner in England. He'll be executed too." There was a war ... what else could I say?

We lived in the Wannsee, right beside the lake, in a house the German government provided for us. A big, beautiful house. I'd never been in one like it. In spite of everything, those times bring back good memories. Perhaps it's just as well that people forget the bad times before the good. All the Red Cross representatives stationed in Berlin, we lived there together. When you came back from a mission, that place was a paradise. It's the little things that make life a paradise: talking to a friend, a walk beside the lake, a flash of humour in harsh times. We never saw the Germans, unless we had to. As little as possible.

It was one morning, we were having one of those conversations that are half work, half chat, and we ended up talking about the man who'd owned the house, a Jew. Nobody had bothered taking down a portrait of him with his wife and daughter. We were talking about the quality of the painting, but we ended up agreeing it was time one of us visited the civilian internment camps.

I don't suppose I need to spell out the difference. You can't point to a Jew, who's been condemned for being a Jew, and say to the Germans: "If you execute this Jew, there's an innocent man somewhere who'll be executed too." We'd nothing to trade. Anyway, we had no authorisation to go anywhere near the civilian camps.

But that morning, standing in front of the portrait of that Jewish family, I decided to go into one of the camps. Though the mere fact of being a Red Cross representative wasn't enough. The little flag on my car might have been a rag for all it was worth. I didn't have a permit, but I did have cartons of cigarettes, nylon stockings and American transistors. That's how I got the necessary papers. I showed them and the barrier in front of the car lifted. I said the same thing at every check-point: "I've come to see the camp Commandant." More than twenty check-points before I got to him.

A man about my age, with blue eyes. I'd thought he'd have been older. "Do sit down. Can I get you anything? Coffee?" He got me a coffee. "Do you have authorisation for the visit?" He knew that sort of authorisation didn't exist. I told him why I'd come. "We can get you medical supplies, for your infirmary." I'm sure you can understand why I said that: it was a pretext, the thing about the medical supplies was the best excuse I could come up with. He recognised my accent. "I like your country. I was on holiday there before the war." I think he wanted me to know that he was from the sort of family that could afford holidays abroad. I wasn't; I'd never had the money to travel. Until the war, that is; that was the first time I ever got the chance to go abroad. So he talked about my country. Every so often, somebody would come in with a file for him to sign. Like in an office. Everyone seemed busy doing something useful. We talked about my country until I managed to change the subject. I had to win his confidence, to play-act. "We'd like to help. I mean, we can send you medical supplies." He paused for a second and said: "Medical supplies ... all right, send them. We'll make the arrangements." I thought it was worth trying to push him a little harder. "We'd need some information before sending them." "Ah, so that's why you're here. You need information." That's all he says. And I think, "That's it, my friend, your number's up." Then: "I don't see why not. You need information."

He lifted the phone: "Our guest is going to tour the camp. Tell Gottfried. Full access." And he turned to me: "The Jews are very ... private. They don't like strangers poking about. More coffee?" I had another coffee. And he told me about how he feels more European than German. He wanted the war to be over as soon as possible, because for him it was like a civil war. He showed me his library: "Calderón, Corneille, Shakespeare ... That's my Europe." I felt uncomfortable. Was he trying to show me what a great man of culture he is? More than I was anyway, that was obvious. From a family that could afford the best schools, afford to travel, to meet interesting people. As we were walking into the camp, he told me that the war was a mistake, a misunderstanding between brothers. We walked away from the wooden huts, towards ones of red brick. Outside one of them, there was a man on the steps, standing waiting for us, smiling, the first man not wearing a uniform I'd seen since I'd arrived. The Commandant introduced him: "This is Gershom Gottfried. The Mayor."

I couldn't speak for a moment. Gottfried, standing there smiling, reminded me of the man in the portrait, in the house in Berlin, so that I had to make an effort not to miss what he was saying. And there was something odd about his tone of voice as well. "If you like, I'll show you round. Take as many photographs as you want."

Of course, I'd a small camera with me. You may well have seen the photographs. I took a lot. Every so often, Gottfried reminded me to feel free to take more. I photographed the streets, tarmacked and clean. The little music stand, where the orchestra plays, in the middle of the square. The park, with its swings in the shape of little animals. The coloured balloons.

The people looked at me in a strange sort of way. I put it down to the fact I wasn't wearing a uniform. They looked at me like somebody who wasn't one of them, but not a German either. I had the unpleasant impression they were avoiding me. It was a sunny day, and people were out and about.

"What did you expect?" the Commandant asked. "Walking skeletons in striped pyjamas? I've heard the same wild rumours. So have you, Gottfried, haven't you?"

Gottfried says he had, he'd heard them too. "Perhaps you'd like to have lunch with us," he said. "Something simple. They're hard times for all of us." We went into one of the red-brick huts and we had lunch with the Gottfried family. I felt relieved that they looked nothing like the family in the portrait. There was a platter of cooked vegetables with white bread on the table. Gottfried gave a Jewish blessing and said, "Take photographs, if you want." Maybe you'll have seen those photographs too. Photographs of a small house, with a window looking out onto a square. The three of us sitting in the window having our coffee: the German, the Jew and me. The Commandant, the Mayor, the Red Cross man. The square was deserted, at lunch time, as though life in the little town had come to a stop for a moment. It was a chance to run over a few practical issues: sewage, the post. But the Commandant wasn't interested. "That's enough politics. It's a beautiful afternoon. No point in letting it go to waste. Gottfried, we can't let our guest go without seeing the station clock."

The Commandant suggested we went through the woods to the station, down by the stream. Gottfried walked beside me in silence, while the Commandant speculated about the future. "This war is the work of all humanity. The peace that follows it will be the work of all humanity too." We were walking through a thick part of the woods; hardly any sunlight came through. The Commandant asked me if I believed in God. And I told him I did, because at that time I still did. He made some reference to the God of Spinoza, and he quoted from Spinoza: "Hatred which is conquered by love, becomes love; and that love is greater than if hatred had not been its forerunner." There was a little girl playing with her doll, in the stream. I stopped to take the little girl's photograph.

The station clock was showing six o'clock exactly. Gottfried told me its history: "It was built about 1502 by Master Peter Henlein, of Nuremberg, the celebrated builder of mechanical figures. Its appearance is deceptive. It doesn't work with wheels. It uses a balance." The clock was still showing six and I began to realise what was odd about Gottfried the Mayor's speech. "The balance is in the form of an iron bar, with two sets of weights, one at either end. There are two arms joined to the bar, which control the rotating action of the wheel." It was as if ... Not just then, when he was explaining how the clock worked, but when he was talking about the weather or when he was passing me the bread. The Mayor spoke like a mechanical figure.

There was a courting couple on one of the station benches. An old man reading a newspaper. Two boys, with a spinning-top. Maybe you've seen those photographs too.

The couple, the old man, the boys, was there not something artificial about them? Was it not like being inside a beautiful toy, from the moment Gottfried had greeted me with his cheery smile? The station still smelled of paint. The orchestra, the swings, everything – all of a sudden – seemed as strange as the Mayor's tone of voice. What had the place been like before I arrived? And what would it be like once I was gone? I'd come here to look. I was the eyes of the world. I was going to leave with photographs, and a report describing what I'd seen.

Let me be clear: I didn't doubt for one moment that they were Jews. They were. But they were behaving like this for a reason. But they were ... doing it badly. They seemed awkward, unsure.

My parents taught me the virtue of compassion. I never close my eyes to the suffering of others. That's why I joined the Red Cross, because I wanted to help. That's why I agreed to work in Germany, and that's why I was here. Because I wanted to help. But I needed one of them, the old man, the couple, the boys, one of them, to give me a signal. I needed a sign. No one gave me the slightest sign. No one said: "I need help."

Instead, they looked at me in their strange way. Even the boys who were playing with the spinning-top. If you've read my report, I talk about them in it, I took photographs of them. Their top span against the Commandant's boots. The boys looked at each other, not knowing what to do, as if that wasn't supposed to happen. Gottfried stopped talking, as though he didn't know what to do either. The Commandant bent down to pick up the top. I wondered if he wasn't just another mechanical figure. Too affable, too cultivated. The Commandant, or the man who had told me he was the Commandant, said to the boys: "In Germany we spin the top a different way." And he went over and he showed them how to spin the top the German way.

The clock was still showing exactly six o'clock. The Commandant was playing with the boys, a few feet away, with his back to us. This was the moment. Gottfried could say it now: "Help me." He didn't even have to say anything. A sign. And he said: "In 1914, more than four hundred years after its construction, the machinery was still accurate to thirty seconds. In fact, the clock's balance derives from an earlier set, manufactured in Toledo in 1492. Which means you're looking at a machine that hasn't stopped for almost five hundred years."

I felt a strange sense of solitude opening up between those Germans and those Jews. I began to feel that I was a toy figure too. But why? Where was I, really? A few feet away from Gottfried, but where?

The Commandant came back over. "People from all over Europe come to this station. But you won't see any trains. Unless you want to spend the night here. They always arrive at six o'clock in the morning." I imagined the sound of trains breaking the silence of the forest. Breaking the sort of silence you only hear deep inside a forest.

On the other side of the rails, I noticed a short concrete ramp, that looked as if it was for unloading cattle. Then another ramp, this one less steep, and longer, rising towards a sort of hangar. The Commandant saw me looking at the hangar. "The infirmary," he said. "The path between the infirmary and the train, we call it 'the way to heaven'." He looked at Gottfried, expectantly. Gottfried nodded: "The way to heaven."

"You can see the whole of our little town from up there," the Commandant said, and he gestured me up to take a look. And you could, from the top of the ramp you could see everything. Things had come back to life again in the square, like a toy that had been re-wound: the children on the swings, the old folk enjoying the sunshine, the balloon seller ... The Commandant pointed out some of the places we'd visited: the football pitch, the theatre, the school. The synagogue. "Religious freedom," he said. "This town is what we call a 'Jewish re-plantation zone'. An experiment in self-determination." Today I'd have asked, "If they look after their own affairs, what are you doing here, Commandant?" But I didn't. Nobody talked to the Germans like that. The Commandant went on: "An experiment designed to solve a problem that no other European nation has been able to address successfully for centuries." He looked as if he expected me to say something. All I could think of was: "Well, I have to say I'm surprised at how difficult it was to get here." The Commandant nodded at Gottfried, as though he wanted him to say something. So he said: "We have people here from all over Europe, which creates a number of organisational difficulties. It's difficult, especially for the older people, but the young ones are full of hope for the future. The young ones know that we're like a ship waiting to enter a harbour that's been sown with mines. The Captain doesn't know the safe route in and he has to ignore all the false signals coming from the shore. The Captain waits for a clear signal. And while he does, it's his duty to be patient."

For the first time, I got the impression that something had annoyed the Commandant. Gottfried's poetic outburst, that thing about the boats, had annoyed him. He suddenly announced: "It's getting dark," and he headed back to the station. Gottfried limped along behind him. Did I mention that, that Gottfried had a limp? And it was just then, as they were going on ahead of me, that I touched the hangar door with my hand. I can still remember the cold on my fingers. And Gottfried's eyes, as he turned to look back.

Did he think I was going to open that door? Because I thought I might. But what if I was wrong after all? Perhaps I was just giving in to prejudice? Or arrogance? The vanity of someone who thought he could see beyond what was there. I stepped away from the door and I rejoined them.

We walked back with Gottfried, the Mayor, to his hut. "Come back any time," he told me. The Commandant and I walked away from the red-brick huts. I glanced back, as I went. Gottfried was watching very intently. Now I know why. He was watching me, thinking: "There goes a man who's alive." The Commandant talked all the way back to my car. "Germany is achieving something remarkable here. One day the whole of Europe will recognise it." His last words were: "Remember what Gottfried said: come back any time."

When I got back to Berlin, I wrote my report. I write it over and over again every night in my memory. People ask me: "Did you not see the ovens?" "Did you not see the trains?" No, I saw none of that. "The smoke?" "The ash?" No. Everything that people say was there, I saw none of it.

Sometimes I think I could have asked Gottfried directly, looked him in the eye. Or I could have asked the little girl who was playing with her doll in the stream. She must have known. That stream was where they threw the ashes. They didn't bury any of them.

But who knew any of that then? Now, it's easy to see me as a fool, but I'm no different from anyone else. Except that I was here, on the "way to heaven."

The wood's overrun everything today, but I can recognise it. Beyond the shadow of a doubt. It was here. The railway line was here. This was where the trains came, punctually, at six in the morning. The trains always came at six in the morning.

It was here. I can feel it beneath my feet: this was the way to heaven. This is where the wagon doors opened to disgorge their passengers into the dazzle of lights and the barking of dogs, before they were herded out along the only path there was: the concrete ramp leading up to a sort of hangar.

I walk up it every night. Every night I dream that I'm walking up the ramp to the hangar door. I open it and there they are, smiling, waiting for me. Gottfried and all the others.

Every night I write my report in my memory. "Hygienic conditions are satisfactory. The people are well dressed, taking into account the normal differences of social status and background. Accommodation is modest, but of reasonable standard. Food appears sufficient."

Don't overestimate what I could do. All I could do was write a report and sign it. Even if I had written something different, what would have changed? Could I have written anything other than I did? My mission was to look and to see.

Now that I'm here again, back in the woods, I can hardly recall the man I was then, but I could repeat word for word what I wrote that night in front of the portrait of the Jewish family. "What I saw is an ordinary town." I hadn't seen anything that was out of the ordinary, and I couldn't invent what I hadn't seen. I would have written the truth if they had helped me. A word, a sign. I wrote: "Each one of us is free to pass judgement on the manner in which Germany is attempting to resolve the Jewish question. If this report serves to dispel some of the mystery which surrounds that endeavour, then it will have served its purpose." Today, standing in this place, I feel horror. But I will not apologise for writing that. I would write it again, word for word. And I would sign it again. I wrote what I saw, and I never said it was a paradise. The next day I arranged for three boxes of medical supplies to be sent. A week later, I got a letter from the camp. It was signed by the Commandant and by Gottfried, the Mayor. Thanking me.

II

Smoke

The following scenes may be accompanied by other silent scenes taken from the preceding narration: children playing on animal-shaped swings, an old man reading a newspaper, a balloon seller, the orchestra, the blessing before a Jewish meal ...

Once in a while the characters look at a spectator, as though conscious of being watched.

Every now and then the sound of a train.

BOY 1 is trying to spin a top, but doesn't know how. He tries twice, three times, with no success. BOY 2 appears behind him.

BOY 2:   You've got to pull the string tight.

          BOY 1 *puts the top away.*

          The tighter the better. Then give it a good tug.

          No reply.

          Tugging's the hard bit. Look, I'll show you. Give it here.

BOY 1:   Go and stick your nose into somebody else's business.
BOY 2:   It's a lovely top. Black and red, isn't it. Will you let me see it?
BOY 1:   Get your hands off me.
BOY 2:   Do you come to play down here because it's flat?
BOY 1:   Go away.
BOY 2:   I followed you down from the hut. I knew you were hiding. You were walking like someone with something to hide. Black and red. Just like the one Leslez lost. He's been looking for it everywhere.

          Silence.

BOY 1:   All right. We'll take it in turns, one day for me, one for you.
BOY 2:   Stick your top. I don't want it.
BOY 1:   So what do you want?
BOY 2:   Tell me what your sister's like. Sarah. You must have seen her having a bath. When she takes her clothes off, what does she look like?

A young couple, on a bench. SHE has red hair. HE gives her a parcel in wrapping-paper. Pause.

HE: Are you not going to open it?

Silence.

You look very pretty today.

SHE: Do I? Today?

HE: What do you mean?

SHE: I was expecting you yesterday.

HE: I left the warehouse late.

SHE: You said you were going to call for me.

HE: The boss asked me to help with the stocklist.

SHE: I was waiting for over an hour.

HE: To listen to you, you'd think I was out getting drunk. I was working.

SHE: There are other things in life, apart from work.

HE: I'm working for us. For you, for me, for everything we've dreamed about. For our future.

Silence.

I'm working for us. For you, for me, for everything …

SHE: The future. I'm sick of the future.

HE: Open it. Please.

SHE: Talk to me about now. Here and now.

HE: I've had to work hard to get a supervisor's job. Do you want me to have to go on breaking my back shifting heavy bags all day? There's a lot of people waiting for me to slip up so that they can take my place. The boss has put me in charge of the weighing-machine because he trusts me. Everything that comes into and goes out of the warehouse, I have to make sure it's weighed. The boss trusts me. He told me that he started at the bottom too, and look how far he's come. If I work hard, I'll be somebody one day.

Silence.

If I work hard, I'll be somebody one day.

She gives him back the parcel. He doesn't take it.

Open it. It's a surprise.

A little GIRL standing in the stream, holding a doll whose head she is stroking.

GIRL: Don't be scared. Don't be scared. I'm going to show you. Just lie forward and you won't sink, I'm holding you. Now move your legs. Like this: one-two, one-two. Now your arms. Stretch them out more. Keep your feet in the water. Now your head. You have to put your head in and breathe through your nose. You do two strokes, like that, one, two, you bring your mouth up, you breathe and again, one, two, very good, you're doing well. Now I'm going to let you go and you keep yourself up on your own. On your own now. Don't be scared.

She looks at a spectator as if suddenly aware that someone is there. She greets the spectator.

Be a good boy, Walter. Say hello to the nice man.

She makes the doll wave a greeting.

BOY 3 is trying to spin the top, but doesn't know how. He tries twice, three times, with no success. BOY 4 appears behind him.

BOY 4:   You have to wrap the string tighter.

BOY 3 puts the top away.

The tighter you pull it the better. Then tug it hard.

No reply.

Tugging's the hard bit. Look, I can show you. Give it here.

BOY 3:   Go and stick your nose into somebody else's business.
BOY 4:   It's a lovely top. Black and red, isn't it. Will you let me see it?
BOY 3:   Get your hands off me.
BOY 4:   Do it again.
BOY 3:   Again? Why?
BOY 4:   You said "Get your hands off me" before I'd even touched you. I still hadn't gone anywhere near you.
BOY 3:   From the start?
BOY 4:   From "Go and stick your nose …".

They take up their positions. BOY 3 starts to laugh, but immediately stifles it.

BOY 3:   Go and stick your nose into somebody else's business.
BOY 4:   It's a lovely top. Black and red, isn't it. Will you let me see it?
BOY 3:   Get your hands off me.
BOY 4:   Do you come to play down here because it's flat?
BOY 3:   Go away.
BOY 4:   I followed you. Down from the hut. I thought to myself: "He's trying to hide something." You were walking like someone with something to hide. Black with a red top. Just like the one Krystow lost. He's been looking for it.
BOY 3:   All right. We'll take it in turns, one day for me, one for you.
BOY 4:   Stick your top. I don't want it.
BOY 3:   So what do you want?
BOY 4:   Tell me what Sarah's like. She's your sister, you must have seen her having a bath. When she takes her clothes off, what does she look like?

Silence.

Prompting.

She's got …

BOY 3:   She's got really white skin. And small feet. Covered in scratch marks because she likes walking in her bare feet when she's on her own.

The young couple on the bench. They speak more quickly than before, so much that at times they cut across each other. HE gives her a smaller present than before, although still gift wrapped.

HE: Are you not going to open it? You look very pretty today.

SHE: Do I? Today?

HE: What do you mean?

SHE: I was expecting you yesterday.

HE: I left the warehouse late.

SHE: You said you were going to call for me.

HE: The boss asked me to help with the stocklist.

SHE: I was waiting for you. I'm tired of waiting for you. I don't want to spend my whole life waiting endlessly.

HE: To listen to you, you'd think I was running about with another woman. I work because I care about the future.

SHE: There are other things in life, apart from work.

HE: I'm working for us. For you, for me, for everything we've dreamed about. For our future.

SHE: The future. I'm sick of the future.

HE: Open it. Please.

SHE: Talk to me about now. Here and now.

HE: I've had to work hard to get that job in the warehouse. Do you want me to have to go on breaking my back shifting heavy bags all day? There's a lot of people waiting for me to slip up so that…

SHE: Do you not hear them? The trains.

HE: There's a lot of people waiting for me to slip up so that they can take my place. The boss has put me in charge of the weighing-machine…

SHE: What do you do not to hear them?

HE: The boss has put me in charge of the weighing-machine because he trusts me. Everything that comes into and goes out of the warehouse…

SHE: Look over there. The smoke. Do you not see it? What do you do not to see it?

HE: There's a lot of people waiting for me to slip up so that they can take my place. The boss has put me in charge of the weighing-machine because he trusts me. Everything that comes into and goes out of the warehouse, I have to make sure it's weighed.

SHE: How long are we going to be here?

HE: I have to make sure it's weighed. The boss trusts me. He told me that he started at the bottom too, and look how far he's come.

SHE:	What if we were to run for it? Once we got into the woods…
HE:	Look how far he's come. If I work hard…
SHE:	I'm going to run for it. Come with me.
HE:	If I work hard, I'll be somebody one day.

She goes, leaving him alone.

Open it. It's a surprise.

Silence.

Our future. That's what's in it. Our future.

The little GIRL, standing in the river, with the doll.

GIRL: Your arms. Stretch them out more. In the water, keep your feet in. Your head. You have to breathe through your nose and put your head in the water. (*She corrects herself.*) You have to put your head in the water and breathe through your nose. Two strokes, you bring your mouth up, you breathe and do it again. One, two, very good. I'm going to let you go and you have to keep yourself up. On your own. Don't be scared.

Silence.

Don't be scared. I'll show you. Lie forward. You won't sink. I'm holding you. Move your legs. One-two. Your arms. Stretch them out. More. Your feet, don't take them out of the water. Your head. You have to put your head in the water. And breathe through your nose.

She looks at a spectator as if suddenly aware that someone is there. She greets the spectator.

Be a good girl, Rebecca. Say hello to the nice man.

She makes the doll wave a greeting. She sings a lullaby to the doll.

You do two strokes, you bring your mouth up. You breathe and you do it again. One, two, very good. I'm going to let you go. You have to keep yourself up on your own. On your own. Don't be scared.

Silence.

Don't be scared. I'll show you. Lie forward. You won't sink. I'm holding you. Move your legs.

She greets a spectator.

Be a good girl, Rebecca. Say hello to the nice man.

She makes the doll wave a greeting. She sings the lullaby to the doll.

One, two. Your arms. Stretch. Keep them in. Your feet. In the water. Your head. Through your nose. Two strokes. Breathe. Again. One, two. I'm going to let you go. On your own. Do it on your own.

Silence. She shivers with cold. BOY 4 is listening to BOY 5.

BOY 5:   She's got really white skin. And small feet. Covered in scratch marks because she likes walking in her bare feet when she's on her own. She's got long arms and small hands. Her nipples are black, at least they look black to me because her skin's so white.

A young couple on the bench. The young man is the same as before, but the woman is different, not a redhead. There is a large package sitting between them, in wrapping-paper.

HE: Everything that comes into and goes out of the warehouse, I have to make sure it's weighed. The boss trusts me. He told me that he started at the bottom too, and look how far he's come. If I work hard, I'll be somebody one day.

SHE gives him back the package. HE doesn't take it.

Open it. It's a surprise.
SHE: It's very light. What's in it?
HE: Our future. That's what's in it. Our future.

The noise of a train. SHE drops the package. It sounds empty.

The little GIRL in the stream, without her doll. She is very cold. She looks at the spectators.

GIRL: Be a good girl, Rebecca. Say hello to the nice man. Don't be scared. I'll show you. I'm going to hold you. Don't be scared. We have to stay here until they tell us. Don't be scared. I'll show you. One – two. One – two. Don't be scared. One – two. Move your legs. One – two. Move your legs. Your head. Your arms. Your feet. Your nose. Your mouth. Until they tell us. Don't be scared. One – two. Say hello. To the nice man. Be a good girl, Rebecca. Say hello. One – two. Be a good girl, Rebecca. Say. Hello. To the nice man. Don't be. Scared.

She sings the lullaby. She smiles at the sound of the train.

III

This Will Be the Silence of Peace

COMMANDANT: Do any of you know who I am? It *is* me. How was your journey? Lovely road up from Berlin. Pity there are so many of those ugly check-points. Damned war. Do have a seat. Can I get you anything? Coffee perhaps? Do you have authorisation for the visit? Yes, yes, I know. You want to send us ... Food? Clothes? Medical supplies? Of course. You want to send medical supplies. Why not? Do send them. We can put them to good use.

If you don't mind me saying so, your accent … For a moment I thought you were … But no, how could I make such a mistake? Your accent is … unmistakable. It brings back so many happy memories. I'm very fond of your country. I holidayed there. Before the war. Beautiful country. Culture everywhere you look. Say something in your own language, please. A single word: "Peace." It is a privilege to listen to such a language. And it will become even more of a privilege, because very soon we'll all be speaking the same language. I say that without arrogance, indeed with a deep nostalgia. Fortunately, we shall always have the past. And we shall always need Spanish to read Calderón, French for Corneille. Take a look at my library. That's what Europe means to me. Take a look while I sign these files. We are inundated with bureaucracy here too. Whenever it gets on top of me, whenever I feel myself suffocating, I jump into the car and drive myself down to Berlin. Out of uniform. I look to see what's on and I go to the theatre. And I breathe again. Ready to come back here and start signing files again. Anyway, take a look while I get on with this. People think we're animals. But look at my library. When I was posted here, I brought a hundred books with me. One hundred exactly. The very best. You'll see some I got while I was in your country. No, I know you haven't come to look at books, you're all keen to begin the visit. I know why you're here. No need to say. The rumours, I've heard them all too. Monstrous rumours. Please don't take it as a reproach. Fantasy overtakes us all once in a while. You have imagined terrible things and you believe you should do something about them. It was your goodwill that brought you here. And your nightmares. Walking skeletons in striped pyjamas. I've had the same nightmares. But who can sleep easy these days? You want to help, but you need information, you can't help blindly. That's what you're all doing here, looking for information, and we intend to provide it. Let's go for a walk. You can take photographs. Please, feel free to take as many as you want. But they have to feel prepared for us. Protocol. Jews can be very private. They don't like strangers poking about. They're not like us, not like you and me. More coffee? As soon as the war's over, I'll go back to your country for a holiday. I'm European before I'm German. We'll all realise one day that this war has been a civil war. A mistake, a terrible misunderstanding between brothers. Take a look at my library. That's my Europe. If we forget that, then the war really will have damaged us. Have you seen what's on in Berlin? Of course, it's a war programme. So, German authors only. I miss my friends: Corneille, Shakespeare, Calderón. But none of you have come here to talk about theatre. Don't worry, I won't let you go without having a walk round. You must see the station clock. We'll go through the woods, down along the stream. You get a wonderful feeling there. You close your eyes, and you can hear the silence. Close your eyes. That's what the silence of peace will be like. Close your eyes. Spinoza says that hatred will be overcome by a love that is as intense as the hatred that preceded it. The world is moving towards unity. This war is an enormous step towards that. A quickening of an inevitable movement towards harmony. One language, one currency, one way. Even if we lose the war, the inevitable will happen. It makes no difference who wins the war. This war is the work of humanity; the first time all humanity has worked together. The peace that ends it will be the second time. The fruits of this war will be for everyone. Each and every one of us, wherever destiny has us. We shall win this war. One day it will be impossible to tell the victors from the vanquished. In the meantime, there will be pain, but such pain is necessary. Spinoza said: "Hatred which is conquered by love, becomes love; and that love is greater than if hatred had not been its forerunner." *Ethics*, Proposition Forty-four. No, don't waste your time looking for it in my library, I only brought a hundred books with me, the best. What Spinoza means is that there's a sense to all this suffering. Birth pangs. A new world being born. Even the slightest twinge of pain is absolutely necessary. Better to suffer for a thousand years than to go back for one instant to the old world. To go from one world to the next demands huge reserves of courage. Courage to do what's necessary. And many will fall along the way, they become the way. They are the way. But enough politics. It's a beautiful day. Let's not waste it here. You haven't come to discuss politics; you're here to visit. I wondered whether you'd be able to find us. If perhaps I'd have to go and look for you. How did you know which road to take? Did you follow the shadow of the smoke? Did you know that, that smoke throws its own shadow? Not everyone does know that. Or had you been here before? Of course, you knew the way because you had been here before. How did I not recognise you until now? I knew you'd come back one day, it was only a matter of time. As you can see, things have changed somewhat. As we foresaw. The huts were made of cheap wood, so they would rot and disappear. We've planted trees. It's not easy today to get a clear idea of what this was like before. The swings were over there, that's where the football pitch was, the synagogue over there. There was a theatre. And here, of course, the "himmelweg:" do you remember it? I don't know if it was them or us who first called it that. Can you say it in German? Him-mel-veck. Say it in your language: "way to heaven." There's none of it left now, but they're still here. All of them, every single one. The swings, the synagogue, everything was swallowed up by the woods, but they're still here. Them and the station clock, showing six o'clock exactly. If it wasn't for them and that old clock, these woods might well be the same as any other ones. I wondered if you would find the right woods, if the shadow of the smoke would be enough. Yes, these are the woods. Welcome. Once again. And once again, let me counsel caution. Do not trust the evidence of your eyes. For generations, they have been schooled in deceit. They are a people who, for centuries, have realised the value of painting themselves as victims. But none of you will be taken in. You all have good memories. Then remember: who was it started this war? Do not be deceived for one moment. Before you pass judgment on us, remember that we are addressing a problem that has confronted the whole of Europe for centuries. It was us who first realised that it is, fundamentally, a problem of transport. Our great achievement has been the solving of that technical issue. Others had dreamed about it: but we've done it. Do you hear them? Do you hear the trains? Every train in Europe terminates here. If you want to see them, you'll have to spend the night in the woods; the trains always arrive at six in the morning. Always at six, and by six-fifteen they've gone again. Speed is of the essence. We've also solved the problems of hygiene and the disposal of remains. Sparing you the details, I can tell you that we have managed to distribute all the functional elements relative to the problem on a European-wide scale through the coordination of all of the relevant and appropriate parties. You must forgive the use of such bureaucratic language; I find it suffocating too. It's not my language of choice: take a look at my library. It's not my language. But it is the language that is most appropriate in this case, a language of objectives and decisions. The immediate objective is to regroup all the Hebrews scattered across Europe into one place: here. But the final objective is much more elevated. Our final objective is to show that everything is possible. Everything is possible. Anything we can dream, we can do. Here, in this world. Even things we didn't dare imagine. That, ladies and gentlemen, is what awaits you in the woods: that which can be seen but not imagined. For that reason, no matter what you may see here, I urge you not to tell anyone. You would not be believed, and if you persist, people will think you are mad. Let me give you a piece of advice: as soon as you leave here, start to forget. So that, when you get home, you can write a lovely report. Today, just like then. Because that's why you came here today, just like then. You want to prove that your nightmares are a lie. I've had those nightmares too. Who can sleep easy these days? Who can sleep, with so many trains travelling through the night? Trains travelling through the night, that's my Europe. Our nightmares travel on the trains. They've happened. Our nightmares have happened. Dreams come before facts; nightmares behind. Everything we fear has happened inside us already. The nightmares that surround us come from inside our soul, they've been growing inside us, in our heads and our hearts. But that's enough politics. We'll begin the visit straight away. Not yet, we're not quite ready. I am, I always am, but they need a little more time. They're getting everything ready so that your visit will be as pleasant as possible. It may not be paradise, but you are expecting something a lot worse. They're well dressed. New clothes. New shoes. Without laces. They do maths and language at school. History as well, no less. Someone suggested: "We could paint the huts." I said: "No. It would look fake. We'll just plant a garden outside each one." You can touch the flowers. They're real. Take photographs of the flowers, if you want. We want you to take photographs. And, especially, look and see, and tell the world what you've seen. The world has to know. You are the eyes of the world. One of them will show you round. I'll simply accompany you and, if you don't mind, I'll show you how we spin a top in Germany. Like this. You spin it like this: "Himmelweg." Say it in your language: "Way to heaven." Ladies and gentlemen, come this way. And look. Here in the heart of the countryside. In the heart of Europe. And if you do like it, come back whenever you wish. Bear with us, please, they're almost ready. In the meantime, take a look at my library.

IV

The Heart of Europe

1

The COMMANDANT is in his office, reading a file. GOTTFRIED comes in.

COMMANDANT: Sit down.

> *GOTTFRIED sits down.*

> Your name is ... *(From the file.)* Gerhard Gottfried.

GOTTFRIED: Gershom Gottfried.
COMMANDANT: Not Gerhard?
GOTTFRIED: Gershom.
COMMANDANT: I've been misinformed. Coffee?

> *GOTTFRIED declines.*

> Have you been able to rest?

> *GOTTFRIED assents.*

> You must be wondering why I sent for you.

> *Silence.*

> We have chosen you to be an interlocutor. You and I are go-
> ing to work together. You will be, in a manner of speaking,
> my translator. Not in the sense of language, I am not talking
> about languages. In the psychological sense. I shall tell you
> what we want, and you will transmit those wishes to your
> people. You will find the right words. You are more familiar
> with the psychology of your people than we are.

> *Silence.*

> Your cooperation will be rewarded. Naturally, if you choose
> not to assume this responsibility, we shall find someone else.
> However, a negative reply would prove very disappointing.
> You came to our attention because we could see that you
> enjoy the respect of your people. Coffee?

> *GOTTFRIED declines.*

> For the time being, we want your people to rest, to eat and
> to rest. Your journey has been an arduous one. We regret
> the circumstances of that journey, we are embarrassed. You
> were treated like animals, we are aware of that. Unfortu-
> nately, not everyone who wears this uniform comes under
> our direct control. The uniform brings out the worst, even

in decent family men. I promise you that those responsible will be held to account. But we're not here to talk about the past, Gottfried. We have received orders that will benefit all of you. You have been chosen by Berlin. And, I can say it with pride, so have we. We have a joint project. Berlin wishes to lay certain prejudices to rest. Prejudices concerning the relationship between our two peoples. You did say Gershom, didn't you? Perhaps Gerhard is the same as Gershom in German?

GOTTFRIED: It's not the same.

COMMANDANT: Well. It's not. There is much about your people we don't know. You are an enigma to us. Not just to Germany, but all of Europe. But my people, the German people, we are no less of an enigma. There are many strange stories about us, going from mouth to mouth. The world hears those stories and wonders: is this possible? Is this possible in a people of poets and thinkers, in the heart of Europe? That's why we're here: to get our project underway.

He spreads out a map in front of GOTTFRIED, and points to various locations on it.

Do you see where you are? This is the station, and here's the stream. We're just here. This is where we're building the school. There'll be a football pitch here. And look what it says here, Gottfried: the synagogue.

Silence.

As you can see, we are going to transform the whole area. But much more important, and more difficult, is the way in which we transform ourselves. All of us, you and us. We must learn to deal with each other in a new way. We must learn to look at each other in a new way. Have you read Pascal?

GOTTFRIED shakes his head. The COMMANDANT takes a book down from his library, opens it and finds the passage he is looking for. He reads.

Pensée two hundred and fifty-two: "We are automata as much as spirits." He goes on: "We must engage the dual elements of our being: the spiritual, through reason, and the mechanical, through habit." Do you understand Gottfried? What Pascal's saying is, if you pray, you end up believing. Or put it another way: smile and you'll end up happy. The wisdom of actors. May I ask: have you any experience of the theatre?

GOTTFRIED shakes his head. The COMMANDANT goes to offer him coffee, then thinks better of it.

As a spectator, at least …?

GOTTFRIED: I've been … not very often. By the time I got out of work …

COMMANDANT: Pity. It would have saved me the trouble of explaining a few things. You'll have a clearer idea once we get to work. I won't keep you today. Try and rest. You'll need a clear head tomorrow. Tomorrow, you and I will plan what has to be done. You might say, we have a script to write.

2

COMMANDANT: Composition. That's the key thing. Composition. How do I get you to understand that?

He takes a book down from his shelf and thumbs through it.

Aristotle's *Poetics*, Chapter Seven.

He sets the open book in front of GOTTFRIED, who reads in silence. Pause. The COMMANDANT waits for GOTTFRIED's reply. But GOTTFRIED can't think of anything to say.

What Aristotle's saying is that the beauty of a work of art is in direct proportion to its complexity, always providing that that complexity is under control.

He takes the cord from a spinning-top, and makes a knot.

A knot is more interesting than a bit of string, but if the knot is too complicated …

He makes the knot increasingly complicated.

If it gets too complicated, then the eye perceives it as chaotic and loses interest. A melody …

He hums a series of tunes, of increasing complexity.

A melody is of more interest than a monotone, but if the melody is too complex, all the ear hears is noise, and it shuts it out. Do you see what I mean?

GOTTFRIED: I thought I heard a train last night.

COMMANDANT: A train? Not as far as I know. Perhaps you dreamt it.

GOTTFRIED: A few of us heard it from the hut. I'm not sure what time it was. Near dawn. We couldn't open the windows to see. The windows and doors in the hut are bolted on the outside. We thought a train had come and that there'd be new people in the camp. But nobody came.

COMMANDANT: If there'd been a train, I would have known. I'll make inquiries. Where were we? Composition. The same story can be told in any number of ways: forwards, backwards, according to a particular point of view or –

GOTTFRIED: People are asking about the shoes.

COMMANDANT: We've given them new clothes. Do they not like them?

GOTTFRIED: They want to know about the shoe-laces. Why the shoes don't have laces.

COMMANDANT: Their shoes don't have laces. That's what you want to talk about. Really? Is this an example of your famous Jewish humour? We're working, Gottfried. Do you need a break? No. Then focus on what we're doing. I think we should begin with classical composition: Act One, the city; Act Two, the woods; Act Three, the station.

3

Coloured pins have been inserted into the site map. The COMMANDANT has a number of personal files in front of him; GOTTFRIED as well. The COMMANDANT is reading from the first page of a notebook that we shall call the "text."

COMMANDANT: Balloon seller.

GOTTFRIED hands a file to the COMMANDANT who, after looking at it, inserts a pin into the map.

Boys with spinning-top.

GOTTFRIED hands him two files. The COMMANDANT glances at them and inserts two pins into the map.

Boy with toy figure.

GOTTFRIED hands him a file. The COMMANDANT looks at it. Silence.

A girl? I thought a boy.

GOTTFRIED: Because of her voice. She has a lovely voice.

Pause. The COMMANDANT inserts a pin into the map.

COMMANDANT: Couple on the bench.

GOTTFRIED hands him two files. The COMMANDANT studies them. Silence. He hands one back.

She's too pretty.

Pause. GOTTFRIED hands him another file. The COMMANDANT looks at it and inserts two pins into the map.

Good. You've done well. Although I'm worried about the scene in the square. I still wonder if we shouldn't scale it down.

GOTTFRIED: Less people? What if it's sunny? Everyone should be there.

COMMANDANT: Yes ... but with so many people you can't ... In this particular scene what matters ... how can I put it? ... is community

spirit. We'll have to coordinate attitudes, gestures, looks …
And some of my men will be there too. So how do we deal
with the mutual distrust? It won't be easy, for us or for you.
Bear in mind this is new for us too. It certainly is for me.
At the end of the day, I'm a military man. A soldier. Are you
listening to me, Gottfried? What are you looking at?

GOTTFRIED: The smoke.

4

*The COMMANDANT is trying to spin a top, but doesn't know how. He tries
twice, three times, with no success. GOTTFRIED is watching, the text in his hands.*

COMMANDANT: He's doesn't notice the other one behind him until he hears
him speak. "You've got to pull the string tight." Then he puts
the top away.

He does this.

All of his senses are focussed on protecting the top.

*He passes the top to GOTTFRIED. He pretends not to know
how to spin it. Twice, three times. The COMMANDANT
stands behind him.*

You've got to pull the string tight.

GOTTFRIED puts the top away.

The tighter the better. Then give it a good tug.

No reply.

The tugging's the hard bit. Look, I'll show you. Give it here.

GOTTFRIED: Go and stick your nose into somebody else's business.

COMMANDANT: It's a lovely top. Black and red, isn't it. Will you let me see it?

GOTTFRIED: Get your hands off me.

5

COMMANDANT: Get them out of my sight. Tell them to go back to their huts.
Everyone. You too.

Silence.

Did you not hear me? You too, Gottfried.

GOTTFRIED: We can do it better.

COMMANDANT: I'm going to telegram Berlin. "Mission impossible. Stop.
Awaiting new orders."

GOTTFRIED: We can do it. We just need time.

COMMANDANT: I'm disappointed, Gottfried. Very disappointed. Your people don't listen to what they're told. It must be one of two
things: either I don't make myself clear, or the translator isn't
doing his job. Do I not make myself clear? Because we're not
making any progress. The lunch was awful. Those women
were dangling their spoons like dead rats. And what about
the scene with the spinning-top? How many different boys
have we tried? And your monologue? The clock monologue.
Gottfried, your clock monologue!

Silence.

The redhead still doesn't know what she's doing. What is
she? A girl having a row with her boyfriend? A lonely young
woman looking for company? A whore arguing with her
pimp? What's her objective in this scene?

GOTTFRIED: I thought she would do it well. And she will. She worked for
two years in a theatre in Warsaw.

COMMANDANT: She's a professional actress? Why didn't you tell me? You
should have told me, Gottfried.

Silence.

The fat boy, he's terrible. He doesn't know how to articulate
clearly. At least you can understand the other one. Not that
he sounds convincing.

GOTTFRIED: It's not the way boys talk.

COMMANDANT: Not the way boys talk? What do you mean?

GOTTFRIED: There are things they say. "You were walking like somebody
with something to hide." A youngster doesn't talk like that.
People don't talk like that. People don't say, "I'm working for
us. For you, for me, for everything we've dreamed about."
Not in real life.

Silence.

COMMANDANT: You always defend them. You find some excuse for every last
one of them. Remember: you're my translator, Gottfried, not
some barrack-room lawyer.

Silence.

Of course you don't talk like that in real life. Of course you
don't.

Pause.

There's your problem, Gottfried. That's why you can't do
your monologue. You're looking for life in the words. But
life isn't in words. It's in the gestures we make when we say

them. Let's have a look at the monologue, Gottfried. You have to find a relationship between the words and the gestures. Watch me.

He is about to start acting, but stops.

I'd forgotten: the balloon seller. He really won't do. He goes left when he should go right. The man can't tell left from right.

GOTTFRIED: The man doesn't sleep. The man gets up every few minutes during the night to make sure the hut's locked. He gets up, makes sure everything's locked and goes back to bed. And he does it again and again and again. He never sleeps.

COMMANDANT: He gets up to make sure the hut's locked? That's ironic, isn't it?

He laughs.

There's no doubt about it, your people have an enviable sense of humour.

He laughs.

Get me another balloon seller, Gottfried. One who can tell left from right at least.

GOTTFRIED: Tadeusz will do it. He's an intelligent man. He taught history at university.

COMMANDANT: The balloon seller taught history? What sort of history was it if he can't tell right from left? They'll give him something in the infirmary to make him sleep. Right, the monologue. It's your big moment, Gottfried, and you can't just throw it away like this. You don't know what to do with your hands, anyone can see that. If you need a prop, get one. A book, a stick ... a walking-stick! That's it! A walking-stick! You need a stick to walk! It'll hide a multitude of sins. Nobody ever notices the colour of a cripple's eyes.

He pretends he has a stick. He shows GOTTFRIED how to limp.

But the key is to find a link between words and gestures. Don't tell me that nobody talks like that in real life. I know, Gottfried, I know. But I also know that you can find real gestures to go with the words. I've been reading your file. You have a wife, a daughter, a life. You have a previous life, Gottfried. Use it. Look inside your life. Listen: "It was built about 1502 by Master Peter Henlein, of Nuremberg, the celebrated builder of mechanical figures." You're not doing some sort of oral examination at school. You're talking about your own town clock. You're proud of it, very proud.

Watch me: "It was built about 1502 by Master Peter Henlein, of Nuremberg ..." Think how Anthony describes Caesar's torn mantle – *Julius Caesar*, Act Three, Scene Two. I told you to read it … Did you? "If you have tears, prepare to shed them now. / You all know this mantle: I remember / the first time ever Caesar put it on – "

GOTTFRIED: I keep hearing trains. We all hear them. None of us sleep because we're waiting for the noise of the train. Staring at the ceiling every night, waiting for the train.

COMMANDANT: You're tired. Is that what you're trying to tell me. You're not doing it well because you're all sleepy.

GOTTFRIED: Today a lot of people didn't want to leave the hut.

COMMANDANT: What do you mean, don't want to leave the hut?

GOTTFRIED: They don't understand … they don't know what it is we're doing here.

COMMANDANT: What you're doing here? How many times do I have to tell you, Gottfried? This is a model experiment. You've been given special status. Berlin has chosen you.

GOTTFRIED: They don't see the sense to this.

COMMANDANT: They don't see the sense. So they need sense? Would it not be your fault, Gottfried, that they don't see the sense? You're the translator. You know what you say to them, and how you say it.

GOTTFRIED: I don't know what to say to them anymore.

COMMANDANT: I can't help you. Your people are an enigma to me. You know the psychology of your people. That's why you're here. They listen to you, they trust what you say, that's why you first came to our attention. Listen carefully, Gottfried, and try to understand. A few weeks ago, while you and your people were travelling here, I received a telegram. A message from Berlin. Just in time, barely minutes before your train pulled into the station. Believe me when I say that if that message hadn't arrived exactly when it did, you and I wouldn't be having this conversation. Do I make myself clear?

Pause. GOTTFRIED nods his head.

GOTTFRIED: The people need to know what to expect.

COMMANDANT: What to expect? They need to know what to expect? We'd all like to know what to expect. Life is uncertainty. Can anyone sleep easy these days? Maybe the train doesn't let them sleep. But there is one thing they know for certain: they're not on that train.

GOTTFRIED: The people are wondering what'll happen if they do it well.

COMMANDANT: Focus on one thought, Gottfried. "I'm not on that train. As long as I'm here, I'm not on that train." Focus on that thought, go back to the hut, and tell your people what they need to hear. You're their translator. It's up to you to find the right words. I can't help you. What do I know about what goes on inside your people's hearts? They need sense? Give them sense. Go and talk to them. And when you're choosing your words, remember: "As long as we're here, we're not on that train."

6

COMMANDANT: Something's not working. I don't know what, but it's not working.
GOTTFRIED: It's like …
COMMANDANT: Like what, Gershom. Go on.
GOTTFRIED: Like the scene grinds to a halt. And the girl suddenly changes, without you knowing why.

Silence.

COMMANDANT: You're right. Good, Gershom, good. Let's make a few changes.

He opens the text. He thinks, scores out, and writes in silence. He gives the text back to GOTTFRIED. He reads it in silence. Pause.

GOTTFRIED: What's the difference between "pause" and "silence?"
COMMANDANT: It's about rhythm. Where it says "silence," count to three in your head. Where it says "pause," count to five.

Pause. GOTTFRIED counts in silence, first to three, then to five. The COMMANDANT pours two cups of coffee. They drink.

Another thing: I want the little girl to sing. It'll be a strong finish to the walk through the woods, before we go to the station. Do you think you can get her to sing?
GOTTFRIED: I think so.
COMMANDANT: Well, if not, there are plenty of other children. I know you're concerned about them, Gershom. I am too. The children. I've been informed that you take the children down to the school every evening.
GOTTFRIED: Only once we're finished. In our own time.
COMMANDANT: Yes, yes. I know it's in your own time. That's not what worries me. You take the children down to the school. They sit at the desks and write down what you put up on the blackboard.
GOTTFRIED: We teach them.
COMMANDANT: What do you teach them?
GOTTFRIED: Maths, language, history … some of us are teachers.
COMMANDANT: Maths, language … history!

Silence.

This is very irregular. This is not why Berlin chose you.

Silence.

You have my permission to continue bringing them to the school for lessons. It is irregular, but you may continue. As long as you don't forget what your real purpose is here. History, or whatever you want. Take it as a gesture of goodwill. Of gratitude, Gershom. Why not? Everything's starting to come together, and I can see your hand in it. I know that you've managed to find the right words at last.

Silence.

So now we embark upon the most important phase of our project. As from tomorrow, some of my men will walk around the camp in civilian clothes. They will behave as if they were visitors from outside. Your people have to get used to such visitors. Full access. They can go anywhere, Gershom, they can ask anything.

7

COMMANDANT: Good, good, good. Much better, Gershom, much better. The girl on the bench has found the right tone. And I think we've eventually got the right boys for the spinning-top, a good pair. Your monologue's come along well too. "It was built about 1502 by Master Peter Henlein, of Nuremberg ..." Very good. The only thing that's still worrying me is the scene in the square.

GOTTFRIED: The scene in the square? The people are doing their best.

COMMANDANT: I know they are. I'm not complaining. They're doing everything they can. It's not a question of effort. Nor of understanding: they know what they're doing. But ... it still lacks shape. I've been thinking it over. Why is that scene not coming together, even though we've gone over it so many times?

Silence.

GOTTFRIED: I think they'd do it better if they knew who he is. The man who's going to come.

Silence.

COMMANDANT: That's not the issue. There's something else. It's impossible to draw so many threads together: the children on the swing, the old people coming out of the synagogue, the balloon seller ... Do you remember what we said about Aristotle? If a knot is too complicated, the eye loses interest. If a melody is too complex, the ear dismisses it as noise. That's why the scene isn't working.

GOTTFRIED: I wouldn't say it's not working.

COMMANDANT: There are too many people.

GOTTFRIED: But you can't blame them if …

COMMANDANT: I'm not blaming them. Who said anything about blame?

GOTTFRIED: But …

COMMANDANT: Too many people. I told you from the start.

Silence.

GOTTFRIED: How many?

COMMANDANT: I've done some calculations. The scene would work best with a hundred. A hundred is the ideal number.

GOTTFRIED: What about the others? The ones who aren't in the scene.

COMMANDANT: The ones left over? All right, Gershom, but you must admit there's no room for them in our project. We can't have them floating about the place like ghosts. And you wouldn't want them to dress up as German soldiers. The best thing is to take them to the infirmary. Yes, that's the best solution for them. The infirmary.

He sets a pile of files in front of GOTTFRIED: the people from the scene in the square.

A hundred. Keep the proportions right: men, women, old people, children … And please, get them to smile every now and then. Your people seem to find it so hard to smile.

He chooses a book from his library. GOTTFRIED sits in front of the files. Silence. The COMMANDANT finishes the page and turns it over.

8

GOTTFRIED looks at the files. He makes no choice. The COMMANDANT reads.

9

The COMMANDANT closes the book.

COMMANDANT: You'd rather I did it? You want me to choose the best one hundred.

He is about to lift the files. GOTTFRIED stops him.

GOTTFRIED: What if we refuse?

COMMANDANT: What?

GOTTFRIED: If we refuse to leave the huts? He arrives, and there's no one there, the streets are empty. Or he arrives and people don't behave how you want them to. We turn our back on him, or we throw stones at him. Or we tell him the truth. What if we don't do what you want? If we don't go along with your wishes?

Silence.

COMMANDANT: My wishes? You think I have wishes, Gershom? Berlin has chosen me. Just as it has you. Berlin has chosen us.

Silence.

Clearly the possibility exists that you won't leave the huts. Let's suppose the visitor does arrive and you don't come out. Or you do come out and do something outlandish, you start weeping and wailing, or you say who knows what to him. Let's suppose you say who knows what. Something like that may have a certain symbolic value. That is if the man, our visitor, understands the symbol, if he can interpret it. It would be a gesture, that's true. In the midst of so many gestures, it would be another gesture. But would it be understood? What would happen if the man didn't understand your gesture?

Silence. GOTTFRIED begins to choose some files from the pile in front of him.

10

The COMMANDANT checks that there are one hundred files.

COMMANDANT: And yours? Have we left you out, Gershom?

He goes to add GOTTFRIED's file to the chosen pile, and hesitates.

But then, if I put yours in, there'll be one too many.

He pulls another file out.

Done.

He adds GOTTFRIED's file to the others.

Gerhard Gottfried.

He removes a number of pins from the map, until there are only one hundred left.

You're all ready. And now, me. Watch me and tell me what you think. Tell me if my gestures match the words.

He acts as though receiving a visitor.

If you don't mind me saying so, your accent … For a moment I thought you were … But no, how could I make such a mistake? Coffee? Your accent is unmistakable. It brings back so many happy memories. I'm very fond of your country. I holidayed there. Before the war. Say something in your language, please. Just one word: "Peace."

11

The COMMANDANT, with the top.

COMMANDANT: You've heard of the melancholy of the actor? Now you know. The curtain falls and, suddenly, that world of words and gestures, that whole world disappears. The curtain falls and the actor's left with nothing.

Silence.

An actor is hammering a nail. The curtain falls. And he realises. At that instant he understands the most terrible thing. He understands that when an actor is hammering a nail, he's hammering a nail and, at the same time, he isn't doing anything.

Silence.

The curtain falls and the actor's left holding a hammer. He doesn't know what to do with the hammer.

Silence.

The curtain falls and the actor comes back to life. And life isn't always pleasant. You know as well as I do, that life isn't always sweet. We don't live in a paradise, Gerhard. Perhaps some day. But not yet.

Silence.

The curtain falls and life has to go on. Life has to go on.

Silence.

"We are such stuff as dreams are made on; and our little life is rounded by a sleep." Suddenly, the spell's broken. The spell's broken, and everything goes back to life. Only life's worse.

Silence.

Could you imagine if the acting went on for ever? It was wonderful while it lasted, wasn't it? There were wonderful moments. Beautiful monologue: "More than four hundred years after its construction, this machine was still accurate to thirty seconds." Almost perfect. Pity about the girl with the doll.

Silence.

She nearly ruined everything. So many children to choose from, and you had to go and pick a half-wit. What did you see in her? She started off well enough. And she did have a pretty voice. The song was pretty. Did you choose it?

He hums the GIRL's song. Silence.

I didn't understand the thing about the boats, Gerhard. Do you think he did?

Silence.

He was a man of little culture. When I quoted Spinoza, I had the impression it was the first time he'd heard the name. He handled my books as though they were bricks.

Silence.

"We're a ship waiting to go into harbour, but the mines stop us. The Captain waits for a true signal. In the meantime, he has to remain patient." That wasn't it. What did you mean? There are times I don't understand you, Gerhard. Another example of your famous Jewish humour? I thought I would manage to work you out, but it hasn't happened. We've been working together for a long time, and we're still an enigma to each other.

Silence. He hums the song. Silence.

For a moment, I thought you might try something. Start screaming or something like that. Would you believe me if I said that, for a moment, I wanted you to? I felt like screaming too. On the "Himmelweg." All of a sudden, I felt ... weighed down. Knowing every word, every gesture, it was suffocating me. Hearing every word before it was spoken. And each gesture, being able to anticipate even the slightest gesture. I felt like screaming. And when you started about the boats, I thought: "At last. Gerhard's really going to do it." For just a moment, but for that moment I wanted you to.

Silence.

"We're a boat that the mines stop from entering harbour. The Captain remains patient while he waits for a true signal." That wasn't it.

Silence.

What is the boat? What does the harbour stand for? Who is the damned captain? You? Me? Him? I don't think he understood it either. There was incomprehension written all over his face. We'll see if he mentions the thing about the boats.

Silence. He hums the song. Silence.

So many children and you went and picked the most stupid one. Just when she was supposed to say, "Be a good boy, Walter, say hello to the nice man," she throws the doll in the water and cries, "Run away, Rebecca, the German's coming."

Silence.

A pity. Such a lovely moment, just as we were coming out of the woods. Apart from that, it was perfect. I hope he doesn't mention it in his report.

He hums the song. Silence.

That's what they call it, the melancholy of the actor. The curtain falls and life has to go on. Life has to go on, but how? The curtain falls and there's nothing left. You're holding a hammer. You have your hands. Your feet. Your body. But what do you do with it all once the curtain falls? Actors know everything there is to know about life, Gerhard. Behind the words and the gestures, there's nothing else, that's the only truth. When a man's hammering a nail, he's hammering a nail and, at the same time, he isn't doing anything.

V

A Song To Finish

GOTTFRIED is practising his limp, with the aid of a stick.

He turns to BOY 1 and BOY 2. BOY 1 has a black top with a red head.

GOTTFRIED: *(To BOY 2)* You're still coming in too quickly. You're not listening to Klaus: "We'll take it in turns, one day for me, one for you." Listen to him, and then react with some gesture before you speak. For example, look disgusted. And that's when you say your bit: "Stick your top. I don't want it." Don't get too close to him at the start. Come closer slowly so that he feels threatened. Let's try it.

He places BOY 1 as though he were playing with the top. GOTTFRIED acts out the words.

You come on from the right, move towards him, and say, "You've got to pull the string tight," Klaus hides the top, you take a step forward and you say: "The tighter the better …" Another step and you say: "The tugging's the hard bit, blah, blah, blah." Take your time. Listen to Klaus, make a gesture and take your time before you reply.

Silence. To BOY 1.

You still look uncomfortable. Very uncomfortable. The Commandant thinks you're not going to be able to manage. I told him what happened to your sister, and I asked him to let you have one more go. I promised him you'd get it right. I'm sure you will get it right, Klaus. Try not to look straight at Franz. "She's got really white skin. And small feet. Covered in scratch marks because she likes walking in her bare feet when she's on her own." Don't look straight at him. "She's got long arms and small hands. Her nipples are black, at least they look black to me because her skin's so white."

Pause. He turns to the YOUNG COUPLE: the man and red-haired woman.

There's a change. A small one. Where you say, "I was waiting for over an hour," and you reply, "To listen to you, you'd think I was out getting drunk …" Now it's:

He produces the text and reads.

"I was waiting for you. I'm tired of waiting for you. I don't want to spend my whole life waiting endlessly." You count to three and say: "To listen to you, you'd think I was running about with another woman. I work because I care about the future." The rest's the same.

Silence.

Yes, I know no one talks like that in real life. Forget about how you talk in real life.

Silence.

I know you can do it. It won't be the first time. At work, at home, we've all had to pretend some time, haven't we? I remember my first boss, Herr Baumann, he made my life a misery. But I pretended to like him. I'd ask how he was: "How's your leg, Herr Baumann?" and I'd smile at him. Everyone puts on an act some time. Every evening for years when I got back home, I'd pretend everything was great, no matter how bad the day had been. Everyone puts on an act some time. There's nothing to be ashamed of.

Silence.

Focus on what you're doing. I know it's difficult, because of the trains. Try not to hear them. Focus on your words and gestures.

He acts.

"It was built about 1502 by Master Peter Henlein, of Nuremberg ..." Focus on the words and gestures and you won't hear the trains.

He gives them the text. The man tries to learn his new lines. GOTTFRIED turns to the little GIRL. She's sitting on the floor, with her head between her hands and legs. The doll lies abandoned at her feet. GOTTFRIED caresses her head.

We have to wait a little bit more. We have to keep waiting for that man to come. When he does come, you take Walter and you say:

He lifts the doll.

"Be a good boy, Walter, say hello to the nice man." If you do it well, we'll see Mummy again. She'll come on one of those trains. If we do what they ask. We're not going to lose patience, are we Rebecca? We'll do it as many times as we have to, until Mummy comes back. We'll do it as often as we have to, won't we? If you can, I can too. And if I can't, if I lose my patience, you won't, will you? You'll keep on going right to the end. For Mummy. For Mummy and for me, if I lose my patience. "Be a good boy, Walter, and say hello to the nice man." And then a song. They want you to sing a song. That's nice, isn't it? Do you remember what Mummy used to sing at bedtime. A song to finish.

He sings her the song. She stands up, takes the doll and sings to it.

2   *The Boy at the Back*

Translated by David Johnston

Translator's Note

This is a play about translation, about how we interpret the world and how we represent what we see there. In particular, it focuses on the imaginative resources that we bring to our acts of interpretation, for better and for worse. The lives of others are here a source both of infinite fascination and the metaphorical road-kill on which carrion-crow writers feast. In that sense, the house, the home of others, becomes the embodiment of privacy, not merely as an extension of selfhood, but the theatre in which private lives play out the tragicomic incongruencies of the major and minor dramas that are the frequently hidden stuff of life. For that reason, French director François Ozon called his 2012 film adaptation of the play *Dans la maison* (*In the House*), which won the Golden Shell at the San Sebastián Film Festival that same year. And it was this idea of the secret life of the indoors that the 2015 BBC Radio 3 production (called in this case *The Boy at the Back*) re-created with its sense of fragmented and punctured enclosure, evoked atmospherically through its award-winning soundscape.

We observe, we decide what the object of that observation might mean, and we draw those decisions into the ambit of our own lives. If translation is a hermeneutics, set out here as a simple tripartite stage of knowledge-making, then so too are theatre and life itself. There is a moment in the play when Germán and Claudio, teacher and pupil respectively, are sitting looking into a block of apartments. They speculate on what the lives inside, silently exposed to the gaze of the outside world, might really be like. Hitchcock's *Rear Window* seems to be at the heart of this, but Hitchcock's is the gaze of the voyeur in search of the gratification that comes with sight of the heightened dramatic. This is more Pedro Almodóvar than Hitchcock – although, of course Almodóvar's scene, from *Mujeres al borde de un ataque de nervios* (*Women on the Verge of a Nervous Breakdown*), when Pepa gazes into apartment windows, is also designed as an act of homage to the great English film-maker. But Pepa's life is in chaos and viewing the privacy of others, now made public, gives her an opportunity to reflect on how the reassuringly normal and the blatantly strange invariably interweave in the fabric of the individual life.

DOI: 10.4324/9781003228301-4

Juan Mayorga's theatre invites us all to become translators of others. There is a particularly appropriate instance of this in *The Boy at the Back*, requiring the sort of hermeneutic analysis that is the foundation act of translation and of our interactions with others alike. The Spanish word *aburrido* can mean both "bored" and "boring," depending on how it is paired with one of the two verbs 'to be'. However, in the several usages relating to one particular character that occur in the play, the grammatical constructions in which the adjective is encased do not dictate a hard and fast meaning, leaving the question of interpretation open to other characters, the audience – and of course the translator, whom it leads into explicit consideration of the hidden channels between boredom as a coping strategy and the ossified assumptions that bulwark the predictability of the boring person. This is not the place to explore this in more detail, but the reader or spectator of this translation should be aware that, in the case of Mayorga's theatre in general, and of translation in particular, they are invariably in the stimulating, but also disturbing, presence of the provisional.

In that vein, some comment on where the action of the play actually takes place is called for here. The answer, of course, is in the imagination of the spectator. Notionally, however, it appears to be set in a Madrid that is only made vaguely explicit by almost passing references to the Prado and Real Madrid. The setting in Spain more generally is supported by character names and through, for example, various references to specific languages understood by the characters or particular cultural details of the urban landscape. In a sense, however, these are almost accidental and, while the setting is that of a large city, any future production of this translation might want to engage its spectators' imaginations differently by re-thinking how and where the action of the translated play is located. Both theatre and translation are, let us remember, actions that take place through constant negotiation and re-negotiation.

Finally, this is a translation written at a time when practitioners and audiences alike are increasingly sensitised to the representation of race, identity, gender, and sexuality. The Black Lives Matter and #MeToo movements have, in particular, coalesced around wider social justice movements that have further galvanised, and in many ways drawn together, different sets of identitarian politics. How we think about and try to understand the complex lives of others, of course, extends into the concern with the politics of recognition that, as noted elsewhere in this book, is one of the ethical touchstones of Juan Mayorga's theatre. In *Boy in the Back* there is a constant return to western views of China and the Chinese as a sort of mini exemplar of the ways in which we impose our own narcissistic perspectives on the lives of others. Racism rears its ugly face in this (sexism is also at work at different moments in this play). In times of increasing offence and outrage, we need to remember that a play can offer conflicting views almost simultaneously, that what is voiced on stage is not conceived of as a final statement on any issue, least of all in the multi-layered theatrical world of Juan Mayorga. Such views are both held up to the mirror of critical scrutiny and offset by the character by whom they are spoken. There is also an issue of translation here, and it is the duty of every translator – so that is of all of us – not to indulge in the manufactured naivety and artlessness of taking every word at face value.

The Boy at the Back (*El chico de la última fila*) first premiered under the direction of Helena Pimenta on 14 October 2006 in the theatre Tomás y Valiente in Fuenlabrada, Madrid. It was first published by the publishing house Ñaque in 2006. It won the prestigious Spanish theatre "Max" Prize, for best author in 2008, among other prizes. In 2012, the French director François Ozon adapted the play for his film, *Dans la maison* in 2012, which won several prizes as well.

Characters (in order of appearance):

Germán
Juana
Claudio
Rafa
Rafa Father
Ester

GERMÁN is reading a hand-written sheet of paper, which he is marking in red.
He is first amused and then outraged by what he reads. He marks the page with
a zero, puts it on the pile to his right and picks up another one from the pile on
the left. He reads the opening sentence and immediately marks an unmistakeable
zero on the page before putting it on the pile to the right. He lifts another sheet. He
is growing angry again as JUANA arrives.

GERMÁN:	So how did it go?
JUANA:	You could have come with me.
GERMÁN:	I haven't been to mass since I was fourteen.
JUANA:	It wasn't mass. It was a funeral.
GERMÁN:	Nobody I knew. I barely knew Bruno.
JUANA:	For company. Someone to talk to.

Silence.

I met the twins. They were just like Bruno had said. Shall I get changed and we'll go out and see a film? A comedy?

GERMÁN: You look fine the way you are. Let me finish this first. Take a look. Funnier than any comedy.

He returns to his reading. JUANA leafs through the pile on the right.

JUANA:	Nought. Three. Nought. Wow, a five. Two. Nought. That bad?
GERMÁN:	Bad's not the word. Worst year ever.
JUANA:	You said that last year. And the one before.

GERMÁN puts a one on the page, gives it to JUANA, and picks up another one.

GERMÁN: *(Reading)* "I watched TV on Saturday. I was tired on Sunday so just stayed in and did nothing." Full stop. They had half an hour to write that. Two sentences. Forty-eight hours in the life of a seventeen year-old. Saturday, TV, Sunday nothing.

He puts a zero on the page, hands it to JUANA and picks up another.

It's not like I asked them for a sonnet. I asked them to write about their weekend. To see if they could string together two sentences. Turns out they can't.

He reads.

"I don't like Sundays. I like Saturdays but this Saturday my father wouldn't let me go out and he took my phone."

He puts another large zero on the page and adds it to the pile on the right.

I tried to explain "point of view" to them. Talking to them about point of view is like talking to monkeys about the evolution of the species. I read the opening of *Moby Dick* to them, assuming they'd know what it's about because they'd have seen the film. It's a story narrated by a sailor, I say to them. "So what would happen if the story was told by a different character, Captain Ahab for example?" They sat in stunned silence, as if I'd asked them to solve the riddle of the sphinx. "All right, just write me an essay about what you did this weekend. You've got half an hour." And they give me this. What evil fate led me to this profession? Can you imagine anything worse than teaching literature to teenagers? I wanted to be a teacher because I imagined myself living and working with books. I'm living and working with horror. They are unbelievably ignorant – but that's not what the worst of it. The worst of it is the future they're going to create. These kids are the future. You've only got to meet them once and you lurch into despair. Catastrophists predict the return of the barbarians: well, they're back now. They're in our classrooms.

He lifts another sheet.

JUANA: I didn't know what to say to the twins. I was about to leave and one of them came over, I don't know which one, they're identical. She said they'll call by the gallery tomorrow to talk about the future. "To talk about the future." Are you listening …?

GERMÁN is lost in his reading.

What have you found?

Silence.

GERMÁN: *(Reading)*. "Last weekend, by Claudio García. On Saturday I went to Rafael Artola's house, to study. It was my idea, because I've been wanting to get inside there for ages. Every evening last summer I'd go to the park opposite his house and watch … one night his father almost spotted me. So on Friday, because Rafa had just failed Maths, I suggested an exchange: 'You help me with Philosophy and I'll help you with Maths.' It was a pretext, of course. I knew if he said yes, it would be in his house because where I live Rafa wouldn't be seen dead. So at eleven o'clock I rang the doorbell and up the house opened. I followed Rafa up to his room, which was exactly how I'd imagined it. I left him struggling with a trigonometry problem and said I was going for a Coca-Cola, so I could have a look round the house. I was finally inside, the house I'd imagined myself in so often. It's bigger than I thought. You could fit my house in four times over. Everything's clean and neat and tidy. 'Ok, enough for today,' I thought, and I was just about to head back to Rafa when I noticed it ... the smell ... the scent, that unmistakeable scent of a middle-class woman ... I followed the scent, into the lounge. There she was, sitting on a sofa, looking through some magazine on interior design, the lady of the house ... I watched her until she looked up, her eyes matched the colour of the sofa. 'Hello, you must be Carlos.' What a voice ... where do these women learn to talk like that? 'Claudio,' I answered, looking her straight in the eye. "Are you looking for the loo?' 'Kitchen.' She showed me where it was. 'Do you want ice?' I looked at her hands while she was getting the ice-cubes: wedding ring on the right, diamond on the left. She poured herself a martini. 'Help yourself,' she said. 'Make yourself at home.' She went back to the sofa and I went up to Rafa's room. I showed him how to do the trigonometry. He's going to need a lot more help if he's going to get through maths this year. To be continued."

Silence.

JUANA: Is that what it says, "to be continued?"
GERMÁN: He even uses brackets.

He gives it a seven and lifts another one.

JUANA: Seven?
GERMÁN: No spelling mistakes, good grammar, good vocab. It's hardly Dickens, but compared to the rest ... What would you give it?
JUANA: I'd take it to the Head.
GERMÁN: Why? Because Rafa's mother has sofa-coloured eyes?
JUANA: Who is he?
GERMÁN: I think he sits at the back, but I'm not sure. I don't know their names yet. It's only week two.
JUANA: So you give him a seven and that's all right? To be continued.
GERMÁN: Would you be happier if I gave him a six. It couldn't be any less.
JUANA: He's taking the piss and you give him a seven.
GERMÁN: He's taking the piss? Out of me?
JUANA: Out of everything, you, his friend Rafa, Rafa's mother

She reads.

"Claudio," I answered, looking her straight in the eye. Who does he think he is? Why don't you ask him to read it out in class, and watch the other lad, Rafa, how he feels about it. Unless Rafa ... is just a ...

She reads.

"Rafael Artola" … He might just be made up.

GERMÁN looks through the pile of essays on the left. He finds the one he's looking for.

GERMÁN: (*Reading*). "Saturday morning I studied maths with my friend Claudio. In the afternoon I went with my father to play basketball. It was a close game but we won and the whole team went out to celebrate. Sunday …"

He continues reading in silence. He gives it a five and puts it on the pile to the right.

JUANA: Five. He seems a nice lad. The other one gets a seven and he gets a five.

GERMÁN: It's Language and Literature, not Ethics or Religion.

He lifts another page.

JUANA: So you're not even a bit concerned? If I were you I'd have a word with him at least. Will you?

CLAUDIO: You wanted to see me?

GERMÁN: Pull up a seat.

CLAUDIO sits down.

GERMÁN: It's about that essay … the one about the weekend. I'm a bit concerned.

CLAUDIO: The punctuation? I'm not good with full stops and commas.

GERMÁN: The punctuation is okay.

CLAUDIO: I'm better at science, but want to do better this year in Lang. Lit.

GERMÁN: It's the content. It's another boy in the class and his family you're talking about. Someone might not like it.

CLAUDIO: You mean you? Or someone else? Did you give it to someone else to read?

GERMÁN: Not yet. I thought I might give it to the Head, to see what he says.

CLAUDIO: I didn't write it for the Head. I wrote it for you.

Silence.

GERMÁN: How do you think Rafa would feel if he read it …? (*He reads*) "because Rafa had just failed his Maths … when I noticed it … the smell … the scent, that unmistakeable scent of a middle-class woman." And it's not just what you say. It's what it implies. The tone. What if I made you read it out in front of the class? How would Rafa feel listening to that?

CLAUDIO: How would I know? I didn't write it for him either. You told us to write about the weekend. It was your idea.

Silence.

GERMÁN: Let's leave it there. I don't know what you thought you were do-ing, but whatever it was, let's move on.

CLAUDIO is about to go.

CLAUDIO: The adjectives exercise, can I hand it in now?
GERMÁN: It's not due until Monday.
CLAUDIO: I sat down and did it last night. That is if I understood what we were supposed to do. Write an essay using all the adjectives on the list. Right?

He produces the exercise.

GERMÁN: It's just something to get you writing.
CLAUDIO: I wasn't sure if you had to use the adjectives in the order they were on the list, or if you could swap them round. I did it in order.
GERMÁN: The order's not important, I said that.
CLAUDIO: I wasn't sure either if you could use other adjectives, apart from the ones on the list. And I had to repeat two. I used "dark" and "normal" twice.
GERMÁN: It's for Monday. Take another look at it.
CLAUDIO: I'd rather hand it in now. I'm doing maths this weekend.

He leaves the exercise and goes. Silence. GERMÁN picks it up and reads. JUANA is taking down an exhibition and wrapping the various pieces. GERMÁN arrives, puts down his briefcase and helps her.

JUANA: Do you think this is art for sickos?
GERMÁN: Art for sickos?
JUANA: That's the bottom line, according to the terrible twins. They had a good look at the accounts first though. They asked for the ac-counts, then they became art critics. If it was selling, they wouldn't think it was art for sickos, I'd an idea they were a bit on the con-servative side, just from the odd thing Bruno would say. Two peasants who've inherited an art gallery; it might just as well be a butcher's for all they care. How can they call this art for sickos?
GERMÁN: Well, you know what I think about exhibitions like this … I need to see faces. People. I feel an infinite solitude in the midst of …
JUANA: Stop quoting at me. I'm about to lose my job. So keep your theo-ries about modern art to yourself. All I need you to say is that those two are fucking philistines.
GERMÁN: They're going to close it – close the gallery?
JUANA: They've given me a month. A month to show it can make money. To find something they said will sell in an art gallery … like a pound of fucking sausages! And if I don't … they'll close it down, rent it out to someone else, and goodbye.

She continues her work in silence.

They touched the pieces ... with faces like spades. "Art for sickos." So how's your day been?

GERMÁN: All right. Oh, I spoke to that boy.

JUANA: And?

GERMÁN: We talked and he handed in the adjectives exercise, the one I set every year.

JUANA: Your Use the Following Adjectives one?

GERMÁN: Yes.

JUANA: And?

GERMÁN: Well, he's done it again. He turned it into the second instalment. It's what he said, remember: "to be continued?"

Silence.

JUANA: Do you have it with you?

GERMÁN: Yes.

Silence.

JUANA: But you don't want me to read it?

GERMÁN: I don't know if you should.

JUANA: I've been reading your pupils' work for thirty years.

GERMÁN: This is different though ... don't you think?

JUANA returns to her work. GERMÁN opens his briefcase, takes out the exercise and hands it to JUANA, who reads it.

CLAUDIO: Write an essay using the following adjectives: happy, same, our, exact, normal, dark, old, well, busy, little, bigger, fantastic.

Silence.

I went over to Rafael Artola on Monday and suggested studying together. He'd just done well in trig. and he was HAPPY, like he'd got the Nobel Prize, so he wanted to start that SAME afternoon. On the way we talked about the sorts of things boys of OUR age are supposed to talk about: girls, what we were going to study, that sort of thing, until we got to his house.

Why Rafa? Why choose him? Because he's the EXACT opposite to me. He's NORMAL. There are other ones in class who're the opposite as well, but last year there was something that made me notice him: I used to see him leaving school. and his parents would be waiting for him ... holding hands. The others would have died of shame if their parents came to pick them up or if anyone else had seen them. Not Rafa though, he was okay about it. And I thought: What sort of house does he live in: what sort of house does a normal family live in?

A woman opened the door, she was DARK, I couldn't tell how OLD she was, she could WELL have been fifteen or fifty-five. His mother was in the lounge, with a copy of *House and Garden* in one hand and a tape measure in the other. She didn't notice us at first because she was BUSY measuring a wall.

Rafa, she said, and gave him a kiss. And your friend ... Carlos, isn't it?

Claudio.

There was a photo in a frame on the television, beside a little green Chinese dragon, of when Rafa was LITTLE, with the holy family on the beach: mum, dad, little boy and a BIGGER girl. The dragon was looking at them as though it was going to pounce on them.

I got a VG in maths Rafa announced.

VG! FANTASTIC! Do you want something to eat?

The dark woman got us something to eat. His mother stayed in the lounge, with her magazine in one hand and her tape-measure in the other, floating like a ghost. To be continued.

JUANA: Awful.

GERMÁN: Awful?

JUANA: You don't think it's awful?

GERMÁN: Since when have you been living on the moral high ground? You, with some of the stuff you've had in here – that exhibition of blow-up dolls – you're horrified by a seventeen year-old thinking whatever he wants to think.

JUANA: It's not what he's thinking, it's what he's writing. That exhibition of blow-up dolls. You'd think I'd turned the gallery into a sex-shop. They'd been altered ... one looked like Stalin, the other one like Franco. They had a meaning. For anyone who cared to look. You should speak to the Head.

GERMÁN: If I did, the boy would be suspended, or expelled, or locked up, or shot. What good would that do?

JUANA: Then your colleagues, his other teachers. And the parents, that goes without saying, you should talk to the parents.

GERMÁN: So they stop him coming to their house?

JUANA: Claudio's parents, the writer. That boy needs a psychiatrist. He could be dangerous. He could be capable of anything. You need to put a stop to this before it's too late.

GERMÁN: He's an angry kid, that's all. At odds with the world. Who can blame him? Better dealing with anger like this than setting fire to cars. It's his classmates who're terrifying. They're the dangerous ones. No respect for anything, for spelling, or grammar or common sense. Apart from Claudio, the ones who make fewest mistakes are two Chinese girls who've only been in the country six months. That last time I organised a theatre trip, I was humiliated right through the whole performance. And if you even dare look sideways at them, then every educationalist in the country is down on you like a ton of bricks.

JUANA: You talk about them like they were all the same. Get to know them, put your prejudice to one side, don't condemn them out of hand.

GERMÁN: Educationalists?

JUANA: Very funny.

She looks at CLAUDIO's exercise.

Either he's got a problem or he's trying to get your attention. What's he like?

GERMÁN: Sits at the back. Doesn't speak. Doesn't join in. Doesn't make trouble, Middle of the road in everything except maths.

JUANA: So you've asked about him.

GERMÁN: I think he's good at maths. Are we going or what?

JUANA: They give him the run of their house and he … He's shameless.

GERMÁN: He's strange. God knows, he has every right to be.

JUANA: Did you used to sit at the back?

GERMÁN: Best place to sit. No-one sees you, but you see everyone.

JUANA: What if someone finds these essays, you'll get the blame.

GERMÁN: Blame for what?

JUANA: Well, you've made yourself his accomplice.

GERMÁN: Accomplice in what?

JUANA: If you can't see it, I can't make you.

She takes down another piece and looks at it.

Art for sickos.

GERMÁN: I want to talk to your parents. Would you prefer me to call them or will you tell them I want to see them?

CLAUDIO: You can call them. She's not there and he never answers.

Silence. GERMÁN produces the exercise with the adjectives.

GERMÁN: "Well" isn't an adjective here, it's an adverb. (*He reads*) A woman opened the door, she was DARK, I couldn't tell how OLD she was, she could WELL have been fifteen or fifty-five. "Well" modifies "could," so it's an adverb. As for style, it's a hotchpotch between Hermann Hesse and Jules Verne. It's understandable at your age, you read anything you get your hands on.

He takes a book out of his briefcase.

This isn't a library book, it's my personal copy, so no underlining, no turning down the pages and don't leave it open face down.

CLAUDIO: All that? Do you not have anything shorter?

GERMÁN: Read the first page, if you're not interested, give it back.

CLAUDIO takes out some sheets of paper. He leaves them in front of GERMÁN.

CLAUDIO: If you're not interested, give it back.

He sits down at RAFA's desk, in front of the maths exercises. GERMÁN reads the sheets of paper.

RAFA:	So why do you have to change the sign?
CLAUDIO:	Because you've put it on the wrong side of the equals.
RAFA:	So what was it doing before?
CLAUDIO:	Multiplying.
RAFA:	Multiplying?
CLAUDIO:	Times three.

RAFA gazes at the problem, perplexed.

RAFA FATHER:	You must be Carlos.
CLAUDIO:	Claudio.

RAFA FATHER is wearing a tracksuit. He is still out of breath and struggles to speak. He offers his hand to CLAUDIO.

RAFA FATHER: Team work. Sharing information. Distribution of responsibilities. Delegation. I pass to you when you're under the hoop, you pass to me when I'm free of my marker. The game is on at eight, Grizzlies and Clippers. Will I phone for a pizza, Rafa? Join us ... Claudio?

GERMÁN stops reading.

This is a parody?

CLAUDIO:	A what?
GERMÁN:	The way you describe him coming in, how he speaks ... you're exaggerating to make the reader laugh.
CLAUDIO:	I'm not exaggerating. That's what he's like.
GERMÁN:	He can't be like that.
CLAUDIO:	I swear.
GERMÁN:	It's realistic?
CLAUDIO:	Realistic?
GERMÁN:	As though you were recording everything with a hidden camera. That's what you're trying to do? Fly on the wall. Or are you stylizing it?
CLAUDIO:	Stylizing?
GERMÁN:	Are you writing what you see or are you changing it?
CLAUDIO:	I don't include everything. I don't put the colour of the tracksuit. I don't care, blue ... green ...

Silence.

GERMÁN:	Why so much in the present tense? Why do you keep slipping into the present?
CLAUDIO:	It's like being there again.

Silence. GERMÁN goes back to his reading.

RAFA FATHER: Join us ... Claudio?

CLAUDIO: I accept the tracksuit's invitation. An hour later we're sitting with him in the lounge, although I don't recognise him at first, he looks different without his tracksuit, but I can tell it's him because of the way he takes over the remote control: head of the house. He supports the Grizzlies. There's a Korean playing for the Clippers, which makes us talk about China. In the second half the mother comes in, to watch the game or maybe to find out about China. In the fifteenth minute the Grizzlies power forward is sent off for five personal fouls and at the same time the father gets a phone call.

ESTER: The airport at this time, what a nuisance.

RAFA FATHER: Work before leisure.

CLAUDIO: Without him the Grizzlies lose the game, even though they had 52 per cent possession, according to the commentator's figures. It's all because, in his opinion, they had their star player sent off. To be continued.

Silence.

GERMÁN: Good, pretty good, if all you want is to make people laugh at your characters. Not much ambition in that, though, is there? The first thing a writer should ask himself is who am I writing for? Who are you writing for? It's easy to shine a light on the worst of everything, to give your mediocre readers something to feel superior to. It's easy to take someone and look at their ridiculous side. What's difficult is to look at them close up, without prejudice, without condemning them out of hand. To find their reasons, their hurt, their small hopes, their despair. To show the beauty of human pain ... only the true artist sees that.

He gives him another book. CLAUDIO goes off to read and write.

JUANA: What exactly are you trying to do?

GERMÁN: Teach him.

JUANA: Teach him what?

GERMÁN: Literature. And through literature, other things.

JUANA: Literature doesn't teach anything.

GERMÁN: Does it not?

JUANA: *Bartleby the Scribe*, the nutcase that shot John Lennon had it in his pocket. What did literature teach him?

GERMÁN: It was *The Catcher in the Rye*.

JUANA:	Same difference. The point is that literature doesn't teach anything. It doesn't make us better people.
GERMÁN:	Unlike your exhibitions. People leave them genuinely improved. That is if they manage to find the exit.
JUANA:	My exhibitions don't make you a better person either. Art doesn't teach you anything.

CLAUDIO gives some pages to GERMÁN. He reads them sitting beside JUANA.

RAFA:	Why change the sign?
CLAUDIO:	Because you've got it on the wrong side of the equals.
RAFA:	So what was it doing before?
CLAUDIO:	Before it wasn't adding. Now it's multiplying.
RAFA:	Multiplying, how?
CLAUDIO:	Multiplying by three. Rafa looks glumly at the exercise. Suddenly an adult dressed in sports clothes comes into the room.
RAFA FATHER:	Carlos?
CLAUDIO:	Claudio.
RAFA FATHER:	Teamwork. I pass to you when you're under the basket, you pass to me when I'm free of my marker. They Grizzlies games is on. Will I phone for a pizza, Rafa? Join us …?
CLAUDIO:	Claudio.
RAFA FATHER:	But first things first, eh? Work before leisure. I'm going to jump in the shower.
CLAUDIO:	So while one Rafa struggles with the maths, I imagine the other Rafa jumping in the shower. An hour later all three of us, the two Rafas and me, are on the sofa eating a Four Seasons pizza, while the Grizzlies are all over the Clippers. The Clippers have a player from Korea.
RAFA FATHER:	There are two types of Chinese …
CLAUDIO:	He spent a week in China ten years ago. He knows everything there is to know about China.
RAFA FATHER:	The worst thing you can say to a Chinese …
CLAUDIO:	In the second minute of the second half, the Grizzlies shooting guard scores three points and the Rafas go crazy. In the fourth minute, Ester sits down to watch the game, but with no real interest so she opens issue 215 of "House and Garden," and gazes at a Victorian-style mansion, a converted Dutch windmill, Catherine Zeta-Jones' holiday home in Mallorca, a whole procession of houses that she'll never own … In the seventh minute she takes out a pencil and does a sketch of some building work she'd like done, she has a whole notebook full of sketches, she spends the whole day in the house but she's not happy with it and there are lots of home improvements she wants to do even though she hates the idea of having workmen trampling through the place. In the tenth minute she bites her pencil and looks into space:

the great question: how can she fit another bathroom in? In the twelfth minute, Rafa Father suggests buying a plasma TV. In the fifteenth minute the Grizzlies shooting guard is sent off for five personal fouls, much to the disgust of the Rafas who give him a standing ovation as he leaves the court, and why shouldn't they, his match statistics are fabulous.

RAFA FATHER: Thirty points, seven assists, four rebounds ...

CLAUDIO: The phone. Rafa Father looks at his watch. He almost decides to let it ring.

RAFA FATHER: *(Answering)* Yes ... I can hear it in your voice. Have you seen a doctor? What time does he get in?

He takes ESTER's pencil to note the details.

BA0423, ten fifteen, terminal two ... A little board with his name? Huang Li, Li or Lee, double e? He's bound to speak English, no? ... the hotel at the business park. Sure, I'll take him somewhere, maybe a Spanish restaurant? Don't worry, take it easy. No problem.

He hands the phone back to ESTER.

I have to go to the airport to pick up a client.

ESTER: At this time of night. That's a nuisance.

RAFA FATHER: Work before pleasure. I might have to take him to dinner, Or maybe not, and I'll be back in a couple of hours.

ESTER: Chinese?

RAFA FATHER: Here to sign a contract, to extend it. Mariano was going to meet him, but he's got 'flu.

ESTER: What time does he get in?

RAFA FATHER: Quarter past ten.

ESTER: You've plenty of time.

CLAUDIO: He sits down to watch the last of the game, but he's distracted now and doesn't enjoy it.

RAFA FATHER: What should I wear? Business suit or go casual?

CLAUDIO: He goes off to meet the Chinese visitor, the Clippers fight back and in the last second steal the game thanks to a really bad decision by the referee.

ESTER: So, who won?

CLAUDIO: To be continued.

JUANA: He's toying with you. The second version is even more cruel. You're trying to teach him and he's running rings round you.

GERMÁN: So what's next, them gossiping about the neighbours? We know all about the infinite mediocrity of the middle class. We know the middle class is ugly, banal, stupid. So was the Russian aristocracy, but Tolstoy still wrote *Anna Karenina.* And Dostoevsky, do you know what his secret was? He turned vulgar people into unforgettable characters. But you're a cartoonist. Is that what you want to do, write caricatures?

CLAUDIO: You told me to look at them close up. The closer I get, the worse it gets. I write what I see.

GERMÁN: If that's all you see, then don't bother!

He flings three books on to the table.

Dickens! Chekhov! Cervantes!

JUANA: What do you think?

She shows him a catalogue. GERMÁN is lost for words.

GERMÁN: It's … interesting.

JUANA: But imagine you're people. Will people buy them?

GERMÁN: Well, they're sort of normal things … a kitchen clock, an electric fan …

JUANA: They are normal things, but changed so as to create a sense of strangeness. Look, the clock has thirteen numbers. The artist has intervened in our domestic space highlighting those features we've grown so accustomed to that we don't even notice any more. That's how he shows our lives growing mechanical, and he challenges the frontiers between the internal and the external, between the private and public.

GERMÁN looks at the catalogue, lost for words.

And this one? Listen.

She gives him a set of headphones, which he puts on. Silence. He takes them off, confused.

GERMÁN: What's it supposed to be?

JUANA: Listen.

She puts the headphones back on him.

JUANA: Verbal painting. It's the voice of the painter, describing the picture. The spectator, or the listener, imagines it. So the spectator becomes a sort of co-creator who transfers the world of their imagination onto the empty wall. The artist suggests you should hang the headphones on a wall, or in an empty frame. To mock the cultural industries with their obsession with product, he opts for poetic, ephemeral, non-material interventions. The paintings really exist, or they did, but as soon as the painter recorded his descriptions, he destroyed them. Thirteen watercolours.

GERMÁN removes the headphones.

GERMÁN: I couldn't see anything. Why was he speaking English? Do you need a degree in languages to enjoy art nowadays? And he had a strange accent.

JUANA: He's Chilean. From Valparaiso.

GERMÁN: Honestly, I can't see it selling. I wouldn't buy it. Or if I did, I'd get a pirate copy from the market.

JUANA: You're not taking me seriously. I've got twenty days. Twenty days and I'm out.

GERMÁN: Look, if it meant saving the gallery, I'd let you put me in the window, Happily. But don't ask me to accept this sort of nonsense.

JUANA snatches back the catalogue, the headphones and the other things which she had intended to show GERMÁN, but which she no longer will. GERMÁN takes an essay from his briefcase.

GERMÁN: Do you want to read it?

JUANA makes no reply, but finally comes over to read.

RAFA: *(To CLAUDIO, reading from his notes).*
              "Your father has been given a traffic fine. He considers it unjust and is contemplating not paying it. What would Socrates advise?"

GERMÁN: What on earth's this?

CLAUDIO: Philosophy. The teacher wants to prove how useful philosophy is. He gives us a case, which he calls a moral dilemma, and then tells us about Plato or Hegel or whoever. Everyone tries to convince us that what they teach is useful. Everyone except the maths teacher. He told us on day one that maths is useless.

GERMÁN: Maths is important. So's philosophy. Although neither of them has any answer for the really big question.

CLAUDIO: What really big question?

GERMÁN: Tolstoy or Dostoevsky? That's the really big question, because it contains every other possible question.

RAFA: Socrates was innocent, and they ordered him to drink hemlock. A friend told him to run away. Socrates replied: "Athens has fed me, it's given me shelter, it's educated me. I can't obey Athens when it suits me and disobey her when it doesn't." And he knocked it back. Get it?

CLAUDIO: I don't get philosophy; like Rafa doesn't get maths.

RAFA: The square root of minus one. I can't get my head around that.

CLAUDIO: It's not a real number. That's why it's called an imaginary number: like the root of minus five, the root of minus seven … They only exist in your head. But they can be added up or multiplied … or drawn! You can do things with them even though they don't exist.

RAFA: I can't memorise the formulas. I learn them and then they go out of my head.

CLAUDIO: It's not about memorising. It's about understanding.

He sets him three exercises.

I set him three exercises, an easy one to encourage him, another one not so easy, and finally a hard one so he gets bogged down. While he's battling with his imaginary numbers, I take a walk round the house. There are four Paul Klee watercolours in the hall – reproductions.

ESTER:	What time did you get back? I didn't hear you come in.
RAFA FATHER:	We were talking half the night. Huang, or Johnny as we call him, is pretty open, I mean for a Chinese. A couple of bottles of red helped. He's not happy with us. He thinks we don't respect him. He was a bit off at the start, as though he was annoyed that it was me picking him up instead of Mariano. He didn't believe the 'flu thing.
CLAUDIO:	I needed somewhere I could listen without being seen. If I could I'd have become that fly on the wall. But I can't become a fly, so the next best thing is to go into the hall and look at the Klee reproductions, with my ears pricked up.
RAFA FATHER:	We talked about working together. He's not happy with the cut we give him. He wants 15 per cent.
ESTER:	I don't understand.
RAFA FATHER:	I've been mulling it over all day … why not take the plunge now? Go out on my own.
ESTER:	But you like the company, you're doing well.
RAFA FATHER:	I'm doing well, but I've hit a ceiling. All my ideas go through Mariano, and he picks up the plaudits.
ESTER:	You always said teamwork was your style.
RAFA FATHER:	Teamwork, yes, but in a team there are passers and scorers. I've spent too many years sweating into my shirt so that others get the glory. I was talking to Johnny about the opportunities out there …
ESTER:	And he was happy to talk about it, so openly?
RAFA FATHER:	They never talk openly. But if I give him 15 per cent he'll be my man in China. Someone I can trust. Well trust, not that you can ever trust the Chinese, they're two-faced like no one else, and he'll find some way of screwing 20 per cent from me, but even so. Transport at current costs would hardly even amount to 10 per cent. The real costs are in the labour, but it's dirt cheap there. Johnny showed me a picture of a shop window with those dolls, you know Barbies: "Thlee eulos." You'd get more than three times that for a Barbie here.
ESTER:	But leaving the company … wouldn't that be risky?
RAFA FATHER:	Well, until we've set the whole thing up, I would stay on, there's no reason why they have to know. I'd be fair, I'd work on a different line. We email the plans to Johnny, we say one hundred like this for whatever date, and he always gets them. It's like having a factory without any workers. Even easier: you send him a photo and they copy it. Not an exact reproduction, that would be illegal, so a few modifications here and there.
ESTER:	That sounds good.
RAFA FATHER:	Of course, there'd be some outlay at the beginning. An investment.
ESTER:	Outlay?

RAFA FATHER:	I've looked at the figures and with what we've got put aside and a small loan …
ESTER:	And the work in the house?
RAFA FATHER:	But you said we don't even have enough to get the lounge done.
ESTER:	Concha was telling me about some Romanians who're good workers, cheap. Cash in hand.
RAFA FATHER:	I know how much it means to you.
ESTER:	And just when I'd decided to have the terrace closed off.
RAFA FATHER:	Look, Ester, at my age I need something to aim for. I'm standing still. I remember the energy I used to have; not so long ago, I was ready to take on the whole world. I think we lack drive. I look at what my boss does and I think to myself why not me. I want to be my own boss. You could help me. Choosing products, setting up contacts … We've got to do the rounds of the shops, talk to traders, see what they need, and then sell them the idea: I'll get you what you have in the window, but ten times cheaper.
ESTER:	You want me to work for you?
RAFA FATHER:	I'm saying we could work together.
ESTER:	You know I was thinking of going back to finish my degree. I've only got one module outstanding, and then I could go into practice. Now the kids are grown up.
RAFA FATHER:	This would be something of ours. Ours. If it goes well, and there's no reason why it shouldn't, you could do more than redesign the lounge. You could have a new house.

Silence.

ESTER:	Would you like some olives?
RAFA FATHER:	Okay.

ESTER goes out. She meets CLAUDIO who is looking at the pictures.

CLAUDIO:	They all end in "ung." "*Zerstörung,*" "*Unterbrechung,*" "*Hoffnung,*" "*Rettung.*"

ESTER goes back into the lounge with two drinks and a bowl of olives.

ESTER:	That boy, does he not get on your nerves here every evening?
RAFA FATHER:	He seems sensible enough, sort of shy.
ESTER:	That lost look of his, does it not make you uncomfortable?
JUANA:	Is this what he really hears, or is he imagining it? Do they really talk about him in front him?
GERMÁN:	They're not in front of him. He's in the hall looking at pictures.
JUANA:	And he can hear them from there?

GERMÁN:	The odd sentence ... and he can see them, their expressions, their gestures ...
ESTER:	He's got an exam next week. If he doesn't pass, we should get him a private tutor.
RAFA FATHER:	Claudio?
ESTER:	A proper tutor, Not someone who's as clueless as he is.
RAFA FATHER:	He seems a bit lost that boy. This matters to him. I don't think he has many friends.
ESTER:	We need to put our own son first. What's best for him.
RAFA FATHER:	Of course we should. Listen, I've been thinking about a name. It's got to be memorable and easy to pronounce in any language. And the logo has to be recognizable to everyone. Like the apple.

Silence. ESTER thinks about the apple.

ESTER:	What apple? Oh, that apple!
RAFA FATHER:	That's it. Shall I email Johnny and tell him we're on? Trust me, Ester, it's now or never.
ESTER:	I'm not sure, Rafa, I'm really not. Nice these olives, aren't they?
JUANA:	He's starting to remind me of my cousin from Alicante, you meet him at all the weddings and he tells you the family gossip. A lot of people love that, poking around in other people's lives. TV's full of it.

Pushing the essay away.

	He's starting to bore me.
GERMÁN:	You're losing the surprise effect. Seeing an outsider in the house, sharing his point of view, it's not enough any more. You're starting to be like that boring cousin who tells you all the family gossip. If I was somebody who was reading the book ...
CLAUDIO:	Is somebody? Reading it? I don't mind. Show it to anyone you like.
GERMÁN:	It's not worth showing to anyone. I'm not going to waste anyone's time with this.
CLAUDIO:	If it's not worth it, then don't.
GERMÁN:	I won't, but if somebody did read it like a novel, there are things missing, uncertainty, conflict ...
ESTER:	Has your friend gone?
RAFA:	He had to get his bus.
ESTER:	Olive?
RAFA FATHER:	Your mother and I, we think what you're doing with that boy is very kind. When you get the opportunity to help someone, you should.

RAFA: He's helping me too.

RAFA FATHER: In exchange. He helps you with maths and you help him with philosophy.

ESTER: Have you met his family?

RAFA: I don't know very much about him. He doesn't say a lot. He hardly speaks to anyone at school.

RAFA FATHER: That's not good. Tell your friends to talk to him.

RAFA: It's him that doesn't talk.

CLAUDIO: Conflict?

GERMÁN: A character wants something but things stand in the way. Rivals, enemies. Antagonists. Ulysses wants to go home, but the Cyclops wants to kill him, Calypso kidnaps him, the sirens hypnotise him … Sometimes conflict isn't the hero, or other people, but inside yourself. I don't mean choices between re-doing the lounge or setting up a business in China. I mean the struggles of the heart. Achilles: do I go to Troy or do I stay with my beloved Deidamia? So that the reader wonders whether the hero will overcome these obstacles and succeed. That's the golden question: the question you have to plant in the reader's mind: what's going to happen? You don't let the reader relax, you keep him on tenterhooks. The reader is like Scheherazade's sultan: if you bore me, I'll cut your head off. But tell me a good story, and I'll give you my heart. The sultan and everyone else. People need stories. Life's not worth living without them.

Silence.

CLAUDIO: Thank you, master.

GERMÁN: Don't call me master. And another thing: you've got to participate in class. When I call for volunteers or ask a question. open your mouth once in a while. Otherwise I'll have to fail you.

CLAUDIO is about to go. He turns round.

CLAUDIO: We've a maths test on Wednesday. Rafa won't pass, and if he doesn't they'll get him a private tutor and get rid of me. We need to get hold of the paper.

GERMÁN: You're asking me to steal the paper?

CLAUDIO: There's no other way. He can't make head or tail of imaginary numbers.

Silence.

GERMÁN: You don't actually need to be there to write, Use your imagination.

CLAUDIO: I've tried, but it doesn't work. I need to see them. From the staff room, the maths cupboard, the photocopier, wherever. Unless you want them to get rid of me.

RAFA FATHER:	Eighty out of a hundred! See what you can do when you try!

RAFA and RAFA FATHER do a high five.

	Eighty out of a hundred! What did you get, Claudio?
CLAUDIO:	Sixty-five.
RAFA FATHER:	Pretty good too. Eighty! We'll have to celebrate. Does your mother know? Ester, eighty out of a hundred in the maths test.

RAFA and RAFA FATHER do a high five.

CLAUDIO:	My sixty-five seems pretty good to them too. They begin thinking of me as one of the team.
RAFA:	Why don't you come this Saturday? We play every Saturday, in the sports centre, from 6 to 8. They're great lads, you'd get on well with them.
RAFA FATHER:	Come on, it'll be great. We don't take ourselves too seriously.
CLAUDIO:	Thanks, but I've other things arranged. As I walk away from the house I try and picture myself and my father bouncing a ball together and throwing it through a hoop with a little net hanging from it. I can't, I can't picture myself and my father bouncing a ball together and throwing it through a hoop with a little net hanging from it. But that's what they do, Rafa son and Rafa father, every Saturday afternoon in life, and they're happy when the ball goes in and are upset when it doesn't. And what about her, what does she do when they're doing that? So Saturday at half past five I'm sitting on the bench in the park where I watched them from this summer. At quarter to six the athletes leave the house. I ring the bell at six – with its naff ding dong sound. The door opens and there she is, the most bored woman in the world.
ESTER:	So you changed your mind? They've just gone. I'll call them and they'll come back for you.
CLAUDIO:	No thanks, I left my book here yesterday. My maths book.
ESTER:	I haven't seen it. Come in and look.
CLAUDIO:	She takes me to Rafa's room. The book isn't there unsurprisingly.
ESTER:	I'll ask Eliana on Monday if she's seen it.
CLAUDIO:	My mother had ones very like those, I say, pointing to her earrings. She left when I was nine. She couldn't stick my father. I don't suppose she could stick me either. My words hit the target. Never fails, I tell them about my mother, and I have people eating out of my hand. It creates a bond. They want to make it up to me. They want to mother me.
ESTER:	Would you like a coke?
CLAUDIO:	She has a martini. We talk about Rafa, about maths, about how bad she is at maths. She studied law.

ESTER:	I gave it up to have children. But now they're growing up I thought I might do the module I need to finish.
CLAUDIO:	At eight o'clock I think that's enough, we'll continue next Saturday. In the hall I stop in front of the Klees – *Zerstörung, Unterbrechung, Hoffnung, Rettung*.
ESTER:	Pretty, aren't they?
CLAUDIO:	They don't speak German. They've no idea what they have in their house. They bought them for the wall. When they re-paint, they'll buy new pictures. These angels are extraordinary.
ESTER:	You think they're angels? I never thought of that.
CLAUDIO:	They're angels, but like they were painted by a child. Their wings are like claws. They're not flying, they're being carried in the wind. *Zerstörung* means destruction. *Unterbrechung*, interruption, *Hoffnung*, hope, *Rettung* salvation. I leave the house at ten past eight. Just after half past eight I'm in the park watching the Rafas come home. They're happy, like they'd won the game. To be continued.
JUANA:	This is not going to end well. It's going to end badly.
GERMÁN:	What on earth are you playing at?
CLAUDIO:	A character wants something and there are obstacles. Conflict. The golden question: what happens next?
GERMÁN:	So what does? You meet her in some cheap hotel?
CLAUDIO:	No. It's got to be in the house. Everything has to happen in the house.
JUANA:	Rein him in before he crashes. Imagine the game's called off and they find them together on the sofa, the mother and the son's friend.
GERMÁN:	He doesn't mention a sofa. You've made that up.
JUANA:	Wherever, him with his coke and her with her martini. Rafa would kill him.
GERMÁN:	Which Rafa?
JUANA:	Both Rafas. They'd both kill him.
GERMÁN:	So you are taking it at face value. Surely you can tell half of it's made up. He's fantasising.
JUANA:	He's fantasising? Well if he is, it's pretty good fantasising. It's believable.
GERMÁN:	He's a good story teller. I've never had a pupil like him before. I don't want him to know it, but with a bit of guidance he could … Sometimes when I'm talking, I think he's the only one listening … I get the impression he's the only one who understands what I'm saying.
JUANA:	The only one?
GERMÁN:	The only pupil.
JUANA:	Rafa's your pupil too. Do you not have some responsibility towards him?

GERMÁN: Of course I do.

JUANA: You think it's wonderful because you think you've discovered Kafka? There he is at the back, listening open-mouthed. I've no idea if he is Kafka. But I do know it's going to end badly. This is one of those stories where everyone ends up losing.

GERMÁN: I don't think you know what you're getting yourself into. What on earth is this meant to be? A middle-class satire? A parody of some cheap love story? A *Bildungsroman*?

CLAUDIO: A what?

GERMÁN: I thought you could speak German All that *Zerstörung, Hoffnung* stuff …

CLAUDIO: I asked my father. He lived in Berlin when he was young. He told me who Paul Klee was as well.

GERMÁN: Then he'd be able to tell you that a *Bildungsroman* is a novel that describes the emotional development of a boy or young man. That's what I thought this was, the rites of passage from boy to man. But I'm not sure any more what you're doing. Do you know what you're doing?

CLAUDIO: I'm doing what you tell me to, master.

GERMÁN: I didn't tell you to poke fun at some frustrated woman old enough to be your mother. And don't call me master.

            Silence.

            Sixty-five in maths. Your father must be proud of you. Not so good in other subjects though. You haven't been to History for days now. Or English. Why are you not going to your English classes?

CLAUDIO: I don't see the point.

GERMÁN: And History?

CLAUDIO: Even less.

GERMÁN: So if you're not in class, where are you?

CLAUDIO: In the library, writing.

GERMÁN: Does your father know?

CLAUDIO: My father knows everything.

GERMÁN: And what does he say?

CLAUDIO: My father doesn't say anything.

GERMÁN: I'd like to meet him. Why don't you tell him to come and see me?

CLAUDIO: My father isn't a character in this story. My father doesn't appear.

            He hands some pages to GERMÁN, who gives him a book. They each go off to read. GERMÁN puts the pages in his briefcase. As soon as GERMÁN disappears, JUANA opens the briefcase, takes out the pages, and begins to read. GERMÁN surprises her reading them.

JUANA: What gets me is …

GERMÁN: What gets you?

JUANA: What gets me is how he treats poor Rafa.

GERMÁN: Well, he's teaching him maths, he got him 80 per cent He's harder on her. An hour on the phone with her friend Concha discussing the price per square metre. That's some topic: the price per square metre. Might we have something a little bit more metaphysical, please!

He pulls a book from his shelves.

JUANA: *The Magic Mountain*. Really? He's only 17?

GERMÁN: I read it when I was 14.

JUANA: I'd give him *The Three Musketeers*, maybe that would help. Pointless dialogue, talking about nothing. … This is getting like … absurd theatre. Her gabbling on the phone while the father's tuning the plasma TV while the son reads the instructions to him … in German, because they can't find the other ones, and none of them speak German. Is that what he's trying to say. That their lives are absurd? They're a normal family.

GERMÁN: What is a normal family? Is there not something abnormal, monstruous even, in the very idea of a family?

JUANA: His handwriting's changing. Less childish. He's doing a lot of writing.

GERMÁN: I reckon there's about fifty pages.

JUANA: Please tell me you're not thinking about trying to get it published. Sending it into some competition or other. Don't do that.

GERMÁN: It's better than most things that get published today. Agile dialogue, sparky situations … Nothing that can't be found in a dozen or so TV programmes. Is that what you want, to be a TV writer? The writing's lazy, you can feel it, the laziness.

He takes his pen to it.

The red circles are clichés. Good going: twelve clichés in three pages. "A passing look of impatience flits over her face." A million writers have said that before you. The word pathetic appears three times. What's pathetic is your vocabulary. And that insistence on every last detail. Trust the reader to use their imagination. Don't describe how your character is feeling, let us get to know them through their actions. Show not tell. I'm still worried about Rafa Son. Each character has to be necessary. Rafa only exists as a ploy to Claudio. But not just him, Rafa Father and Ester are buried under the voice of the narrator. You're not that interesting, stay in the background so we can see them. The scene should begin when the father comes in with the box Made in China, and end on what Claudio says to Ester when they're on their own: "The day my mother left, my father threw the television through the window." That's the secret of a good scene, allow the action to build up at its own pace, and then suddenly, bang. The opening sentence is fantastic, the best you've ever written, but it doesn't work here.

He scores it out.

The final paragraph is just drivel.

He scores it out.

You want to imitate Poe, but all these pages put together aren't worth one of Poe's commas.

He gives the pages back to CLAUDIO, covered in red marks.

CLAUDIO:	If you know how to do it, why don't you?
GERMÁN:	I tried. Years ago. Until I realised I wasn't good enough. Neither are you. But you might be. You have a gift. Respect that gift and you might be a writer one day.

Silence.

There's something we still haven't talked about. We've avoided it up to now, but we can't keep putting it off. The title. The title commits. The title establishes a pact with the reader. The title directs the reader towards what needs to be judged, what needs to be noticed. *War and Peace. The Brothers Karamazov.* What about *The Boy at the Back*?

Silence.

CLAUDIO: I thought *Imaginary Numbers*.

Silence.

GERMÁN: The title's not the place for literature, the literature missing from the rest of the book. *Crime and Punishment. Uncle Vanya.*

CLAUDIO: I like it. *Imaginary Numbers*.

GERMÁN: We'll leave it there. You look tired. You fell asleep in class this morning. Were you bored?

CLAUDIO: I was up all night, writing.

He gives GERMÁN some pages. In return he receives The Magic Mountain.

Maybe we should do this someplace else. The others are beginning to talk. Why does he always stay behind? People have a lot of imagination.

He goes. GERMÁN reads the pages.

CLAUDIO: They're so happy with eighty out of a hundred they invite me to dinner. The father makes the starter – soup he learned in China.

RAFA FATHER:	They cook everything. I was in a restaurant right beside the Wall and they brought a little slice of something, lovely, but you couldn't tell if it was fish or meat. Do you know what it was? The web off a duck's foot.
RAFA:	There are two Chinese girls in our class.
CLAUDIO:	Kafka's got a story called "The Building of the Great Wall of China." Germán lent it to me, you know, the literature teacher.
ESTER:	Rafa says he's a bit of an oddball, never happy with anything.
CLAUDIO:	Eliana brings in the main course. Ester glares at her. Eliana takes away the dirty dishes in silence.
RAFA FATHER:	What's wrong?
ESTER:	She knows what's wrong.
RAFA FATHER:	What?
ESTER:	My suede coat, I put it in a bag with other things for the church. Well, on Sunday, I go into town with Concha and there's Eliana …

JUANA comes in. GERMÁN looks up.

JUANA:	I thought we were going to have lunch together.
GERMÁN:	We lost all track of time talking about the title. Do you know what he wants to call it? *Imaginary Numbers.* I'm trying to get the idea out of his head, although you know what a mule he can be … What's wrong with you?
JUANA:	When I went in this morning there was a For Rent sign. I called them and said they'd given me a month. And whoever it was, Rosario or Eugenia, I can never tell the difference, said yes, I'd got to the 30th. But the fact is the sign's up already.
GERMÁN:	It's to put pressure on you. Ignore it. They've made you a promise.
JUANA:	Perhaps the problem isn't what we're selling. I told Bruno hundreds of times it's the name. The Minotaur's Labyrinth. It doesn't exactly draw people in. What do you think of this?

She takes something out of a box.

GERMÁN:	It's like a bag.
JUANA:	It is a bag. African crafts. And there are backpacks, purses …
GERMÁN:	It's nice.
JUANA:	Bah.
GERMÁN:	Why bah. It is nice.
JUANA:	I don't want to be a shopkeeper.
GERMÁN:	What's wrong with being a shopkeeper? At least shopkeepers know exactly what they're selling: a pound of sugar, two yards of fabric, a leather backpack … They know what they're selling.
JUANA:	Bah.

She sits down beside GERMÁN to read.

ESTER:	Well, on Sunday, I go into town with Concha and there's Eliana wearing it. It was Concha who said straightaway is that not your coat?
RAFA FATHER:	It's her day off.
ESTER:	Did you hear what I said, Rafa? She was wearing it, my coat.
RAFA FATHER:	She must have thought you'd thrown it out. You'd given it to the church.
ESTER:	That's not the point.
RAFA FATHER:	Why are you so annoyed? You'd given it away.
ESTER:	That's not the point.
RAFA FATHER:	So talk to her. Tell her you're annoyed.
ESTER:	I'd rather you did.
RAFA FATHER:	Right, I'll talk to her. I'll tell her after dinner.
CLAUDIO:	Which ruins the rest of the meal for him. He looks anxious. He goes into the kitchen. By the time he comes back, his meat's cold. He puts the TV on at ten o'clock, to watch the news.
ESTER:	It was a better picture on the old one.
CLAUDIO:	The first item is about French people setting fire to cars.
RAFA FATHER:	No future, those boys. No way out. That's how they vent their frustration at the system.
CLAUDIO:	Rafa Father's a member of Amnesty International, Ester of Médecins Sans Frontières and some Animal Rights Group that her friend Concha got her involved with. After the sports news, Rafa Father goes out onto the terrace for a smoke. I go out with him. Last summer I used to watch the three of them having dinner out there, and now here I am, looking at the park from the house. The streetlights are on and I can see the drunk who gives water to the ducks, the junkies, the black guys still trying to sell sunglasses … Rafa Father runs four miles a day in that park, but now he's staring way beyond it, all the way to China.
RAFA FATHER:	People are frightened of China. But China's a great oppor…
CLAUDIO:	A door slams. Then Ester comes out onto the terrace.
ESTER:	Did you see that? Eliana. She's gone. Taken her bags with her.
RAFA FATHER:	Gone?
ESTER:	Without a word.
RAFA FATHER:	It can't be what I said to her about the coat. I didn't say anything she could take offence at.
ESTER:	She's left it there, in the kitchen. She might have said goodbye to Rafa at least.
CLAUDIO:	I see Eliana from the terrace, walking down the street with her bags. To be continued.

Silence.

GERMÁN:	I'm not convinced. The whole thing about the coat, what does it bring to the story? Cut the scene and what do you lose? Unless … is Claudio trying to get closer to Rafa Father?
JUANA:	Do you think so?
GERMÁN:	I do, trying to get closer to him.
CLAUDIO:	Me, trying to get closer to him?
GERMÁN:	Whole dinner scene, like Banquo's ghost. You can see you don't know what to do with him. The truth is, Claudio, you've got a real problem with that character.

Silence. CLAUDIO is watching RAFA. He discounts a number of ideas before he begins to write.

RAFA:	It was like stripping me bare. I've never felt so stupid.
CLAUDIO:	Concentrate on this and forget that wanker. Seven x squared plus sixteen y squared equals a hundred and twelve. You don't need to draw it to see it's an ellipse. Do you see that, an ellipse?
RAFA:	Yes, I think so.
CLAUDIO:	What do you mean you think so? It has to be an ellipse, look at the sign. Change the sign and what is it?

Silence.

CLAUDIO:	It would be a hyperbola. But this is an ellipse – look at the sign. Let's calculate the foci. So what do we do first?
RAFA:	It was like he stripped me bare in front of the whole class.
GERMÁN:	He did take it badly.
CLAUDIO:	He shouldn't have done that. And he shouldn't have gone on when the rest started laughing. As soon as he heard them laughing he should have stopped. But the laughter made him worse.
JUANA:	Did you say something nasty to Rafa? You can be really cutting.
GERMÁN:	All I did was point out a number of his syntactical and conceptual errors.
RAFA:	I'd like him to feel how I felt. I'd smash his face in. I'd smash his face in and I'd set fire to his car.
CLAUDIO:	He doesn't have a car.
RAFA:	I'd smash his face in.
CLAUDIO:	You could do something even better. An article in *Spotlight*. Telling what happened, giving your side of it.
GERMÁN:	You encouraged him to write an article against me?
JUANA:	It's your magazine. Are you going to publish it?
GERMÁN:	Depends how it's written.
JUANA:	But an article against a teacher.

GERMÁN: Anyone can publish in *Spotlight*.

JUANA: But not just anything. I'm assuming you couldn't write any-
            thing that was racist or sexist or bullying. It's not the right
            place for debating teachers and their methods.

GERMÁN: I certainly wouldn't want to do anything to tarnish its huge
            reputation as a high-quality publication – School Today, School
            Trip Snaps, Teachers Gone But Not Forgotten, Jokes and Pas-
            times, and its pull-out supplement of vomit-inducing poems and
            stupid stories. Nobody could accuse it of censoring its content.

JUANA: Why don't you just have a word with him, with Rafa? To defuse
            the situation. For his sake, in case he writes something stupid.

GERMÁN: I don't know if he's going to write anything at all. The prob-
            lem is I'm not supposed to know.

CLAUDIO: Do you know what you could call it? "The Blank Blackboard."

RAFA: "The Blank Blackboard." Brilliant.

CLAUDIO: Let's concentrate on this for the time being. So what are the
            foci of these ellipses?

He writes three equations; Rafa sets to work on the problems.

I go for a walk. In the drawing room they have shelves full of
really good books, arranged by size, and photograph albums,
labelled by year. I look for the year I was born. The first
photo is of Marta, his sister, holding the baby. I go back to
Rafa's room. Ok, how are you getting on? I give him a hint
how to solve the second ellipse and I continue my exploration. I go into the study. The Grizzlies power forward smiles
up at me from the computer's screensaver. There are so many
drawers you wouldn't know where to start. Let's try this one:
a stapler, glue stick, files "Bianjan Toy Project,' "Junjin Jew-
ellery Project"… Let's try this one instead: the deeds of the
house, postcards from Marta, the last one three years ago, an
X-ray … I hold it up to the light. It's a spinal column. Noise
behind me. I spin round. Luba. When Eliana left, Ester went
into crisis as though her own mother had abandoned her, until her friend Concha found Luba. Luba, who was brought up
under communism somewhere, pretends not to see me and
keeps brushing. The X-rays of a woman, definitely a woman.
I put it back in the drawer and go on down the corridor. The
master bedroom. The bed. I lie down on the bed. Two bedside tables, with the books they really read. Hers: *The Secret
of Happiness: How to be Your Own Best Friend*. His: *Who Took
the Cheese? Adapting to a World in Flux*. A wardrobe with a
mirror door. Seven pairs of women's shoes. Their bathroom.
A little cupboard with shaving things, anti-wrinkle cream,
codeine, paracetamol, Lexatin … I put on a splash of Rafa

Father's after-shave and I go back to the boy. He can't make head or tail of the third exercise. That's because it isn't an ellipse. It's a hyperbola.

RAFA: Ah.

CLAUDIO: But can you see why?

Silence.

CLAUDIO: A key turns in the lock. "Did you get the fish done, Luba?" "There's no white wine." "Pop down to the Chinese supermarket." Her footsteps coming closer. She gives Rafa a kiss. She gives me a motherly smile. Her footsteps disappearing towards the lounge.

RAFA: Could it not be a circumference?

CLAUDIO: After a while, he arrives too. He comes in to say hello, and I can see he looks anxious.

ESTER: Are you all right?

RAFA FATHER: Do you remember Johnny, the Chinese guy? Well, I only found out today he didn't sign. Apparently, they were arguing right up to the last minute. They couldn't agree on a percentage. So this afternoon Mariano calls me in about the restaurant bill, could I not have found one even more expensive. But it was him who said look after him. It wasn't as if it was exorbitant.

ESTER: So how much was it?

RAFA FATHER: On top of everything, it was him who phoned me, saying he's in his sickbed …

ESTER: So how much?

RAFA FATHER: Two hundred and seventy euros. I admit the wine got a bit out of hand. But I wanted to look good. Not me, the company.

ESTER: Well, pay it yourself and forget about it.

RAFA FATHER: It's not the money. They're pissed off because the Chinese bugger didn't sign. If he'd signed they wouldn't have thought twice about the bill.

CLAUDIO: They lower their voices when they see me. I'm looking at the water-colour *Zerstörung*, which means Destruction.

ESTER: So what are you going to do?

RAFA FATHER: Wait until it dies down. As soon as they forget him they'll forget about the dinner and the three hundred euros.

ESTER: Three hundred?

RAFA FATHER: Including the tip.

Silence. ESTER looks at RAFA FATHER.

ESTER: Rafa …

RAFA FATHER:	What?
ESTER:	Do you think we read enough?
RAFA FATHER:	Read enough? What?
ESTER:	Doesn't matter.

Silence.

JUANA:	Ester's not well.
GERMÁN:	How do you know?
JUANA:	Lexatin is for anxiety.
GERMÁN:	I take Prufax. Half of my colleagues are on anti-anxiety pills. How do you know it's hers, not his?
JUANA:	He's more balanced. I don't know why Claudio doesn't open the computer. What difference is there between a computer, a drawer, a door?
GERMÁN:	Why doesn't Claudio open the computer?

CLAUDIO has no answer.

JUANA:	Maybe it's because … because what Claudio's looking for won't be on the computer. It's Rafa Father's. Claudio's only interested in Ester. In Ester's secret.
GERMÁN:	Ester's secret? That woman doesn't have secrets. She's an open book.
JUANA:	When Claudio first went into the house, he thought he knew everything about her. But he's discovered he doesn't know her at all.

Silence.

GERMÁN:	The way Claudio talks about Ester. The way he looks at her. Something has changed and he doesn't understand why. But she's still the most boring woman in the world.

Silence.

JUANA:	I think he said bored.
CLAUDIO:	I realise: there's a scene missing. An earlier scene to explain why Claudio has changed.
GERMÁN:	I'm not saying there's anything missing. The opposite, there's too much. Too much Ester. And that X-ray – one of the things I hate, that I hate most in the world, is playing with the reader's emotions. Tear-jerking: there's nothing worse. Please, Claudio, don't let her have cancer.
CLAUDIO:	A few days earlier, on the terrace. She's staring out at the park. Eating an apple.

He writes.

GERMÁN:	Rafa, do you mind hanging on for a moment?

RAFA comes over.

GERMÁN: The other day, when I brought you up to the board ... I got the impression ... I don't think you understood what I was trying to ... Do you like basketball?

RAFA: Yes, I do.

GERMÁN: Think of it like the trainer working on your shooting or your bouncing ... I don't know, I don't know anything about basketball.

He gives him a book. RAFA looks at it and hands it to CLAUDIO.

RAFA: I think he wanted to talk to me, but he had nothing to say. And then he goes and gives me this.

Mimicking GERMÁN.

"No underlining, no turning down the corners, no leaving it open face down."

CLAUDIO: You lent him *Letter from Berlin*. I don't believe it.

GERMÁN: What do you not believe? Lending him *Letter from Berlin* or lending him a book? He's one of my pupils too. *Letter from Berlin* is the story of a misunderstanding. Something that was only meant as a ... well, the protagonist spends the rest of his life feeling insulted.

JUANA: Got it! At last!

She shows GERMÁN a catalogue.

Everyone's talking about her, but she's never had an exhibition here.

GERMÁN: Chinese?

JUANA: That's her background, but she was born in Los Angeles. She revises traditional calligraphy from a gender-based perspective.

GERMÁN: You know what I think of gender-based perspectives ... boy girl, homo hetero, black white, vertebrate invertebrate ... Perspectives don't matter when you look at a Velázquez.

JUANA: What do you think? Most people would get this, wouldn't they?

GERMÁN: What's the difference between Shanghai Sky 6 and Shanghai Sky 7?

JUANA: No two pieces are the same. There are tiny variations, generated at random by a computer.

GERMÁN: But what does it represent? What does it mean?

JUANA: It doesn't represent anything, it's just there. It doesn't mean, it is. Do you not think its sheer presence, its materiality, are really imposing?

GERMÁN: Actually I do think they are, it's a bit overwhelming.

He leafs through the catalogue.

Can I hang on to this?

JUANA: Yes, look at it in your own time and let me know what you think.

GERMÁN puts the catalogue into his briefcase. CLAUDIO finishes writing his scene and hands it to GERMÁN to read.

CLAUDIO: The terrace is open. She's staring out at the park. Eating an apple. It's cold.

ESTER: I like days like this.

She bites the apple.

CLAUDIO: It's a different park at night. During the day children on swings, pensioners doing Tai-Chi, the black guys selling … well, they're there all the time, day and night.

ESTER: That's where Rafa learned to walk. And Marta, the three of us used to spend the whole day there. The swings were different. They were made of iron.

CLAUDIO: She points to the swings. The evening light slips down her arm. Do you see that bench? I saw you from there so often this summer.

Silence. ESTER passes her hand over her back with a look of pain. CLAUDIO takes her by the arm, as though to support her.

ESTER: It's my spine. I had an operation. There's no cure, just a temporary fix. Sometimes it feels like needles. I can't be too long on my feet. And I can't run, I used to go out running with Rafa. And I can't dance.

CLAUDIO: I think about the seven pairs of shoes in the wardrobe. Which ones did she dance in, when she still could? I imagine her dancing in the red ones. I imagine her dancing in the park, barefoot on the yellow autumn leaves.

CLAUDIO takes the apple from the ground, bites it and gives it to ESTER.

GERMÁN: I imagine her dancing in the red ones. I imagine her dancing in the park, barefoot on the yellow autumn leaves. When you wrote that had you just swallowed a whole tin of peaches in syrup? The apple, is that a symbol? A fucking symbol? Or just an apple? Barefoot. Yellow leaves. Do you want to end up writing art catalogues?

He takes out JUANA's catalogue and reads.

What is it we see in Feng Tang's work? Silence. Born in a no-place between East and West, these mute presences oppose the world's noise, the deafening babble of blah-blah-blah. Is that what words are for? The worst writing is in contemporary art catalogues. Junk poetry, worthless jargon, fairy tales. All to sell this, look at the photo. It's art because someone has written this, otherwise it would just be shit. Can you think of a sadder job for a writer? Actually, I can: writing speeches for the Minister of Education: Title of task: Run two hundred words together to justify this pile of crap. My wife sells this type of thing in her shop. The Minotaur's Labyrinth, a place to lose yourself in. It's been inherited by two women with a bit of nous, the sort who call a spade a spade, and who've told her to stop trying to sell art for sickos or they'll close the whole she-bang. It's fraud: it begins with the title: Shanghai Sky. It could just as easily be Seville Sky or Any Sky or Shanghai Footballer. It's the devil's pact: talentless artists and dishonest writers. I imagine her dancing in the park, barefoot on the yellow autumn leaves. No, Claudio, that's not the way, and you know it.

Silence.

CLAUDIO: Anything else?
GERMÁN: The bit about her shoes? It's not just pseudo-romantic, it's incongruous. If that scene takes place before the bedroom, Claudio still hasn't found the seven pairs of shoes. It would make sense if you set it more in the past.... The narrator blends memories, confuses moments ... but setting it in the present ....

Silence.

CLAUDIO: What else?
GERMÁN: This mania of yours for lists. List of medicines you find in the bathroom cupboard, list of people you see in the park, the list of
              ...
CLAUDIO: I learnt it in Scott Fitzgerald, *Tender is the Night.*

Silence.

GERMÁN: I've not read that.
CLAUDIO: It takes you into the character's eyes. Into their point of view. By the way, have you read Rafa's article? We've made a bet.
RAFA: A tenner on he doesn't have the balls to put it in.

GERMÁN gives JUANA a copy of Spotlight *open at the article "The Blank Blackboard"*

JUANA: "The Blank Blackboard."

She reads it. RAFA FATHER and ESTER come closer to read it too.

You made him write his essay on the blackboard and rubbed out one by one the sentences with mistakes. Sentence by sentence until there was nothing left on the board. Was that it, was that what you did?
GERMÁN: Yes.
JUANA: Then he was right to be angry with you.
GERMÁN: Was he?
JUANA: It was like stripping him in front of everyone. First you take off my shirt, then the trousers ...

GERMÁN: Look, you know what I think about symbolism. I don't understand symbols. For me an apple's an apple, and correcting an essay on the board is correcting an essay on the board.

JUANA: And you did it while his classmates sat and laughed.

GERMÁN: All right, maybe I should have stopped when they started laughing.

JUANA: It's not badly written. Or constructed. The boy can think.

RAFA: Some parents decide to take their son out of school and let him learn on the Internet. How would Aristotle respond?

Silence.

Aristotle thinks that education is too important to be left just to the family. According to Aristotle …

CLAUDIO: Philosophy puts me to sleep.

He closes his eyes.

Aristotle. Family. Destruction. *Zerstörung.* Germany. Greece, China …

GERMÁN: What on earth's this?

CLAUDIO: Claudio's consciousness. Interior monologue.

Silence.

GERMÁN: So you've found him at last: James Joyce. No one has inflicted more damage. Words like piles of rubble. Is that what consciousness is? Art should illuminate the world, not spread confusion. The twentieth century: two world wars and James Joyce. You won't find him in my library.

RAFA: … from which may be deduced, according to Aristotle, that the parents should be put in jail.

CLAUDIO: In revenge, I set him ten problems. In the first one, in triangle BDE BD is three metres long, DE four metres, BE five. Calculate the distance of AD, on the basis that the angles shown in the drawing are obtuse. He doesn't know where to begin. But he's too proud to give up.

RAFA FATHER: Have you lads any idea of the time?

RAFA: I can't get my head round these.

RAFA FATHER reads the problem. To CLAUDIO

Stay over if it helps you to get these done.

To RAFA.

He can bunk down in Marta's room.

To CLAUDIO.

Do you want to call home to let them know?

CLAUDIO: I don't need to, thanks. At midnight we're still working on them. There's a light on in the lounge, the TV's still on. Rafa takes me to Marta's room, which is now the ironing room.

RAFA: She's in Ireland, studying English.

CLAUDIO: It's the room of a fourteen year-old girl, though Marta must be in her twenties by now. There's a shelf full of Barbie dolls … Although they're … One's only got one arm, another one's lost an eye – they're all mutilated, poor sad things. Rafa lends me some pyjamas, which are too big for me. That makes him laugh, seeing me in pyjamas that are too big.

RAFA: You should come some Saturday to play basketball. It doesn't matter if you're no good, it's about having a good time. Having a laugh. Getting annoyed with the referee. Going out afterwards.

Silence.

Thanks for helping me with the article. You're helping me a lot. You're a good friend.

He claps him on the back.

Do you know what I feel like sometimes when it's late? Like going out and doing something, like those French kids, going out to set fire to cars or whatever, when I feel really hacked off.

CLAUDIO: At last he goes to his room. I lie on the bed and look at the ceiling. I hear voices in the corridor.

RAFA FATHER: We should have got him a private tutor. There's still time.

ESTER: He's doing better in maths than anything else.

RAFA FATHER: It's taking him too long. He's falling behind in everything else.

CLAUDIO: The house falls silent. I wait for a while before going out. I feel my way along the corridor until I get used to the dark. The four angels are there, hanging like bats from the wall. I go into Rafa's room.

He goes over to RAFA, who's sleeping.

CLAUDIO: He's restless, he looks agitated.

He covers him up.

GERMÁN: No, it's not realistic. It's a pity because as an image it's powerful. Claudio moving about the still house like an angel or vampire, while they're asleep. Powerful, but not realistic.

CLAUDIO: It might not be realistic, but it's real. It's what's happening.

GERMÁN: If it's not realistic, it's no good, even if it is real.

CLAUDIO tears up the pages. Pause. GERMÁN picks them up and reads.

CLAUDIO: I go into the master bedroom. On his bedside table: "Basketball for Managers" and "Confucius for Managers." On hers "The Building of the Great Wall of China."

He goes closer to the sleeping couple.

CLAUDIO: He's asleep with his arm round her waist. He's breathing heavily. She's smiling. Her skin's very pale. She's got tiny feet, like a little girl.

He caresses ESTER's feet.

JUANA: Do neither of you have any respect for anything? He's seventeen years old. If you care about him at all, get him out of that house before something goes badly wrong. I told you from the start, he's not going to stop until someone makes him.

GERMÁN: You've gone too far. This has got to stop.

CLAUDIO: You want me to stop?

GERMÁN: No more writing.

CLAUDIO: It was you who got me into this. That morning I was on the verge of throwing away my books and running away. Each class was worse than the one before. But you told us to write that essay. You told us to write and now I can't stop.

GERMÁN: You can't stop writing? Then write. Write about your own family.

CLAUDIO: I like these characters. I have to keep writing about them.

GERMÁN: Well I'm not going to keep reading.

CLAUDIO takes out some pages, leaves them in front of GERMÁN and goes. After a while GERMÁN lifts them and reads.

ESTER: You look fed up. Are they still going on about Johnny or whatever his name was?

RAFA FATHER: Turns out it was my fault he didn't sign.

ESTER: Your fault?

Silence.

RAFA FATHER: That night, after dinner, we went on out and Johnny, who'd already had too much, started a whole commotion. He lost his temper with some girl, he almost hit her in the middle of the dance floor. I got him out of there the best I could otherwise they'd have battered him – they nearly hit me instead. So now it seems I didn't treat him very well, and that's why he didn't sign.

ESTER:	On out where?
RAFA FATHER:	He wanted a drink.
ESTER:	How did you find somewhere else to go? Somewhere you'd been before?
RAFA FATHER:	First time.
ESTER:	Then how did you know?
RAFA FATHER:	Everyone knows the sort of areas they're in.

Silence.

	That's how these things work. You've got to keep your visitor happy. Some visitors want to go to the Prado, some to see Real Madrid, some are pigs.
ESTER:	A brothel. You went to a brothel. No matter how much of a visitor he was, I don't understand it, it wouldn't occur to me.
RAFA FATHER:	It's not a brothel. It's a bar where women go.
ESTER:	A bar where women go. Lovely.
RAFA FATHER:	I'd never been there in my life. I don't go to places like that. Mariano does, he goes for that sort of thing. Not me. I went as a colleague, I couldn't say no. Look where it got me.
ESTER:	So you were there against your will. You didn't drink, you didn't dance. Or did you, dance?
RAFA FATHER:	I had a couple of drinks to keep him company.
CLAUDIO:	She puts on the TV, and turns up the volume. He goes out onto the terrace for a smoke. It's the right moment. I know it's the right moment but for the first time since this started, I'm afraid.

CLAUDIO gives ESTER a piece of paper and leaves. ESTER reads it.

JUANA:	I don't know what price to suggest to the artist. This piece, for example, how does six hundred seem?
GERMÁN:	Who'd pay six hundred for that?
JUANA:	Is that the problem, the price? What if it was sixty?
GERMÁN:	Sixty … still too much. Maybe if it was six … Have you thought about the Chinese? The real Chinese, the Chinese in China?
JUANA:	The Chinese in China?
GERMÁN:	The Chinese in China would do this for you a hundred times cheaper. Then you'd have no trouble selling it. Avant garde to suit every pocket. Avant garde six euros a go. That Johnny, Rafa father's friend, he can copy anything. No, not copy, that's illegal, small modifications here and there … like the title, changing the title's the main thing, the title.

CLAUDIO: Every hour a leaf transpires two milligrams of water per square centimetre. The edges of the leaf are limited by the curves of equations y equals five x increased by one half and y equals one fifth of x squared, where x and y are expressed in centimetres. Calculate the quantity of water the leaf will transpire in one day. While Rafa is calculating the quantity of water the leaf transpires, I go for a cold drink of water. I've got the ice cubes in my hand when she comes into the kitchen. She doesn't look at me. She pours herself a martini. I drop the ice.

ESTER: Not even the rain dances so barefoot. What does that mean?

CLAUDIO: It doesn't mean anything. It's what you feel. It's the effect on whoever reads it.

ESTER: I couldn't sleep.

She takes out the paper given to her by CLAUDIO.

Not even the rain dances so barefoot. My son's done a lot for you. Rafa likes you too. Could you imagine if they read this?

CLAUDIO: I didn't write it for them.

ESTER: If they read it, they'd kill you. I understand the rest of it, I think, but this bit about the rain. I don't know what it means. Not even the rain dances so barefoot.

A tear runs down her cheek. CLAUDIO dries her tear.

GERMÁN: Bastard. You gave her a poem. Nobody's ever written that woman a poem in her life. You're abusing her. They're almost illiterate. There's not a drop of poetry in that house. You give her a line of poetry and it's like setting off a bomb. They couldn't recognise a symbol if it stood up and screamed at them. Not even the rain dances so barefoot. Are you talking about that woman? You can't be talking about her.

CLAUDIO: I see her differently now.

GERMÁN: Aha. Our young iconoclast has developed a taste for middle-class living.

CLAUDIO: You told me to look close up, free from prejudice. I'm going to take Ester away from that house.

GERMÁN: So you're not laughing at her scent any more, her way of talking. You're going to get a job, take out a mortgage and buy a house with a nice big lounge?

CLAUDIO stands up.

GERMÁN: Don't be deceived by your own words. As for the poetry: A) it's no good. B) it's plagiarised.

CLAUDIO goes back to ESTER.

ESTER: I understand the rest of it, I think, but this bit about the rain. Not even the rain dances so barefoot.

A tear runs down her cheek. CLAUDIO dries her tear. They kiss.

JUANA:	How's Claudio?
GERMÁN:	Okay, I suppose.
JUANA:	You've not shown me anything of his for a while now.
GERMÁN:	It's been five days. He hasn't brought anything since Thursday. Just as well. That boy has really disappointed me. He started off well "That unmistakeable scent of a middle-class woman." Such a disappointment.
JUANA:	I saw them. The two Rafas. And Ester.
GERMÁN:	Where?
JUANA:	I was sitting in the car, in front of the house. I saw the boy. Then them. They were arguing. I thought she'd be prettier.
GERMÁN:	Come in.

He invites RAFA FATHER to sit down.

	What can I do for you.
RAFA FATHER:	It's about that article, Rafael's article, in the magazine.

He takes out Spotlight.

GERMÁN:	Oh, the article. Don't worry, it's all in the past.
RAFA FATHER:	I couldn't believe it when I read it. He hadn't said a word, although I noticed he'd not been himself. It hit him for six. My wife doesn't think it was important. What worried me was the symbol of it. Standing up there in front of a blackboard getting blanker and blanker. The symbol.

Silence.

	What I want … what I think is that Rafa deserves … You humiliated him in public. He deserves a public apology, in front of his classmates.
RAFA:	In a match, an opponent strikes one of your team-mates, injuring him. What would Immanuel Kant suggest you do? What would he suggest?
CLAUDIO:	No idea.
RAFA:	Kant would probably say you can't right a wrong with another wrong. Heraclitus and St Augustine give revenge a bad press as well. But as far as I'm concerned, touch someone on my team and I'll go through you. My father, for example. My father and I are a team.

Silence.

	When you left yesterday, I followed you. I know where you live. I saw you through the window with some man.
CLAUDIO:	You're joking.
RAFA:	Thin, glasses. Something on his skin? What's wrong with your old man's skin?

Silence.

I don't give a flying fuck about Kant. Or Seneca or St Thomas of Aquinas. But if some little smartass hurts my father, then I'll knock the shit out of the smartass, and the smartass's father. That's my philosophy. The philosophy of Rafael Artola.

Silence.

Okay, enough philosophy. Let's go over our imaginary numbers. Final class: imaginary numbers. If you even think about moving your smart arse from that chair, I'll stuff these notes down your throat, understand poet? I've got them now, those imaginary numbers. It's like playing without a ball.

He plays basketball without a ball.

In basketball it's how you play without the ball that really matters.

He moves round CLAUDIO, his elbow jutting dangerously.

GERMÁN:	What happened to your eye?
CLAUDIO:	You wanted to see me?
GERMÁN:	You haven't given me anything for ten days now. Are you still angry?
CLAUDIO:	I've stopped.
GERMÁN:	You don't go to the house anymore?
CLAUDIO:	I study on my own. Maths. You can trust maths.
GERMÁN:	But you can't leave it like that. You need an ending.
CLAUDIO:	Option A: the Rafas kill Claudio. Option B: Claudio kills the Rafas and moves in with Ester and keeps the house. Option C: Ester sets fire to the house with the three men inside. You choose. Write it yourself.
GERMÁN:	I will if you don't. Do you know what makes a good ending? Two things: the reader has to think I didn't expect that, and yet it was inevitable. That's the hallmark of the good ending. Necessary and unforeseeable. Inevitable and surprising. You've got to find one – an ending that comforts or one that hurts. Perhaps you haven't got the guts. Perhaps you don't dare end it? You want me to do it?

CLAUDIO is about to go. He turns round.

CLAUDIO:	Option D: Ester keeps saying over and over again Not even the rain dances so barefoot … Not even the rain dances so barefoot … Life becomes a living hell in that house, in that horrible house, with her horrible husband and her horrible son. She sees no sense in anything, she feels she can't breathe, she goes out to the terrace. Suddenly she sees him. He's there, in the park, on the bench, waiting for her. She goes down to the street, runs towards him, they kiss.
GERMÁN:	Write that and I'll fail you.

CLAUDIO goes. Rehearsing.

A few days ago, while I was endeavouring to point out his syntactical and conceptual errors to Rafael Artola, I may have wrongly … The other day. when I brought your classmate Rafael Artola up to the blackboard, I may have misjudged …

JUANA: Can I help?

Silence. GERMÁN nods.

I've been thinking about how Rafa must have felt standing in front of the blank blackboard.

GERMÁN: I've been thinking about how Rafa must have felt standing in front of the blank blackboard.

JUANA: Rafa, I owe you an apology.

GERMÁN: Look …

JUANA: Rafa, I owe you an apology.

Silence.

GERMÁN: I've been thinking about how Rafa must have felt standing in front of the blank blackboard. Rafa, I owe you an apology.

ESTER: *(Rehearsing)* Rafa, I've been thinking about you and me, about our life … Look, it's better I just come straight out with this … Rafa, the truth is for years you and I …

RAFA FATHER comes home from work. ESTER goes to talk to him. RAFA FATHER interrupts.

RAFA FATHER: He brought up the bill again, in front of everyone. I was in two minds about throwing the three hundred euros in his face. But I didn't.

ESTER: Just as well.

RAFA FATHER: I set fire to his car. On my way out. I saw it parked there and …

ESTER: Rafa, did anyone see you?

RAFA FATHER: I don't know, I don't think so, but there's cameras everywhere nowadays.

Silence.

ESTER: We've got savings. We can hold out until you find something else. I'll get a job. If we have to sell the house, then we sell it.

She hugs him. They hug awkwardly.

CLAUDIO: They hug awkwardly. They sleep in each other's arms that night, hugging awkwardly, sleeping badly. I don't sleep well either, today's a different sort of day, today's the ending. I get up at seven, like every day, I make my father's lunch and leave the house at eight, like every day, but knowing today I have to find an ending that's necessary and unforeseeable.

Inevitable and surprising. It's Wednesday so I have History at nine, English at ten, break from eleven to half past, Maths at half eleven, Lang. and Lit at half twelve. But I pack a case and walk in the opposite direction, in search of an ending. The case is heavy, but it's got wheels, I catch a bus and before nine I'm standing in front of the two signs: The Minotaur's Labyrinth and For Rent. She's inside, but doesn't open until ten. When I go in I have the feeling, although she's never seen me before, that she recognises me at once. I feel she knows a lot about me and I know almost nothing about her. Well, I do know something. I know what sort of man she's married to. I know they've no children. I know what her husband thinks of everything in her world: shit and art for sickos.

JUANA: Shouldn't you be at school?

CLAUDIO: I've left school.

JUANA: You've left? What are you going to do, if you don't mind me asking?

CLAUDIO: I can earn my living doing private tuition. People have problems with maths.

JUANA: Don't leave school. You'll be sorry.

CLAUDIO: I can write contemporary art catalogues as well. My language teacher says I'm good enough for that.

He looks at a piece. He reads its title.

CLAUDIO: Shanghai Sky 5. Do you know what I see in these – presences? Silence. These mute presences oppose the world's noise, the deafening babble.

JUANA: I haven't sold a single one.

CLAUDIO: Would you have them in your own house?

JUANA: My husband doesn't like them.

CLAUDIO: People don't want art. They want decoration. That's what people want.

He hands her ESTER's magazine House and Garden.

JUANA, pointing to the case.

JUANA: Are you going somewhere?

CLAUDIO: It's for my language teacher. I don't know where he lives, but one day he told me his wife has a shop called The Minotaur's Labyrinth. Have you never thought about changing the name? It doesn't draw people in.

JUANA: You can leave it here. Or go to school and give it to him there.

CLAUDIO: I prefer to take it to his house. You know how much he likes surprises.

Silence. JUANA points to Shanghai Sky 5.

JUANA: Would you help me out to the car with this?
CLAUDIO: I get in beside her. The whole journey she doesn't say a word.

GERMÁN goes into class. He talks to the audience as though they were his pupils.

GERMÁN: I've been thinking about how Rafa must have felt standing in front of the blank blackboard.

Silence.

Rafa …

Silence.

Rafa, the thing is, point of view: you try to help someone else but they see you insulting them. It all depends on your point of view. Sometimes I wonder what *Moby Dick* would be like if the narrator was Captain Ahab. How would it end? Ah, a solitary death after a solitary life. I shall pursue you fixed on your body, damned whale. Here is my harpoon!

He pretends to throw a harpoon at an imaginary whale. Silence.

Okay, let's get to work. Books open, page ninety-five.
JUANA: Come in.
CLAUDIO: It smells of books, there are books everywhere, it's a labyrinth of books. I open the case and I take out the books. She helps me to put them back, it's not easy because they're arranged by period. Meanwhile we talk. About mathematics, about how she met Germán, about the books she likes.
JUANA: Russian stuff, no. Too heavy. I could only get through ten pages of *Anna Karenina* – the first five and the last five. So many books here … do you not find it oppressive? Germán is like Noah in his ark here. Outside, the floods. He was like that even at your age. You remind me of him. You like reading and writing. You're going to be miserable.
CLAUDIO: The phone rings: it's him. Juana doesn't tell him I'm here with her, in their house. She asks me to stay for lunch. After lunch she lies down on the sofa and falls asleep. I'm writing this beside her, while she sleeps. Her feet are pale.

He leaves the pages reside her feet and tiptoes out, so as not to wake her up. When she wakens, she reads what CLAUDIO has written. GERMÁN comes in with his briefcase.

GERMÁN: I did it. Not easy, but I did it. I've been thinking about how Rafa must have felt …
JUANA: Claudio wasn't there though.

GERMÁN: How do you know?

JUANA points to the book shelves. GERMÁN gazes at the books he lent and which have now been returned.

JUANA: He left this for you.

She hands him CLAUDIO's last essay. GERMÁN reads in silence. Meanwhile, JUANA hangs Shanghai Sky 5.

GERMÁN: What's that?
JUANA: Shanghai Sky 5.
GERMÁN: Does it have to go there, right in front of Dostoevsky?
JUANA: Yes.

Silence. GERMÁN lifts the file full of essays, inserts the final instalment, and goes out. CLAUDIO is sitting on the park bench. ESTER arrives. Silence.

ESTER: I saw you from the terrace.

Pause.

I wanted to give this back to you. I didn't know what to do with it. I didn't want … to just throw it out.

She returns the poem to him. Silence. ESTER hugs him maternally. Embracing, they seem to begin to dance. But ESTER pulls away from CLAUDIO and goes back the way she came. Pause. When he sees GERMÁN, CLAUDIO dries his tears. Silence.

CLAUDIO: Have you ever thought about all the windows you can see from here, all the people? I sit here and wonder what life's like in that house. That one, for instance. Those two old women.
GERMÁN: They're arguing. Two sisters squabbling over an inheritance …?
CLAUDIO: Two lesbians about to break up …?
GERMÁN: Two sisters arguing about the house in the village. The fair-haired one wants to sell, the dark-haired one says no way. Dragging up everything from the past.
CLAUDIO: Two lesbians. Thirty years living together out the window because the fair-haired one has fallen in love with her rheumatologist. The dark-haired one says, I introduced you to her! Look at her hands.

He moves them, imitating her.

I introduced you to her! So that's why you never wanted me to come with you to your appointments!

GERMÁN: No, she's saying:

He moves his hands, imitating her.

Our father's house. He fought tooth and nail to keep this house!

CLAUDIO: Third floor right.

GERMÁN: Forget it. I doubt whether they need a maths teacher.

CLAUDIO: There'll be something they need. There's always a way to get in. There's always a way to get in to any house.

Silence. GERMÁN gives the file back to CLAUDIO.

GERMÁN: The ending's terrible. Change it.

CLAUDIO: It's not the end. To be continued.

GERMÁN: Stay away from my house.

CLAUDIO: You do have James Joyce. What would he have called it – "Imaginary Numbers," "The Blank Blackboard," "The Minotaur's Labyrinth?"

GERMÁN: Stay away from my wife. If you ever go near again, I'll kill you.

CLAUDIO: Ever since I met you, I've wanted to know how you lived. From the very first class. What's his house like? Who could live with someone like that? Could there be any woman crazy enough, so crazy that …

GERMÁN hits CLAUDIO. Silence.

CLAUDIO: That's it, master. That's the end now.

He gestures in the final fade.

3   *Perpetual Peace*

Translated by Jerelyn Johnson

Translator's Note

The so-called "War on Terror" that has dominated our geopolitics since September 2001 has been punctuated by brief counter-shocks – like the 2004 images of U.S. military personnel abusing prisoners at Abu Ghraib, or news that detainees in Guantanamo Bay were subjected to "enhanced interrogation techniques" – like water boarding – to obtain intelligence, practices sanctioned by the U.S. Government. It is against this horizon that Juan Mayorga's *Perpetual Peace* takes its place. Mayorga wrote this play after Gerardo Vera challenged him to write about terrorism soon after the Madrid Atocha train bombings on March 11, 2004, that killed 191 people. Mayorga chose to place the decision of whether or not to use torture to acquire information in the hands of his three dog protagonists instead of humans. This choice underscores the moral complexity of the choices that the characters face in the play: dogs are specially trained and inclined to obey, so what would it mean to disobey? One of the dogs – Immanuel – questions, hesitates, and tries to use his reason to negotiate his way through the conflict. Yes, if we torture a man to make him talk, then we have abandoned civilization. On the other hand, are we so certain that civilization will survive – the theater, philosophy, democracy – if we aren't prepared to inflict pain now and then in order to defend it?

I first translated the play to produce it with Fairfield University's Academy Players in 2011, in Fairfield, Connecticut, which was its North American premiere. Mayorga encouraged us to explore the field of the play in our Fairfield production – that we use Odin, Emmanuel, John-John, and their struggles as a medium for thinking deeply about this dilemma, and not to rush toward a self-flattering conclusion. Because *Perpetual Peace* is a play, these difficult questions are further complexified by nature of the characters – who they are, and the unique qualities each actor brings to the role. Each night, at any performance, we may find ourselves leaning one way or the other, swayed by our own passionate natures, by what we heard on the evening news moments before, or by how we identify with each character's desires. Philosophically, there may be "right" answers, and Kant's state of perpetual peace may indeed

DOI: 10.4324/9781003228301-5

arise one day. But history does not make a strong case for moral progress. Existentially, there are only people – and dogs – limited in their understanding, self-interested, frightened, angry, in over their heads, and yet required by circumstances to make difficult decisions in the here and now. How, then, should *Perpetual Peace* be interpreted? What is the play's ultimate message? Mayorga's own reflection on these questions when we met may be fitting here: "I don't know. I am not the wise man of my own plays."

Perpetual Peace (*La paz perpetua*) first premiered at the Teatro María Guerrero in Madrid on April 24, 2008, under the direction of José Luis Gómez. Mayorga has revised it significantly since its first publication in the Spanish theater magazine *Primer Acto* (*First Act*) in 2007. It won a prestigious Spanish Prize, the Premio Valle Inclán in 2009. This play continues to resonate with audiences and most recently its last scene was adapted into an opera and performed in Madrid at the Reina Sofía Museum on June 6, 2022. This translation is based on the most recent unpublished changes sent to me by Juan Mayorga in the summer of 2019. The profanity I use most likely represents the most American English characteristic about the play. Additionally, I changed all measurements from metric to imperial.

Characters (in order of appearance):

Odin (Rottweiler Mix)
Immanuel (German Shepherd)
John-John (Mixed Breed)
Casius (Labrador)
Human Being

Any closed space with two doors. ODIN, IMMANUEL, and JOHN-JOHN are sleeping. JOHN-JOHN is wearing headphones. ODIN wakes up not feeling well. He doesn't know where he is, who the others are. Guided by his sense of smell, he looks for water, finds it, smells it, drinks. He observes the other two, who are still asleep. He looks for water around the enclosure. IMMANUEL wakes up. He doesn't know where he is, who the others are.

IMMANUEL:	Can you help me, friend? I'm sick.
ODIN:	I'm not your friend and you're not sick.
IMMANUEL:	Someone gave me something to drink, and then... I don't remember anything after that.
ODIN:	Take a sip; it'll make you feel good. It's good. The dizziness, the sour taste in your mouth, the cold in your gut, it'll pass. You're not sick. They drugged us. It's to be expected.
IMMANUEL:	What is to be expected? That they drugged us?
ODIN:	They don't want you to know where you are.

IMMANUEL drinks some water. He starts to feel better.

IMMANUEL:	My name is Immanuel.

He extends his hand to ODIN, who ignores it.

ODIN:	I don't remember seeing you in the stadium, Immanuel.
IMMANUEL:	There were more than a hundred of us.
ODIN:	I do remember sleeping beauty. He was in group C. And you?
IMMANUEL:	In group F.
ODIN:	In F? Are you sure? I don't remember any German Shepherd in F.
IMMANUEL:	You weren't paying attention.
ODIN:	What was your time in the obstacle course?

Music. IMMANUEL and ODIN wait for something to happen. Nothing happens.

	I made it in seven and a half. You?
IMMANUEL:	I didn't finish. I stumbled on the third hurdle.
ODIN:	Were you the guy who skipped the hurdle?
IMMANUEL:	I didn't see it. I was distracted.

JOHN-JOHN: Five point forty-five.

JOHN-JOHN opens his eyes. He doesn't know where he is, who the others are.

Five seconds, forty-five hundredths. Against the wind.

In his earphones he hears something we don't. He marks his territory.

You seriously needed seven and a half seconds? Did they make you run with one leg tied to your back?

The music ends. The three of them wait for something to happen. Nothing happens.

Watch where you put your tail. Don't you see the marks?

Theatrically, ODIN lies down in the zone marked by JOHN-JOHN

I am going to count to three. And later I am going to clean up my zone. I am going to take out all the trash I find in my zone.

ODIN hums the music.

One. Two. Three.

He goes to jump on ODIN when one of the doors opens – we'll call it door A – through which the HUMAN appears. JOHN-JOHN looks at ODIN as if postponing the combat, and goes for the rubber toy thrown by the HUMAN, he returns it to him, so that the HUMAN can throw it again… The HUMAN will communicate with him, as with the others, using monosyllables. The HUMAN and JOHN-JOHN play until CASIUS enters, also through door A, lame and with only one eye; there is an old white collar on his neck.

CASIUS: Did you have a nice trip, gentlemen? Are you comfortable? If you need anything, all you have to do is ask him for it. (*Indicating the HUMAN*) She is here to serve you.

JOHN-JOHN: (*To ODIN and IMMANUEL*) But he's… Don't you recognize him?

CASIUS: You are here because you excelled over the rest of the contenders. You are the best candidates. Our finalists.

JOHN-JOHN: That old Labrador is the great Casius! I didn't know he was alive. Casius is going to judge us!

CASIUS: Three finalists and only one collar available. A collar like this one. Have you ever seen a K9 collar?

ODIN, IMMANUEL, and JOHN-JOHN admire CASIUS' white collar.

CASIUS:	John-John, Odin, Immanuel, the three of you aspire to be a K9, but there can be only one. Only one is the best, and we're here to find him. The final exam will consist of three tests. The first, which starts right now, is a practical exercise.
JOHN-JOHN:	Didn't you hear? Only one open collar. I was destined for that collar even before I was born. My parents have already done this job, and my parents' parents. Don't waste your time.

CASIUS gestures to the HUMAN. He gives each candidate a piece of colored chalk.

CASIUS:	Three days ago, two men had a conversation here. One of them was sick. Reconstruct the sick human's path, from where he entered to where he left. You can sing.

With a gesture from CASIUS, the HUMAN turns on the stopwatch: tick-tock, tick-tock... The candidates sniff the enclosure. JOHN-JOHN, pressured, chaotically, singing; IMMANUEL, methodically, parceling out the space; ODIN, without moving around, only moves his nose. Shortly afterwards, euphoric, JOHN-JOHN marks out a specific route. CASIUS approaches, consults the stopwatch, and writes something down in a notebook. Shortly, ODIN marks out a different route. CASIUS consults the stopwatch and writes something down in the notebook. Shortly CASIUS gestures to the HUMAN to stop the stopwatch, writes this down, and exits through door A, which then closes. Silence.

JOHN-JOHN:	Why?
ODIN:	Why what?
JOHN-JOHN:	Why didn't he stop the clock when I picked up the trail?
ODIN:	Do you know what you picked up? (*He cracks up. He's playing with JOHN-JOHN's expectations*) A worm, that's what you picked up.

JOHN-JOHN sniffs the trail that he marked.

JOHN-JOHN:	It wasn't a worm. I know the smell of a worm.
ODIN:	You have your tail in my space. It's not a man, it's a worm. Get your little tail out of my space.

They go to fight. The HUMAN separates them by tossing them meat. JOHN-JOHN eats it angrily.

ODIN:	It's going to make you sick if you eat it when you're all pissed off. Look at the bright side, sweetheart: you've found your teacher. First lesson: The difference between a man and a worm.
JOHN-JOHN:	There's two tests left. You aren't going to take that collar away from me.

ODIN:	I don't know if I even want that collar. I'll know it once I hear the conditions.
JOHN-JOHN:	Well, if you don't know if you want to win or not, then you won't win.
ODIN:	The truth is I'm beginning to feel motivated. I've never tasted meat like this before.
JOHN-JOHN:	Casius wouldn't like a guy like you. Do you know how he lost that eye? Fighting for something more important than his stomach.
ODIN:	You're right; the old guy wouldn't like me. But I picked up the trail. I don't have your pedigree, princess; I'm the cross of two mutts. But I call a spade a spade, and a worm, a worm.
IMMANUEL:	Maybe there wasn't anything to pick up.
JOHN-JOHN:	Huh?
IMMANUEL:	Maybe it was a trick.
ODIN:	If there was no trail, then you won by keeping your mouth shut. But as it turns out there was. And I found it.
IMMANUEL:	Could be. But maybe they wanted to evaluate other things. Not our sense of smell. Or not only that.
JOHN-JOHN:	Oh yeah? What other things would they want to evaluate?
IMMANUEL:	Our sense of smell isn't that important now. I've read that in Colombia they use rats, and in Israel, pigs.
ODIN:	Pigs?
IMMANUEL:	Apparently, they are easier to train than we are, and cheaper. In any case, every day our sense of smell is worth less. I've read that the Japanese have invented an artificial nose.
ODIN:	A mechanical snout? With or without hair?
IMMANUEL:	You have to get used to the idea: very soon there will be machines with better senses of smell than us. And more agile, stronger. But there are qualities that no machine will ever have.
JOHN-JOHN:	What else would they want to evaluate? Tell us.
IMMANUEL:	Serenity in the face of an extreme situations. Speed of analysis of a complex context. The capacity to observe other individuals.
JOHN-JOHN:	You think you're pretty smart, don't you?
IMMANUEL:	No.
JOHN-JOHN:	Smart guys make me sick. You think I'm only a sack of muscles without a brain, a muscular dumbshit.
IMMANUEL:	Not enough to attack me and eliminate yourself. We're probably being observed. Are you going to make them throw you out because you can't control yourself?

JOHN-JOHN resigns not to hit IMMANUEL. His head hurts.

Is something wrong with you? Are you ok?

JOHN-JOHN takes a pill to alleviate the pain.

ODIN: (*To the HUMAN*) Hey you, I'm still hungry. Bring me more.

JOHN-JOHN: Don't talk to her like that. Some respect.

ODIN: (*To the HUMAN*) Didn't you hear me? Another steak, get a move on.

JOHN-JOHN goes to attack ODIN who prepares to fight. But ODIN turns toward the other door, that we'll call door B. He sniffs it.

There's something there, on the other side. Something alive.

JOHN-JOHN puts his ear up to door B. He confirms that there's something alive on the other side.

IMMANUEL: I already told you: they're observing us. Surely there are microphones all around. (*Pointing at an audience member*). Isn't that a camera?

As if in front of a camera, ODIN makes burlesque gestures at the spectator. The HUMAN puts a leash on JOHN-JOHN, takes his earphones off and takes him through door A, which shuts. ODIN and IMMANUEL hide their confusion.

ODIN: That guy, he's a little weird, isn't he? He has the ears of a boxer, but his snout is Rottweiler. And he moves like a pit-bull.

IMMANUEL: And he talks like a pug.

ODIN: Yes! He talks like pug!

IMMANUEL: They take more and more risks with the mixes now.

ODIN: Those lab rats make my skin crawl. I don't know what the world's coming to.

IMMANUEL: They're looking for the perfect dog. A "ten." They've been looking for it for centuries. I've read that Dobermans aren't real.

ODIN: What, are they plastic??

IMMANUEL: There weren't any Dobermans on Noah's ark. This guy named Luis Doberman, a night watchman, created them by crossing every type of breed.

ODIN: Luis Doberman? You're fucking with me.

IMMANUEL: He was looking for the perfect guard: the aggression of a pinscher, the resistance of a Rottweiler, the jaws of a pointer...

ODIN: So he was mixing it up until he came up with the perfect son-of-a-bitch.

IMMANUEL: He was successful. A Doberman killed him.

Silence

                 This place is...

ODIN: Too clean. I don't like it.

IMMANUEL:	What does it smell like?
ODIN:	They mopped it three hours ago. With disinfectant.
IMMANUEL:	What time do you think it is?
ODIN:	I don't know.
IMMANUEL:	The light has changed three times. And the temperature. Listen. Isn't it…? Airplanes?
ODIN:	It could be.

Silence. Music.

What the hell is happening? Has he won? Or was he eliminated?

IMMANUEL:	For the worm thing?
ODIN:	It's not a worm. I told him that just to fuck with him.

Silence.

I wonder what music this guy listens to.

He picks up JOHN-JOHN's earphones. IMMANUEL doesn't think it's a good idea, and worse yet that he puts them on. What ODIN hears shocks him.

How's his head not going to hurt listening to this shit?

He passes the earphones to IMMANUEL, who allows himself to be convinced into putting them on, but he can't tolerate even three seconds with them on.

Explosions, screams, ambulances… This dude is nuts.

Silence.

No, I don't think they've thrown him out. If this guy is boxer plus Rottweiler plus pit-bull plus pug, and on top of it he's nuts, it's going to be impossible to beat him.

IMMANUEL:	He's a difficult rival, yes.
ODIN:	Unless you and I make a pact. Don't make that little face, you understood me just fine, I am proposing a pact. Let's take him out of the race and then it's just between me and you. That guy's got plenty of muscle, but he has fewer streets than Venice. Between me and you, we'll convince that punk that this isn't the place for a champion like him. That he could get rich in those beauty pageants for faggot dogs. We'll get the freak out of the way and we'll play for the white collar, just me and you, two real dogs. What do you say?
IMMANUEL:	Let the best dog win. If John-John is the best, he should win.
ODIN:	"Let the best dog win." Who are you trying to fool? Ah, you were speaking to the camera. (*To the spectator-camera, parodying IMMANUEL*) "Let the best dog win. If John-John is the best, he should win. And if you need someone to suck

you off, then here I am." (*To IMMANUEL*). Do you think they're stupid? (*To the spectator-camera.*) Mr. Casius, or whoever the fuck is watching us: I know that you appreciate sincerity. If you and I come to an agreement regarding the conditions, you can be sure that...

He shuts up as door A opens. It's the HUMAN, who returns with JOHN-JOHN. The HUMAN puts a leash on IMMA-NUEL, takes him out, and the door closes. JOHN-JOHN puts his earphones on. Silence.

How was the walk? Is it nice out?

JOHN-JOHN: This place is amazing. They have some fucking great machines here, cutting edge technology to measure everything: visual sharpness, reflexes, DNA... Fucking great.

ODIN: So then you're the chosen one. Because all those measurements mean they've chosen you.

JOHN-JOHN: You really think so?

ODIN: What are we going to do, you're the best. You probably stunned them with your statistics: sharpness, reflexes, genetic code...

JOHN-JOHN: Forty percent boxer, thirty percent Rottweiler, fifteen percent pit-bull, fifteen percent pug.

ODIN: But you aren't only genetic. It shows that you've really prepared to get here.

JOHN-JOHN: I should think so. I had the best teachers.

ODIN: An expensive school, I suppose.

JOHN-JOHN: 6,000 a semester.

ODIN: And you were there how long?

JOHN-JOHN: A year and a half.

ODIN: In other words, you are worth 18,000 dollars. I'm with an $18,000 dog! Wow!

JOHN-JOHN: Yes, that's what my education cost.

ODIN: Money well spent. It's a profession with a great future. I'm sure it was tough to snag that spot at the school.

JOHN-JOHN: They select the puppies with the best pedigree. The first three months are probational: if you aren't worthy, you're out. During that time, they condition you to not cry even if something hurts, to put up with hunger and thirst and, above all else, to not be afraid. At all hours they subject you to sounds of explosions, to get your nerves used to them. Then comes the specialization: narcotics, immigration, or homeland security. But you can't choose, they send the best ones to homeland security. You start the practical training right away: embassies, stadiums, airports... They prepare you

	to react in any circumstance. They let you loose in a super-market full of people and you have to neutralize a suicide bomber.
ODIN:	A suicide bomber! How exciting!
JOHN-JOHN:	Well, an actor playing a suicide bomber. In my school, they didn't even think of using dummies, always actors, even though that's more expensive. Actors in all types of roles: suspect pursuits, kidnappings, rubble rescues, protest rallies…
ODIN:	Protest rallies?
JOHN-JOHN:	Lesson forty-one: "A protest rally that turns out badly, soon can change into a revolution." They teach you to be persuasive, and to only use violence as a last resort. Lesson thirty-nine: "If you know how to bare your teeth, you don't need to bite people."
ODIN:	So you miss your school, eh kid?
JOHN-JOHN:	There were difficult moments. But they were always overcome by friendship and camaraderie.
ODIN:	It's a lot different here, right? Here you can't trust anybody. That guy, Immanuel. I don't trust him.
JOHN-JOHN:	Me neither.
ODIN:	His mouth says one thing, and his smell expresses another. He acts as if he were our friend. But he's not here to make friends. He's here because he wants the white collar and there is only one white collar. He knows that you're an invincible rival. That's why he invented that thing about the cameras. Smart dog.
JOHN-JOHN:	There aren't any cameras?
ODIN:	When did he first bring it up? Just when you were about to give him what he deserved. He thinks that with his smooth tongue he is going to defeat you. Do you know what he told me about you?
JOHN-JOHN:	What? What did he tell you about me?
ODIN:	"A lot of muscle but fewer streets than Venice."
JOHN-JOHN:	That I have fewer streets than Venice, that's what the bastard said? What does he mean by that?
ODIN:	Venice. It's a city without streets, it's all water.
JOHN-JOHN:	In school they didn't teach us geography. What a son-of-a-bitch… But what does it mean?
ODIN:	That you are gullible. A dimwit.
JOHN-JOHN:	Sonofabigbitch…
ODIN:	That guy's a hyena. You know why he told you that about the cameras? He wants to deny you your best virtue: your instinct. He knows that he's lost if he lets you guide yourself by your instincts. What is your instinct saying now?
JOHN-JOHN:	To kill him.

ODIN:	I want to see him at your feet, with his neck broken, bleeding to death.
JOHN-JOHN:	Yes. Yes!
ODIN:	But don't get ahead of yourself. When you catch him off guard, you'll throw yourself at him like a bolt of lightning.
JOHN-JOHN:	Like a bolt of lightning.
ODIN:	But don't forget he's a smart dog. Don't allow him to confuse you. Show him that you're smarter than he is. Here they come. Remember, like a bolt of lightning.
JOHN-JOHN:	Yah, like a bol...
ODIN:	Shhh...

Door A opens. It's the HUMAN who's returned with IM-MANUEL. The HUMAN puts ODIN on a leash and takes him away. Before leaving, ODIN exchanges a glance with JOHN-JOHN. IMMANUEL notices something strange in JOHN-JOHN's attitude. Every time that IMMANUEL turns his back, JOHN-JOHN gets ready to throw himself at him. But, every time, IMMANUEL turns around, spoiling the attack...

IMMANUEL:	I hate tests. I can't stand to see blood. Ever since I was a pup, just seeing the needle I'd get dizzy... And making me urinate, I hate it... That apparatus that looked like a speedometer, did you figure out what it was measuring?... And later, they take the print of only one of your paws, the left one.
JOHN-JOHN:	So, I'm a gullible huh? So, a dimwit, eh? So, fewer sidewalks than Valencia.
IMMANUEL:	What's wrong with you?
JOHN-JOHN:	What's wrong with me, know it all, is that I'm going to make chopped meat out of you.

He lunges at IMMANUEL. But much to the surprise of JOHN-JOHN, IMMANUEL counter attacks just like a good fighter. They fight. JOHN-JOHN is gaining on him.

IMMANUEL:	Did you hear that?
JOHN-JOHN:	What?

He points to door B.

IMMANUEL:	Behind that door. Don't you hear something like a prayer? Isn't there someone praying?
JOHN-JOHN:	I don't hear anything.
IMMANUEL:	Do you believe in God?
JOHN-JOHN:	Huh?
IMMANUEL:	If Casius asks you about "God," have you thought of what you'll answer? In the interview, it's a probable topic. These days, you can't do this job without knowing theology. Many of those guys that go around planting bombs say they have

God on their side. They kill in the name of God. But what do they mean when they say "God?" What's in their minds when they speak of "God?" If Casius brings up the topic "Terrorism and God," what will you respond?

JOHN-JOHN: In my school we didn't take religion.

He immobilizes IMMANUEL, who is at his mercy.

IMMANUEL: (*Barely intelligible.*) I'd begin by talking to him about Pascal's wager.

Pause.

JOHN-JOHN: Whose wager?

IMMANUEL: Pascal says: Both God's existence and his nonexistence cannot be proven; for that reason, you must consider the question as a wager. It's like a roulette wheel with two pockets; one says: "God exists;" the other says: "God doesn't exist." According to Pascal, it's a good idea to bet on the "God exists" pocket.

JOHN-JOHN: ??

IMMANUEL: If you wager "God doesn't exist" and God actually does not exit, what would you win? Only those fleeting pleasures that the believer renounces and the atheist permits himself. Those same ephemeral pleasures that you will lose if you wager "God exists" and it turns out he does not exist. On the other hand, if you wager "God doesn't exist" and God exists, you'll regret it eternally in hell. Lastly, if you wager "God exists" and God exists, you'll win eternity.

Silence.

JOHN-JOHN: Could you repeat that?

JOHN-JOHN's pressure has relaxed a bit. Without JOHN-JOHN realizing it, IMMANUEL manages to wriggle out from under him as they converse.

IMMANUEL: It's like dice with two sides…

JOHN-JOHN: Didn't you say it was a roulette wheel?

IMMANUEL: It doesn't matter. Like a roulette wheel with two pockets, or like a deck of cards with only two cards, or like a coin, that's it, yes, like a coin: heads or tails.

JOHN-JOHN: Don't confuse me, don't confuse me, I'm going to…

IMMANUEL: Ok, ok, roulette, two pockets. One says, "God exists" the other says "God doesn't exist."

IMMANUEL uses two objects that he finds to represent "God exists" and "God doesn't exist."

Which do you choose?

JOHN-JOHN: That pocket.

IMMANUEL:	So you're betting that "God doesn't exist?"
JOHN-JOHN:	Isn't that one "God exists"?
IMMANUEL:	No, it's "God doesn't exist."
JOHN-JOHN:	Well, ok, that one then.
IMMANUEL:	Listen to Pascal: "If God exists, you could be condemned for centuries and centuries. If he doesn't exist, everything will go to shit anyway."
JOHN-JOHN:	Pascal's right. The other one.
IMMANUEL:	According to Pascal, that's the intelligent wager. According to Pascal…

Door A opens. The HUMAN brings ODIN, who can't understand what he's seeing.

| JOHN-JOHN: | (*To ODIN*) Do you believe in God? |

ODIN takes JOHN-JOHN aside.

ODIN:	I thought I was going to see him at your feet, with his neck ripped apart, bleeding to death. What the hell happened?
JOHN-JOHN:	Have you heard about a gambler named Pascal?
ODIN:	He's confused you again. You've let yourself get confused.

JOHN-JOHN shows him the objects that represent the two roulette wheel pockets.

JOHN-JOHN:	A roulette wheel: God exists, or God doesn't exist. If you bet here, eternity; if not, what do you lose? What do you lose, eh? No, it wasn't like that, what was it? A roulette wheel. If you bet on this one, you burn eternally. But if there is no God… Everything started because of a whisper behind that door, then he asked me about God and a while later we were talking about some Pascal guy.
ODIN:	That guy's a snake.
JOHN-JOHN:	Pascal?
ODIN:	He's as crafty as a reptile.
JOHN-JOHN:	But it's a likely topic: God. What will you say if Casius brings it up to you?

They shut up as CASIUS enters through door A.

CASIUS:	Gentlemen, it's time to start the second test.
JOHN-JOHN:	What about the first one, sir? Aren't you going to give us the results?
CASIUS:	We only allow one check mark per question. Every wrong answer will count as a negative point.

The HUMAN gives each candidate pen and paper. Following CASIUS' indications, he will start or stop the stopwatch: tick-tock…

One. What is the radial action of seven grams of trinitrotoluene?

a) 300 ft.
b) 65 ft.
c) 1600 ft.

Time.

Time. Two. Upon identifying a vehicle-bomb in motion, what does the dog have to do?

a) Kill the driver.
b) Immobilize the driver, letting him live.
c) Put himself in the path of the vehicle, provoking the explosion.

Time.

Time. Three. In case of a disagreement between a man and a dog, who decides?

a) The man.
b) The dog.
c) There can never be a disagreement.

Time.

Time. Four. In the case of a capture, what should the dog do?

a) Act like he's going over to the enemy's side.
b) Keep quiet.
c) Commit suicide.

Time. JOHN-JOHN takes a pill.

Time. Five. Smell these three garments and tell me which one belongs to a terrorist.

Time.

Time. Six. If the neutralization of a suspect puts an innocent life in danger, what should the dog do?

a) Desist the neutralization.
b) Complete the neutralization.
c) No life is innocent.

Time.

Time. Seven. Faced with the impossibility of simultaneously protecting two possible victims, who will the dog protect?

a) The youngest victim.
b) The weakest victim.
c) The victim with the greatest symbolic value.

Time. JOHN-JOHN takes a pill.

Time. Eight. Where should you bite a suicide bomber?

a) His eyes.
b) His testicles.
c) His left hand.

Time.

Time. Nine. How would you classify the Spaniards that fought against the French invaders during the years 1808 to 1813?

a) Insurgents.
b) Terrorists.
c) Patriots.

Time. JOHN-JOHN takes two pills.

Time. Ten. In less than twenty-five words, define the concept "Terrorism."

Time.

Time. Sign and turn in.

CASIUS collects the exams and exits through door A, that then closes. Furious, JOHN-JOHN bangs on the floor and walls.

JOHN-JOHN:	Shit, shit, shit! In almost all of them, "a" was equal to "b" and the "c" was the same but in another order. "Define 'terrorism'". Where the hell did that come from? Even a puppy knows what terrorism is. But at least I got six right. Well, at least four. "Define 'terrorism.'" What did you put?
ODIN:	I left it blank.
JOHN-JOHN:	Blank? What do you mean blank?
ODIN:	How old are you, kid?
JOHN-JOHN:	Three.
ODIN:	At your age, you should already know what humans do with words. "Terrorism." They use words. They stretch them, they shorten them, they twist them, they move them from one place to another. Don't let yourself get mixed up because of their words.
JOHN-JOHN:	What are you talking about? You, what side are you on?
ODIN:	I'm not on any side, and you aren't either. Dogs, we don't have a side, or a country, or a house. I don't like you, kid, but I'm going to give you a good piece of advice: don't get mixed up in their business.
JOHN-JOHN:	What do you mean we dogs don't have a side? I have a side; I really believe I have one.

ODIN:	Why don't you review Pascal, cutey? It seems to me you don't quite have it yet. But if you concentrate well, you're going to impress the hell out of Casius.

He gives JOHN-JOHN the imaginary roulette wheel elements. JOHN-JOHN begins to talk to himself, trying to reconstruct Pascal's argument.

IMMANUEL:	(*To ODIN.*) You wouldn't talk like that if you had been through it.
ODIN:	I wouldn't talk how if I hadn't been through what?
IMMANUEL:	If you had seen the blood of innocent people, you wouldn't talk like you do.
ODIN:	I don't know anyone innocent.
IMMANUEL:	You're a cynic. Did you know that the Greeks called philosophers who imitated dogs "cynics"?
ODIN:	"Cynic." I like it. It sounds good: "Odin, the cynic."
IMMANUEL:	You haven't been loved much, have you?
ODIN:	You're wrong. My fourth owner, that one adored me. He named me Odin. Can you believe it, that creep? The class of dickhead that names his dog "Odin." Tell me what you've named your pet and I'll tell you what problems you have. He was a neurotic, that one. Owners of Rottweilers are all a mess of neurosis. Actually, no one who has a dog at home is to be trusted. Homosexuality already seems pretty bad to me, but to live with a dog... I look at a dog and I can already tell what his owner's like. Looking at you, I figure that your owner would be a genuine prick.
IMMANUEL:	I'm going to win that collar just so that you don't win it.
ODIN:	You can't win, fatty. The battle is between the pup and me. You might as well just put your tail between your legs and leave us alone. This job isn't for pricks.
JOHN-JOHN:	(*To IMMANUEL.*) Could we review "If God doesn't exist" when God doesn't exist? I can't get it.
IMMANUEL:	Don't try to repeat Pascal's arguments or anybody else's. *Sapere aude*!!
JOHN-JOHN:	What?
IMMANUEL:	Kant's motto: *Sapere aude*! It means think for yourself; don't let anyone tell you what you should think; ask questions, research, trust your reasoning. *Sapere aude*!

Silence.

JOHN-JOHN:	But then, you... Don't you have your own idea of God? Not Pascal's, but yours? How do you see the topic?
IMMANUEL:	I've thought a lot about this lately. Up all night to arrive at the conclusion that God is the idea of something desired but inaccessible.

JOHN-JOHN:	???
IMMANUEL:	An ideal that cannot be achieved in this world, that's how I see God. If there is a God, it's a distant and silent God. He doesn't intervene in History; doesn't give out awards or punishments...
JOHN-JOHN:	A God that doesn't enter or exit, award or punish... What kind of shitty God is that?
IMMANUEL:	You're right, it's a God that doesn't alleviate the pain in the world, a God that doesn't console. At base, it's the smallness of life and reason that is expressed in this idea of a God infinitely separated from men. It's what the Scholastics called *ens realissimum, summun bonum, esentia essentiarum...*
ODIN:	Enough! (*To the spectator-camera.*) Get him out of here, throw out Mr. Know-it-All before he drives us all crazy. (*To IMMANUEL.*) If you say another fucking word in Greek, I swear that I'll, I'll... (*Silence. It surprises him that he's about to hit IMMANUEL.*) Ok, I get it, now I understand. I've been thinking it over this whole time: What is this guy doing here, who doesn't have a sense of smell and can't jump hurdles, how does he fit here? Now I see it: you aren't a candidate. (*To JOHN-JOHN.*) He's not a candidate, he isn't taking the test. He's part of the test!
JOHN-JOHN:	He's part of the test?
ODIN:	He's here to make us nervous and see how we react, same as that damn music and the faint smell of bleach. There are only two finalists, you and me.
JOHN-JOHN:	You and me alone?
ODIN:	You or me.

Silence.

Although I don't have chance. You have the potency of a boxer, the resistance of a Rottweiler, the aggression of a pit-bull, the perseverance of a pug...

JOHN-JOHN:	Well, yes.
ODIN:	Finalist to finalist, John-John, may I ask you a question?
JOHN-JOHN:	Sure.
ODIN:	Are you sure you're all dog?
JOHN-JOHN:	???
ODIN:	How do you know they didn't put ten percent turtle, to make you tough, or seven percent rabbit, to give you agility? Now they have all types of methods: hormones, genes, clones... How do you know they didn't throw in twenty percent human into the mix, to make you twenty percent prick?... Now, now, kid, don't be like that, my family tree isn't all fantastic either. Look at this hand, isn't it canine? My grandmother

was a bit of a slut. But at least I know I'm only dog. Has anyone ever told you have the eyes of a monkey?

JOHN-JOHN furiously attacks ODIN. To protect ODIN, the HUMAN applies electric shocks to JOHN-JOHN until she calms him down and puts a muzzle on him.

(*To the spectator-camera.*) Now you see, Casius, the kid can't control himself. Can you imagine him facing a crisis? He's not the type of employee that you are looking for. Lucky for you, I'm willing to consider a good offer...

He shuts up as door A opens, through which CASIUS enters.

CASIUS: John-John, Immanuel, would you be so kind as to leave?
JOHN-JOHN: (*Barely intelligible, due to the muzzle.*) But who's winning? Aren't they going to tell us who's winning?
CASIUS: At the end of the hallway, you will find three doors: the library, the television room, and the garden. You can wait wherever you want.

IMMANUEL and JOHN-JOHN exit. The HUMAN closes door A and puts a leash on ODIN. During this and the rest of the interviews, the HUMAN will direct the candidate with the leash, forcing him to go to a particular part of the enclosure, adopt some position or do a physical exercise. CASIUS will take notes in his notebook.

You have a minute to introduce yourself.

Silence.

ODIN: I don't know any languages. I hardly know anything. But I know all that I have to know.

Silence.

CASIUS: Your date and place of birth aren't listed on your resumé.
ODIN: I figure I'm probably six years old. No fucking clue where I was born.
CASIUS: There's also nothing listed about your parents.
ODIN: Nope, not listed.
CASIUS: Kids?
ODIN: Not listed.
CASIUS: Is "Odin" your real name?
ODIN: Who has a "real name?" Before "Odin" I had three others, just the same number of owners: "Express," "Fortune," and "Furor." Call me whatever you like.
CASIUS: It's hard to imagine you as a companion animal.
ODIN: Well I was. Until I got sick of caresses and kissing shoes.
CASIUS: And then?

ODIN: The street, my university. In the street I learned to growl to be
            scary, to howl to elicit pity. And, above all else, I refined my sense of
            smell. I learned that the guy who wants to hit you smells differently
            than the guy who is going to pet you.
CASIUS: One has to admit that your sense of smell is formidable.
ODIN: Three judges have accepted my testimony of smell recognition
            in homicide trials. I can tell the difference between two thousand
            smells. I can identify any chemical or biological agent in a 100-mile
            radius with ninety-seven percent precision.
CASIUS: Currently you work in Customs. Can you explain its mission to us?
ODIN: Trucks. From the smell, I determine the carbon dioxide density. A lot
            of dioxide means that there are people breathing. Undocumented.

            Silence.

CASIUS: You were employed in a hospital. But not in security. You worked
            in the oncology section. Can you clarify that point?
ODIN: I used to detect tumors.
CASIUS: You're able to detect cancer with your smell?
ODIN: With a probability of eighty-seven percent.
CASIUS: You saved lives. An emotional job.
ODIN: Four kilos of tenderloin daily and a new female every three months.
            But I received a better offer and I left.
CASIUS: What else can you detect? Happiness? Sadness?
ODIN: Are you messing with me?
CASIUS: My conscience. Can you smell it?
ODIN: No.
CASIUS: You quit that job in the hospital. And others. You've changed jobs
            often.
ODIN: They've never thrown me out of any place. I'm always the one
            moving.
CASIUS: To where?
ODIN: Always in the same direction: toward my well-being. I know what's
            going on here, Casius. Just say it, say the word: mercenary. Look,
            Casius, if you want ideology, choose the kid, he's got enough ideol-
            ogy to fill a train. Or the know-it-all, he has philosophy, and that's
            just ideology for pricks. You want ideology? Pick one of those two.
            But if you want a professional, then I'm your man.
CASIUS: You don't have ideology? It would be the same to you to be with
            us or against us?
ODIN: Who do you want me to be with? Think if you want me at your
            side, Casius. And, when you've thought about it, be sure to make
            me a good offer.
CASIUS: It's all the same to you – us or them?
ODIN: Them? The bad guys? Point out the bad guys, Casius, according to
            you, and I'll act like they're the bad guys, I'll know how to do it.
            I've done worse things. Welcoming home an asshole with his slip-
            pers in my mouth, now that's shit.

Silence.

CASIUS: We don't understand why you want this job, Odin. It's well paid, but it's very dangerous. We don't know why you want it, and without knowing that, we're not going to give it to you.

ODIN: You aren't going to give me or take away anything. It will be your masters who will decide. And if your masters understand that I'm the best, and I am the best, they will pay whatever I ask for. Because they are scared shitless, your masters, and they'll give anything to be a little less scared. If I ask for it, they'll kiss my feet. Of course, it's dangerous, of course I could get blown up, but it's worth it. Now, I'm the master.

Silence.

CASIUS: Put yourself in my place, Odin. Which of your two comrades would you choose?

ODIN: I can't put myself in your place. I can't imagine myself as a cripple who slobbers gratitude because the master doesn't throw me out with the trash, the master.

Silence.

CASIUS: Do you believe in God?

Silence.

ODIN: I spent some time in a dog shelter. One day, some guy points a finger at you. They can take you to a Marquis's mansion, to stuff you with bonbons, or to a laboratory to test syrups, to see if you turn blue or if you kick it. That's my idea of God.

Silence.

CASIUS: Lastly, the man who leads you on the leash, what is he to you?

ODIN: I don't even notice him.

Silence. CASIUS gestures to the HUMAN, who takes the leash off of ODIN and leads him toward door A.

CASIUS: Just a minute, Odin, I almost forgot. In your resumé you don't mention that you worked in a program to purge illegal dogs.

Silence.

ODIN: That was a long time ago. They told me it was to vaccinate and de-worm them. I myself was undocumented. They offered me a collar.

CASIUS: I didn't ask you why you did that job. I only mentioned that you didn't put it in your resumé. We were wondering why. Did it embarrass you? Is it possible that "Odin the cynic" is capable of feeling embarrassment?

ODIN is about to respond, but CASIUS signals to the HU-MAN to take him away. After a gesture from CASIUS the music starts; after another gesture, the music gets softer and softer until we can't hear it anymore, but CASIUS continues to hear it. The HUMAN returns with JOHN-JOHN, on whom he puts a leash, and takes off the muzzle.

You have a minute to present yourself.

JOHN-JOHN: A minute?

CASIUS: We're interested in how you see yourself.

Silence.

JOHN-JOHN: Basically, I agree with Pascal. He convinces me, it seems to me that he set out the topic well. I never would have thought about it like a lottery. Actually, I wouldn't have thought about it in any way. My father never talked to me about it. My father never talked to us, the person who talked was my mom, my dad thought talking was a woman's thing, but about this topic, not even with my mom. But now I know, if I want to progress in this profession, I should face the topic, because many of those bastards spend all day praying, and if we don't know what they're praying to…

CASIUS signals that his minute is up.

CASIUS: You waited your turn in the library. You took down a book and sat down to read.

JOHN-JOHN: Here I've learned that action isn't everything.

CASIUS: Volume 5 of the encyclopedia.

JOHN-JOHN: I looked up "God," but I didn't have time to read it all, I stopped at some Voltaire guy. I didn't know that so many people thought about God, and such different things.

CASIUS: Do you consider yourself impulsive, John-John?

JOHN-JOHN: There are many prejudices about boxers, sir. We know how to think. If we must think, we think.

CASIUS: Do you consider yourself a boxer?

JOHN-JOHN: It's my majority component, sir. Forty percent.

CASIUS: The graphological analysis indicates that yes, that you are impulsive. Do you consider yourself to be violent?

JOHN-JOHN: In this life, you must be threatening so that they don't threaten you. The other guy must know that he'll pay for it if he dares.

CASIUS: Do you enjoy the danger?

JOHN-JOHN: I don't get riled; I don't look for excuses. Just like you. They talked to us a lot about you in school, they gave you as an example. That time, with the hijacked plane. Nobody dared

CASIUS: You want to be like me. Have you gotten a good look at me, kid? Have you asked yourself why I tilt my head to listen to you? It's because my right ear is as dried up as my left eye. I have pain that barely lets me sleep, and when I do get to sleep, nightmares don't let me rest. All my dead show up in my dreams, John-John, and you can believe there are a lot of them, my dead. That's my prize, for never getting myself riled up. And I've been lucky. My best friends have fallen or have gone crazy. You want to be like me? Take a good look at me. Can you believe that I was once a little ball of fur that kids used to pet? Today I scare kids. Today I even scare myself... (*Silence*) Program R. You mention it in your resumé. What does it consist of?

JOHN-JOHN: "R" for "Resistance." A simulation. They give you a secret word and without previous warning, you fall into the enemy's hands, and they take you prisoner. You must resist without saying the word. They tie you up in unbearable positions, they expose you to extreme cold and heat, they forcibly keep you awake, they waterboard you...

CASIUS: Waterboard?

JOHN-JOHN uses his body to explain.

JOHN-JOHN: Board. Inclined just a bit like this so that your feet are higher than your head. Eyes blindfolded, arms behind you. Towel in your mouth, shoved way in, so that it touches your throat. They pour water in your nose and mouth until the towel is soaked. It doesn't fail, you think you're asphyxiating. I lasted one minute and seven seconds.

CASIUS: But you gave them the word. The secret word, to the enemy.

JOHN-JOHN: I was the one who lasted the longest. The others didn't even resist a minute.

Silence. CASIUS writes in his notebook.

I need this job, sir, (*He takes a pill. And another.*) If you don't give me that collar, what will become of me? A gladiator can only be a gladiator. In school they showed us gladiator movies. "You are all preparing for a life-or-death battle. There isn't a place for you outside of this battle." If you don't give me that collar, you should sacrifice me, sir.

CASIUS: Don't be so dramatic, kid. There are other teams. The war against terror doesn't end with the K9.

JOHN-JOHN:	You are the best.
CASIUS:	We suppose we have the best of the best in our ranks. That's why we're so careful selecting new members. Put yourself in my place: Odin or Immanuel? Which one, in your opinion, is worthy of becoming a K9?
JOHN-JOHN:	I'm eliminated? I prepared the psychotechnical to death, but I drew a blank. I messed myself up with that twenty-five words thing, I had twelve words too many, and I wanted to finish, so that's when I made that mess.
CASIUS:	You're not eliminated. It's merely a hypothesis to see how you reason.
JOHN-JOHN:	How I reason... Which would I choose? In a dangerous situation I wouldn't count on either one of them. One has the makings of the traitor, the other, of a coward.
CASIUS:	Years ago, we were infiltrated by a mole. We paid dearly for it; we're still paying for it. If you had to pass along a secret concerning State security, which of the two would you not trust it with?

JOHN-JOHN doesn't know what to say.

Immanuel has killed. Odin has killed. And you, John-John? Have you ever killed?

Silence. JOHN-JOHN denies it.

Tell us, the man who leads you on the leash, what is he to you?

JOHN-JOHN:	Is it him?
CASIUS:	Who?
JOHN-JOHN:	Lesson number one hundred, and the last one: "One day they will turn you over to a man. Brother of that man the dog will be."
CASIUS:	That is what they taught you. Now, look me in the eyes and tell me, who is this man?
JOHN-JOHN:	(*Looking at the HUMAN*) He is me. We will always be together, until the end. If you commit an error, or if I'm wrong, the two of us will fall together.

Silence. CASIUS gestures at the HUMAN, who takes the leash off of JOHN-JOHN and invites him to leave through door A. But JOHN-JOHN turns toward CASIUS.

Perhaps I'm not as smart as those two, but I would be the best with a man at his side. He'll think for me, and I'll feel for him. The Chinese can invent a mechanical nose, but there will never be a machine like a dog with a man. A dog knows if someone wants to kill, a dog knows a man is going to do it even before the man does. Put one of your men at my side, Casius, and I will be that man's instinct.

JOHN-JOHN and the HUMAN exit. CASIUS gestures as if asking for some music that he hears and that we can't hear. The HUMAN returns with IMMANUEL, on whom she puts a leash.

CASIUS: You have one minute to present yourself.
IMMANUEL: I prefer to pass directly to the dialogue.

               Silence.

CASIUS: You waited in the television room. Not in the library.
IMMANUEL: Lately I can't seem to concentrate on what I'm reading.
CASIUS: Is this your normal weight?
IMMANUEL: I've let myself go a little.
CASIUS: "Immanuel" Too long. If you stay with us, we'd have to shorten it. "Imm?" "Manu?"
IMMANUEL: Why even think about it? I'm probably not even going to stay with you.
CASIUS: Probably not.
IMMANUEL: It surprises me that that you haven't already rejected me. Unless you're looking for something besides sense of smell or strength.
CASIUS: Suppose we were only looking for sense of smell or strength. Who should we choose?
IMMANUEL: What's strength worth without reason to govern it? What's a sense of smell worth if it will be at the service of he who pays the most?
CASIUS: Who, Immanuel?
IMMANUEL: If I were my responsibility, I'd choose John-John.

               Silence.

CASIUS: Your resumé is unique. Studies in philosophy.
IMMANUEL: In resumés one always exaggerates. Isabel, my owner, studied philosophy. I learned something by accompanying her to class and listening to the lectures. That's why she named me Immanuel.
CASIUS: ??
IMMANUEL: As a joke, she called me "Immanuel Can-nine." She had that kind of humor. You know, Immanuel Kant.
CASIUS: No, I don't know.
IMMANUEL: *The Critique of Pure Reason.* Well, he has easier books. I suggest you begin with *Perpetual Peace.* "Will there be harmony between people one day?" asks Kant. He's optimistic. According to him, due to pure selfishness, to not all be mutually

devoured, humans will continue to arrive at increasingly more comprehensive agreements. In the end, a universal hospitality will reign, there will be no borders, and no one will feel like a foreigner in any place on earth.

Silence.

CASIUS: Do you really believe this is your place? Do you truly want this job?

IMMANUEL: With all my heart.

CASIUS: Why do you hide that scar?

IMMANUEL: ??

CASIUS: On your neck. It's too big to hide it.

IMMANUEL: I'm not hiding it.

CASIUS: Maybe you do it without knowing, but you do hide it. Does it embarrass you?

IMMANUEL: I don't show it off, but it doesn't embarrass me either.

CASIUS: We'd like to know how you got it.

IMMANUEL: It was a workplace accident.

CASIUS: If you don't want to talk about it, we're not going to force you to.

Silence.

IMMANUEL: Before living with Isabel, I belonged to a guy that made me fight. Underground fights with betting.

CASIUS: You didn't mention any of this in your resumé.

IMMANUEL: I'm not that dog anymore.

CASIUS: Are you a good fighter?

IMMANUEL: You had to be. If you made a mistake, the master would hit you until you howled begging for death. And when he would hit another, he'd make you watch, so you could see what was waiting for you. Sometimes, he would hit you just because, to toughen you up, he'd say.

CASIUS: It's hard to imagine you biting a throat.

IMMANUEL: I didn't have a choice.

CASIUS: Did you kill?

Silence.

IMMANUEL: If I'm alive it means I killed. Those fights only ended in death. Only winning mattered. There were stronger guys, but I knew how to wait for my opportunity.

Silence.

CASIUS: Did you kill?

Silence.

IMMANUEL: One day I lost my patience, I got sick of receiving those beatings. I got him good, but I'm left with this little gift. I was bleeding out, I was dying. It was a miracle that a man gathered me up and took me to his house to be with his daughter. She cured me. When I met her, Isabel seemed strange. She moved strangely, she looked at me strangely. Until I understood what was going on with her. It was difficult for me at first. Not accompanying a blind girl but understanding the new rules. Understanding that she didn't want to use me. That's the most important thing I learned by her side. Apart from other things. Pascal for example. Her father used to read her lessons aloud to her.

Silence.

CASIUS: Any other job, besides those fights and this guide dog?
IMMANUEL: Isabel's thing wasn't a job. It was much more than that.
CASIUS: But you're no longer with her. Did you leave or did they throw you out?

Silence.

IMMANUEL: One morning, when we were on our way to the University... I don't know how I didn't recognize the danger... There was an explosion and... (*His emotion doesn't allow him to continue. Silence.*) I didn't leave her side until her father arrived. Seeing him there, hugging Isabel, hugging what was left of Isabel, I swore I had to do something.

Silence.

CASIUS: Have you thought about visiting a psychologist? He would help you forget. To get that image of the destroyed girl out of your head.
IMMANUEL: I don't want to get it out of my head. I don't want to forget.
CASIUS: We don't want anyone who cannot control his emotions. We don't want anyone who uses this job to settle personal debts.
IMMANUEL: I can't pay that debt. That debt is unpayable.

Silence.

CASIUS: Your definition of terrorism is longer than 25 words.
IMMANUEL: Forty-three. I preferred to be precise rather than comply with the rule.

Silence.

CASIUS: The man who leads you on the leash, what is he to you?
IMMANUEL: I don't know. I don't know him.

Silence. CASIUS is about to leave through door A. The HU-MAN takes the leash off IMMANUEL.

CASIUS turns toward IMMANUEL.

CASIUS:　One more thing, Immanuel. When John-John attacked Odin... You stayed on the margin, watching. Your neutrality surprised us. It surprised us that your decision was to do nothing.

Before IMMANUEL has a chance to respond, CASIUS exits; the HUMAN exits after him. In a while, ODIN returns, and a little while later, so does JOHN-JOHN. The door shuts.

JOHN-JOHN:　And? Who won? How much longer will we have to wait? They prepared me for action, not to be waiting. They didn't prepare me for this, they prepared me for...

ODIN:　(*To the spectator-camera*) Put on the fucking music!! I don't want to hear this cry-baby!!

JOHN-JOHN:　Casius knew that I was waiting in the library. Was it part of the test, to see how we'd entertain ourselves? Where were you?

ODIN:　I went to the TV room, then to the library, later to the garden, and then again to the library. I was chasing a cat.

JOHN-JOHN:　I explained the Pascal thing to him, but I don't know if I made myself understood. My head hurts from so much Pascal. I want to see some action; philosophy gives me a headache.

IMMANUEL:　It's not the philosophy. Do you know why I think your head hurts? Because your brain, when you get excited, is bigger than your skull. I'm sure it also hurts when you're with a female.

JOHN-JOHN:　It's true.

IMMANUEL:　When the brain gets excited, it hurts you. It's due to all those crosses. Probably, you have the brain of a pit-bull and the cranium of a Rottweiler.

JOHN-JOHN:　Did they make a mistake?

IMMANUEL:　Or not. Maybe they think that the more your head hurts during critical moments, the better dog you'll be.

JOHN-JOHN:　So that's why it hurts. Do you think I'll have to stop...?

ODIN:　If you can do it without getting excited...

JOHN-JOHN:　In school they spoke about a fourth test. A special test, in case of a tie.

ODIN:　What tie? Right away, the old guy is going to come and announce my victory.

JOHN-JOHN:　I asked my parents if they had to go through it, but they didn't want to talk about it. In school there were rumors. That they would show you a house with some scumbag in it and you had to fix it all yourself. That it was about neutralizing a dog bomb.

ODIN:	A dog bomb? (*He cracks up.*)
IMMANUEL:	In the old days, miners used donkeys against the police. Donkeys equipped with explosives.
ODIN:	Explosive dogs, explosive donkeys, explosive fleas…

Door A opens, through which CASIUS enters.

| CASIUS: | Congratulations, gentlemen, your grades are magnificent. The three tests haven't been enough to find the winner. We find ourselves obliged to have you face a fourth test. The decisive one. Sir. |

He turns toward Door A, through which the HUMAN enters and has a white collar in his hands.

| HUMAN: | John-John, Odin, Immanuel, we didn't make a mistake selecting you. However, we have discovered that each one of you presents a vulnerability. An Achilles' heel. We can't take risks. We would be risking the lives of our K9 workers. The lives of those people we've sworn to protect. The survival of our world. We need to know that you understand this, that it is an entire world that we are defending: bodies, but also convictions, principles. The chosen one will not only fight for our lives, but also for our values. We need to be sure of this, above all else – your sense of smell, your strength… – they are hardly important. |

He gestures to CASIUS, who opens door B.

Behind that door, you've guessed it, there is life. A human being. He assures us that he doesn't know anything, but we suspect that he has information about an imminent terrorist attack against a civilian population.

JOHN-JOHN wants to lunge toward door B. With a gesture, the HUMAN holds him back.

Before making a decision, we want you, gentlemen, to share our doubts. Maybe this man really doesn't know anything. And even if he does know, if we touch him, if we touch this unarmed man, wouldn't we be justifying his dark worldview? How are we different from him, if we scorn the law? If this man doesn't have rights, aren't mine also in danger, and those of all men, of democracy? We fight for values. And also for those innocent people who could be about to die.

He starts the watch: tick-tock, tick-tock…

| JOHN-JOHN: | I want to be a good dog, but I need clear orders. Throw me at him and I'll put him on his knees in front of you. Is that what |

	you want? Do you or do you not want me to bite him? Is this another wager? My head's going to explode. I'm leaving.
ODIN:	You can't leave, kid. Only one of the three will leave here, with a white collar.
JOHN-JOHN:	What are you talking about? Why doesn't anyone speak clearly in this place?
ODIN:	Listen to me with your thirty percent Rottweiler: two of us will be converted into sausages. Or do you believe that they are going to let us leave to go tell what we've seen? Tell him, Casius; tell him that only the one who wins the collar will survive. He who loses, dies, Spartacus. Isn't that true, master Casius?
JOHN-JOHN:	If we act like a team, nobody will be able to stop us. You guys take care of him; I'll be in charge of the old guy. If we can make it to the garden…
ODIN:	The garden ends in a ditch. The library doesn't have any windows; the television room does, but they're fake. There's no way out.

Pause.

| JOHN-JOHN: | Two pockets. I don't know if he is good or bad. If I act like he's bad and he's bad, I save the good guys. If I act like he's bad and he's good, I kill a good guy. If I act like he's good and he's good, I save a good guy. If I act like he's good and he's bad, I kill the good guys. |

JOHN-JOHN moves toward the door B; ODIN follows him. The HUMAN stops them.

| HUMAN: | They've already made a decision, Immanuel. You, however, doubt. We appreciate your doubts, and your capacity to overcome them. We have a lot of hope placed on you. You don't have John-John's strength or Odin's sense of smell, but you have a wise heart. We want that heart, if we can trust in it. |

Tick-tock, tick-tock…

Are you going to just sit there, watching what the others do? Don't you realize that this test is for you, that this is your test?

Tick-tock, tick-tock.

| IMMANUEL: | You said it yourself: if we touch that man, we justify his dark worldview. How are we any different from him if we scorn the law? If this man doesn't have rights, yours are also in danger. Those of all men, democracy. We are fighting for values. |
| HUMAN: | It disappoints us to hear set phrases out of your mouth. Values, law, rights, democracy. What rights would there be |

without us? What democracy? We save democracy every day here. We love the law so much that, although that man may want to destroy it, we treat him in accordance with the law. Provided that it's compatible with our primary mission, which is to defend the law. In order to save the law, sometimes it is necessary to suspend it. But that decision should only fall in the hands of someone who feels a profound love for the law. Someone that never uses strength to humiliate, to avenge, or to punish. Do you love the law Immanuel? Then, you won't let Odin and John-John get close to that man. And when you are in front of him, ask yourself: what is worth more, this man's rights or the innocent people's right to life? And if this man is innocent?, you ask yourself. Yes, Immanuel, that man could be innocent. But isn't it too steep of a wager, to put innocent lives in danger only because maybe that man isn't guilty? It's about values, Immanuel. Life, doesn't that seem like an important value?

IMMANUEL: We will win his hate, that of his children, of his brothers. Tell her, Casius. Help me, Casius...

CASIUS keeps quiet.

We have to offer him justice, not hate. Socrates says...

HUMAN: No quotes, Immanuel, not to me. Do you know what Napoleon said about the Spanish guerrilleros? "*Il faut opére en partisan partout où il y a des partisans*" "Fight the enemy as they fight." The enemy doesn't expect our justice, nor can he hate us more than he does now. Do you know how he sees us, the enemy? He sees us as monsters, and he won't hesitate to destroy us. Tomorrow, when the danger passes, we'll be judged by the same scandalized hypocrites who today look the other way. We'll accept the punishment the Pharisees impose on us; the true punishment is already in our souls. To sacrifice the soul is the task of today's hero in these dark times. Everyone's life depends on our tormented souls. Remember how *Perpetual Peace* begins? A cemetery is the only place that guarantees perpetual peace. There won't be any other peace than the one we conquer every day. Hopefully one day love will prevail in all hearts, hopefully one day there will be a humanity without enemies. We fight for that day to arrive. This is a metaphysical war, a war of the spirit. Reason or shadow, progress or reaction, civilization or barbarism? What side are you on, Immanuel?

IMMANUEL: I'm just a dog.

HUMAN: To distinguish between the just and the unjust, that can only be done by the heart of a dog. The dog has never been as important for humans. Humanity is in danger, don't abandon us.

IMMANUEL: Let me talk with that man. I will find the words.

HUMAN: How many lives are you willing to sacrifice to your words? Innocent people like Isabel. Isabel would be alive if we would have known that the danger was there, waiting for her. You didn't see the danger in time. What were you thinking about, Immanuel? What are you thinking about, while Isabel approaches her death? Think about her, Immanuel.

IMMANUEL: I don't stop thinking about you. You would be ashamed…

HUMAN: Kant would be ashamed. We work so that people can read Kant. But freedom has a price. We pay that price, in our hearts. We will pay until peace arrives. To the world and to our hearts. It is our dream: perpetual peace.

She releases JOHN-JOHN and ODIN, who go toward door B. IMMANUEL blocks their path, protecting the door. JOHN-JOHN and ODIN attack IMMANUEL. IMMANUEL dies.

4 The Mapmaker (Warsaw 1:400,000)

Translated by Jerelyn Johnson

Translator's Note

In *The Mapmaker*, Mayorga returns to the Holocaust, as in *Way to Heaven*, but this play is centered in both present-day Warsaw and the time of the Warsaw Ghetto. Here he presents the audience with a drama of remembrance of what has been erased, and an encounter with what is present but unspoken, both within the characters themselves and the history that they, and we, have inherited. Mayorga wants us to remember history, but it is more than that: he wants us to realize that there is little separation between ourselves and those who lived before us, that we consider ourselves contemporaries, to keep us vigilant to prepare for and divert the prospect of similar atrocities.

The role and centrality of maps in this play is significant in terms of Mayorga's poetics. He has often commented on the debt to cartography in his work in general. Like a map, Mayorga's plays are constructed through a process that selects points of significance, weighted and chosen, that constellate to create a matrix of meaning. Privileging some moments over others, the play works toward an idea that is presented as a map of significance, rather than a sequential narrative that arrives at a destination. He considers his treatment of the past to be a map for the audience, and he does not strive to make plays that are exact presentations of the past; instead his plays are maps for the spectator to interpret.

While arguing that theater about the memory of the Holocaust is necessary because it strengthens our vigilance of and resistance to current barbarism, Mayorga recognizes that it needs to be handled with care. Mayorga posits that theater about the Holocaust needs to construct an experience of loss more than anything else. We are not witnesses to the past event, we should not pretend that it happened to us, we cannot speak for the victims, nor can the theater simply update the past event given only that which is recognizable about it today.

In *The Mapmaker*, Mayorga presents a story of an event in the past having a flash of its trauma in the present through the character of Blanca. The play opens with Blanca disclosing her sudden realization that nothing remains of the ghetto in present-day Warsaw, save for a couple of monuments and a

DOI: 10.4324/9781003228301-6

museum of Jewish history. The places represented in the photos in that exhibition no longer exist, no traces remain. She is sympathetic to this erasure because she herself is recovering from an erasure of a different sort.

First published in 2010 in the collection *Memoria–política–justicia. En diálogo con Reyes Mates* [Memory–Politics–Justice. In Dialogue with Reyes Mates], *The Mapmaker*'s first staging was a dramatic reading of the text translated into Polish by Marta Jordan, in Warsaw on May 3, 2013, in the Teatr Polski of Warsaw, directed by Andrzej Seweryn. Mayorga himself directed the first full Spanish staging, which premiered on November 11, 2016, at the Teatro Calderón in Valladolid while using just two actors (Blanca Portillo and José Luis García-Pérez) to represent the twelve characters.

In a conversation with Mayorga, I asked him if he wrote the play with the idea that only two actors would interpret all twelve characters, and he told me that, no, it was written as all his plays are – thinking of as many actors as characters. However, Blanca Portillo, a well-known and lauded Spanish film and stage actor with whom Mayorga has worked before, wrote to him to ask if they could stage it using just her and José Luis García-Pérez. Mayorga agreed because, as he told me, the play is about cartography, that is, about representation, and therefore it made sense to stage it in a concise, cartographic way where a simple gesture or object could signal a change in setting or character. Besides, because every scene consists of just two characters, it was possible. The only problem was scene 24, in which Blanca is talking with Deborah, but Mayorga found a "poetic solution" by having José Luis play the character of Blanca. He explained that the Moscow staging had one actor per character, but the Buenos Aires staging had fewer. This is in line with Mayorga's generosity with those staging his plays – he believes that the play knows more about itself than he does, so every production teaches him something new about his work.

This translation is based on the original text as well as unpublished changes from July 2019 sent to me by Mayorga, his revisions from the Barcelona tour of the play, as well as a copy sent via email in 2021. I have changed all measurements from metric to imperial.

Characters (in order of appearance):

Raúl
Blanca
Samuel
Old Man
Girl
Marek
Magnar
Tarwid
Molak
Deborah
Dubowsky
Darko

1

RAÚL:	Blanca! How are you? Are you OK?
BLANCA:	I'm fine.
RAÚL:	What happened? Where were you? I didn't know what to do. I called the police, firemen, I called every hospital in Warsaw.
BLANCA:	I'm sorry. I lost track of time.
RAÚL:	You lost track of time? Did you lose your phone too? I called you a thousand times. We had an appointment, remember? We were invited to lunch at the ambassador's house. We were supposed to meet there at two. I haven't heard anything from you all day.
BLANCA:	I was on my way, to the address you gave me. I left with plenty of time, with that map you gave me. Right next to an abandoned handball court, I thought I saw an old church, I approached it thinking it was a church. I'd never been in a synagogue before. Have you?
RAÚL:	What are you saying, Blanca? You have the whole embassy out looking for you.
BLANCA:	Inside, they're very different from our churches. The way the pews are arranged, the shelves full of books… There were two men talking in English. One was explaining to the other that the Germans used it as a stable, which is why they didn't burn it. When they saw me, they pointed to a small staircase. I understood that it led to the women's section. In a large room up there, they were setting up an exhibition. They were putting up the little cards. Underneath each photo, in Polish and English, the place where they think the photo was taken. Nowolipie 35, Bonifraterska up by Krasinski plaza… Boxers, police officers, prostitutes, bicycle taxi drivers…
RAÚL:	Yeah, I know, we've seen all that in the movies.
BLANCA:	People! A wedding. Children, lots of children. It occurred to me to mark the locations of the photos on my map. I thought the street names would have changed, or wouldn't exist at all, but I

found a lot of them. Look, each mark is a photo, there were a lot on Chlodna Street. As I left the synagogue I started walking toward this mark, because according to the map it was the closest. Nothing's left from what's in the photo. Then I went here. Nothing. On Chlodna I did see a house that could've been from the period, a house…

RAÚL: Blanca, I have to call the ambassador and I can't tell him this story about the photos.

BLANCA: "As she left the house someone hit her over the head, she thinks they shoved her in to a car, and when she woke up, she was in the middle of the countryside." Would that be more acceptable for your ambassador? Or better yet: "She went to a bar, met a man who bought her a drink…"

RAÚL: Forgive me. Sorry. You found a house from that period…

BLANCA: I was looking until I realized that a little girl was watching me from the window, from behind a curtain. I thought I might be scaring her, so I left, until this place and later I went to this one, and later to this one. Nothing. Here there is a monument, the pedestal's covered with flowers and candles, and little stones. They look like shipwreck survivors trying to reach an island. But what really hits you, is the emptiness all around, the emptiness that surrounds the statues. Across from it they've built a museum: "Museum of the History of Polish Jews." I kept going this way, via Zamenhofa, and a little bit later, here, at the intersection of Mila, I saw another monument. Without human figures, only a burnt black stone, from the ruins of the Ghetto. They have engraved names on it. The last members of the resistance are buried underneath, that's where they fell and that's where they are, the stone looks lost in between those apartment buildings. In the photos, the street was filled with kids, it was the happiest street in the world. Here is where I realized it was getting dark and I had spent the whole day walking.

RAÚL: Have you eaten?

BLANCA: It's not just the people that are missing.

RAÚL: Maybe you should go to bed. Tomorrow we can talk more. I'll call to say you're OK.

BLANCA: This house, look at the map. Our house is inside the Ghetto.

2

BLANCA walks following a map.

3

SAMUEL: Can I help you?

BLANCA: I don't understand. I don't speak Polish.

SAMUEL: English?

BLANCA: English, yes.

SAMUEL:	Are you Italian?
BLANCA:	Spanish. Why are you taking them down?
SAMUEL:	You've already seen them. You were here yesterday. And the day before that.
BLANCA:	Why are you taking them down?
SAMUEL:	The exhibit has been shut down.
BLANCA:	???
SAMUEL:	There's some controversy about who owns the photos. The judge has decided to keep them until it's resolved.
BLANCA:	???
SAMUEL:	As he was digging a ditch, a construction worker found an old brass milk can and seven rolls of film inside it. He took the can to the police. The police developed the photos and, seeing what they were of, brought them to us. Now the worker is asking for compensation. There's also the landowner. He's demanding the film cartridges. And there's someone else. A German. He says his father took those photos. Wouldn't that be great, that they end up in one of those guys' houses? The judge is thinking about it. Who does this photo belong to? To the descendants of the guy who took them or to the descendants of the people in the photos? To Poland, to Germany, to Israel? He's thinking it through. But I have faith. You know why you and I are talking about this right now, right here? Why these walls withstood it all? Not even the devil is perfect. He always forgets something, always leaves something behind. They're beautiful, aren't they?
BLANCA:	They're not sad.
SAMUEL:	They're not posing. They don't know they're being photographed. My grandmother lived on this street.
BLANCA:	The teacher Grabowski, teaching violin.
SAMUEL:	The teacher Grabowski?
BLANCA:	That's what I call him. I don't know if it's a Jewish last name.
SAMUEL:	And what do you call those two chubby ladies? How can they be so fat?
BLANCA:	To me, these are Milena and Flora. Prostitutes.
SAMUEL:	I hadn't thought of that.
BLANCA:	There had to be all sorts there, right?
SAMUEL:	Could be. What do you think of Warsaw?
BLANCA:	I've barely seen it. This one doesn't have a card.
SAMUEL:	The ones that don't have a card mean we still don't know where they were taken. Do you know what the most popular music was in Warsaw at that time?…
BLANCA:	The tango? Seriously?
SAMUEL:	Do you like to dance?
BLANCA:	I used to.
SAMUEL:	I know a place in Warsaw where people go who really like to dance.
BLANCA:	I can't.
SAMUEL:	It's called "Utopia." It's not far. I'll finish this and we'll take a walk.

BLANCA: What does this man have in his hand?
SAMUEL: … A watch?
BLANCA: The girl with the pencils, have you put it away already?
SAMUEL: The girl with the pencils?
BLANCA: It was over there… Here.
SAMUEL: The girl with the pencils… Don't ask me to look for it, given all I have to do, the judge is waiting for them… If it was on this wall, then it has to be in that box. No, not that one, the third one. Don't mix them up, don't change the order.
BLANCA: Here it is. Look, they took them in the same place. The map in the background, don't you see? In the two photos it's the same map.
SAMUEL: Could be.
BLANCA: Look at this street. It's a continuation of this one… Can I take them?
SAMUEL: Take them? I have to give them to the judge.
BLANCA: I'm not asking for the rolls of film. It's just a piece of paper.
SAMUEL: Please, put that photo where it was.
BLANCA: That map… What city is it? That city doesn't exist.
SAMUEL: ???
BLANCA: There's no city like that, nor would there have been… Unter den Linden… Boulevard Saint-Germain… Piazza Navona…
SAMUEL: Can you really read those little letters?
BLANCA: I recognize the shape of the streets; I've been on them. If only there were a city like this… You walk up the Gran Vía in Madrid and you arrive at Prague Castle, you cross the Restauradores Plaza and you're in the Acrópolis… A compass, that's what the man has in his hand!
SAMUEL: Mosiek, the mapmaker. Or do you prefer Merkin? Merkin, the mapmaker.
BLANCA: Are you making this up?
SAMUEL: My grandmother. My grandmother would pass the day telling stories about the Ghetto. The older she got, the more stories she told. She told me the one about the mapmaker a thousand times.
BLANCA: The mapmaker of the Ghetto.
SAMUEL: Old wives' tales.
BLANCA: A mapmaker that lived in the Ghetto? A mapmaker that drew the Ghetto?
SAMUEL: In Utopia, if you don't want to dance, nobody forces you to. On the way, I'll tell you that story. My grandmother used to tell it to me like this: "Once upon a time in the Ghetto…"

4

OLD MAN: Something's missing.
GIRL: ???
OLD MAN: You've drawn the girl's route. You've drawn the wolf's route. And the hunter's route?

GIRL:	???
OLD MAN:	The hunter, does he fall from the sky to save the girl?
GIRL:	No, of course not.
OLD MAN:	When you're finished, you'll do *Puss in Boots*.
GIRL:	My father is waiting for me.
OLD MAN:	Well if your father is waiting for you, then go, goodbye.
GIRL:	Goodbye.
OLD MAN:	Wait. Look in the pencil box. Do you see a key?
GIRL:	Yes.
OLD MAN:	That cupboard over there. Open it.
GIRL:	It won't open.
OLD MAN:	Try it again.
GIRL:	Now it does.
OLD MAN:	There should be two folders. Bring me the white one. Open it. Don't you feel like you're right there, right in the battle of Waterloo?
GIRL:	Yes!
OLD MAN:	You don't need to hold it with such respect, they're not the originals. Ibrahim al Mursí drew this one on gazelle skin!
GIRL:	It looks like a painting.
OLD MAN:	As if Dürer drew it. A map is just as much art as it is science. "Egyptian Map of the Afterlife." They left it for you in the sarcophagus to orientate you in the land of the dead. Until we draw them, places scare us. When we've drawn a place and the road that leads to it, only then do we feel like masters of that place.
GIRL:	This one looks like a children's map... "Paradise!"
OLD MAN:	Drawn with complete detail. This map doesn't say much about the world, but it says everything about the world for which it was drawn. In every map you see the world that drew it.
GIRL:	Are they in some sort of order?
OLD MAN:	They are, but you have to find it yourself.
GIRL:	This one's so beautiful!!!
OLD MAN:	You're looking at it upside down. The guy who drew it paid for his mistakes with his life.
GIRL:	???
OLD MAN:	The success of a trip, the triumph of a battle, life or death depended on maps like these. This other one, contrary to what it looks like, wasn't made to orientate the Spanish ships, but to confuse the Turks. Allowing false maps to be stolen, they've been doing that since Rome.
GIRL:	My father is...
OLD MAN:	Look.
GIRL:	A part of France? What's so special about that?
OLD MAN:	It took a century to make it. Four generations of the Cassini family worked to make that map. They covered France in a network of four hundred triangles, and they didn't have the equipment we

	have today. Their weapons were their eyes and math and a nation that spurred them on. The French were the first to understand it: France is the map of France.
GIRL:	France is the map of France?
OLD MAN:	The map creates France. It erases differences. In school, hanging on the wall, France in just one color, so that a child learns to whom she is subject. This map is a triumph of reason and King. A map makes some things visible, and hides others, covers and discovers, gives form, and deforms. If a mapmaker tells you "I'm neutral," don't trust him. If he tells you he's neutral, you already know what side he's on. A map always takes a side. Why was the mapmaker the most important man after the king in Versailles? Why was Servetus burned? Ortelius of Antwerp, Mercator from Rupelmonde, they were all dangerous and they all lived in danger. In this map, the center of the world is Athens; in this one it's Jerusalem. These two represent the same place but look what the Czechs call it and what the Germans do. This is the Mexico that Cortés found according to how the indigenous people saw it; the Spaniards saw it like this. First map of India. India is the invention of English mapmakers; it is a military map, what's important are the strategic landmarks used to conquer the territory. In this one, Africa is asking the whites to occupy it. Lions, chimpanzees... Where are the people? This map of languages, this one of creeds, this one of races. They all prepare attacks that will erase borders. They are weapons against other maps. There are always maps on the desks of the powerful. Maps they display to frighten, and secret maps they never show. New maps filled with delusions and old maps they will clench when they call for war. How many catastrophes have begun with a map! Good times for the mapmaker, difficult times for humanity.
GIRL:	"Retreat of European Forests"?
OLD MAN:	Actually, that's three maps in one. The most difficult thing to represent, and the most important: time. The most important thing about space, is time. Europe 1914; Europe 1918. Time!
GIRL:	...??
OLD MAN:	Those are the Galton Maps of smells and sounds. You can make a map of anything. Happiness. Pain.
GIRL:	...!!
OLD MAN:	That's the first map your father drew. Put the folder where it was. The red one underneath. The key with the pencils. If something happens to me, now you know where they are. They'll be yours; I've already spoken to your father about it. And those on the walls, too. Your grandmother didn't like seeing them there, in between the family portraits, but to me they're part of the family. Warsaw 1874, when they started numbering houses. Don't think they did it to make the mailman's job easier, it was to make sure they could

find everyone. First partition of Poland, in 1772. Map of the German language 1932. Map of the Friendship Treaty between Hitler and Stalin from 1939. How can anybody be surprised by what's happening? Everything occurring today was announced in those maps. Looking at them, don't you feel danger? Don't you feel the catastrophe approaching? We didn't discover how to read them in time. How could we have been so blind? Now I know that all of those maps, and all the ones I've sketched in my life, were only a prelude to the one I should draw today. But this last one, I can't do it alone now. If God would return just a smidgen of my strength, even if I had to drag myself, I would go out there to look and I would make the map of those streets in which men hunt men. But I don't even have the strength to hold a pencil. I need your eyes. Will you be my eyes?

GIRL: ?? My father could…
OLD MAN: Your father, no…your eyes. Grab the ruler. Go over there and take a step… A normal step… Measure from one foot to the other… Write it down… The first thing we're going to draw is the perimeter. You are going to walk along streets parallel to the wall, counting your steps.

5

BLANCA walks following a map. GIRL walks counting her steps.

6

RAÚL: But what are you doing out here? Aren't you cold?
BLANCA: Yes.
RAÚL: At eight o'clock the ambassador is going to say a few words. We should get back inside.
BLANCA: I don't see our house.
RAÚL: Follow my hand. The Sony billboard, the stadium, the glass cupola of the mall. Behind that bunch of trees, that's it.
BLANCA: Is that the park where you go running?
RAÚL: Yes.
BLANCA: Can you remember the addresses of all our houses? You can't.
RAÚL: 312 Ahmed Bouzrina… 45 Choquehuanca…
BLANCA: 65 Choquehuanca. 15 Sloane Square.
RAÚL: … The man you were talking to before at the cocktail hour – who is he?
BLANCA: He said he was a councilman.
RAÚL: I saw you showed him a notebook.
BLANCA: An idea I had. Look.
RAÚL: … Why two colors? That white patch.

BLANCA:	The shadow of the Ghetto.
RAÚL:	??
BLANCA:	The space it occupied. The dotted lines are the successive reductions.
RAÚL:	A map for tourists? "Visit Warsaw. A Journey to Depression."
BLANCA:	A map for those who live here. It's part of the city.
RAÚL:	What did the councilman say?
BLANCA:	He talked to me about that museum of the history of Polish Jews, and about the monuments. But it's not about museums or monuments. I told him an idea I had this morning, walking through there.
RAÚL:	Another one?
BLANCA:	To draw the silhouette of the Ghetto, on the ground.
RAÚL:	Imagine that a foreigner came to Spain, lecturing us. That he had the idea to draw, there on the map, or on the ground, the atrocities of our history. Wouldn't you feel offended?
BLANCA:	He wasn't offended. He said he'll speak to the mayor about my ideas.
RAÚL:	I hope he doesn't. These receptions are mere theater. The only important thing is to not do anything that would bother anyone. We're not Polish, we're not Jewish. What city doesn't have its wounds, its shadows?
BLANCA:	That blue building, that's where the Great Synagogue was. Now it's the headquarters of Peugeot.
RAÚL:	What should be there, in your opinion? A vacant lot?
BLANCA:	I don't know, but not the Peugeot headquarters.
RAÚL:	We have to go in, the ambassador...
BLANCA:	I spoke to him about the mapmaker of the Ghetto. The councilman hadn't heard of him.
RAÚL:	??
BLANCA:	I told you about it. The story the man at the synagogue told me. The councilman promised me he'd look in to it.
RAÚL:	Have you gone back to that synagogue?
BLANCA:	To see the photos. They've taken them down.
RAÚL:	Why did you go in there that time, when you thought it was a church? Did you want to pray?
BLANCA:	No.
RAÚL:	...Blanca, it's only going to be a few minutes.
BLANCA:	Is he going to say something important?
RAÚL:	No. I wrote it. I have to accompany the ambassador.
BLANCA:	I'd like you to see the photos. They're not sad. There's life in those photos.

7

OLD MAN:	So, in total we have...34,812 steps for the wall's length.
GIRL:	The height is about two men. We're not allowed to get near it.
OLD MAN:	You're not going to get near it. So, Zlota and Lucka streets are left outside the wall... What is this?

GIRL:	A footbridge so that the people don't step on this street that's not part of the Ghetto. I can measure the wall without getting too close. With that machine, if you teach me. I've seen you use it. It's called a toedolite.
OLD MAN:	I'm not going to let them see you with it out there. You said the height of about two men. That's enough.
GIRL:	I'll cover it with a rag, as if it were a doll.
OLD MAN:	… It's called a theodolite. Do you know what it's used for?
GIRL:	To measure heights.
OLD MAN:	To measure angles. And, accordingly, to measure inaccessible heights. Your great-grandfather made that one with his own hands. The wall. You point at the base with this, and at the top with this. The semicircle gives you the angle. You take a few steps back and you look again, and you jot down the new angle. A couple of calculations and you have it.
GIRL:	Yes.
OLD MAN:	You'll also take the small compass. We'll begin by determining reference points in order to situate the others. If they stop you, you say you don't know how to use it. "It's a toy I found. I don't know why this needle moves." Do you know why it moves?
GIRL:	… Yes.
OLD MAN:	Machines help you, but nothing can substitute an eye that knows how to see. The strength of the mapmaker is the ability to see and choose the essential. Seeing, choosing, representing: those are the mapmaker's secrets. With just a few signs the mapmaker must reveal a world. Any sign works if it speaks clearly, the map should speak at first sight. We don't make it for ourselves, but for someone who will look at it one day, maybe within a thousand years. What do we want them to see? This is where the scale question comes in. Important things are only seen at a small scale. Two armies about to enter in to combat: it's easy to represent the number of soldiers, their positions, their armaments… But, what about their reasons to die? And a soldier's courage and fear? It's easy to draw a street, but an instant in the life of the street? We'll begin with Nowolipie. When we get to the corner with Smocza, we'll turn right.

8

MAREK:	It's not here, or anywhere.
BLANCA:	??
MAREK:	Ever since I've been working here, I've seen people arrive with all kinds of treasures. We look at each piece in detail, no matter how extravagant they may seem. It's our responsibility, this is much more than a museum. I've seen it all: crudely rigged movies, Anne Frank knockoffs… It's surprising how imaginative memory can be. Who produces this trash? Madmen, people who want to look

important, riffraff looking for a profit... You wouldn't believe the amount of money they ask for. But there are also well-intentioned people. With good or bad intentions, every so often someone shows up with a map of the Ghetto. Do you want to see an authentic map of the Ghetto? Watch the step. I call this storeroom the "Room of Lies." A museum within a museum. Come this way, here they are. Some have... poetic value. Look at this one, isn't it beautiful? But this avenue wasn't opened until after the war. There are many legends about the Ghetto, and the map legend is the most unlikely of all.

BLANCA: How would you tell it?

MAREK: Once upon a time in the Ghetto, while everything was dying around him, an old man insisted on drawing a map. But because his legs wouldn't support him, because he couldn't go look for the data he needed, he asked a young girl to do it for him.

BLANCA: ... Those photos. I've already seen them in an exhibit, in the Nozik synagogue, only smaller. Are they fake?

MAREK: We're analyzing them. At least one wasn't taken in the Ghetto.

BLANCA: Which one?

MAREK: That boxing club was in the Aryan section. I am going to show you two authentic maps. We have them exhibited on the second floor, follow me... This was the sign at the entrance to the Ghetto. Do you know German?

BLANCA: No.

MAREK: "Typhus Threat Area." Typhus was the pretext to build the wall. But much before then, look at these plaques, Jews were prohibited from sitting on benches or entering parks. This is the Warsaw census from 1939; this one, from 1945. Here, take them. Do you feel it? It's people that are missing. This is the first map I wanted to show you, the flames took half of it. By the shape of the borders, you can deduce it was drawn before the war. Do you see what it represents?

BLANCA: ... No.

MAREK: It's a map to escape Europe. Places where you could still flee from: Lisbon, Rotterdam, Trieste... And the possible destinations, with distances from Berlin: Cape Town, Havana, Shanghai... There in front you have, yes that one, an authentic map of the Ghetto, the only one drawn during those dates, that I know of. It is full of interesting information: number of occupants per building, number of children... The enemy always makes the most precise maps. The Ghetto from the murderers' point of view. They were convinced they were going to finish the job. All across Europe they collected pieces to create a Museum of the Extinct Jewish Race.

BLANCA: How do you know the story about the mapmaker is fake?

MAREK: Why do you want it to be true? What are you looking for in that map?

BLANCA: How do you know it's fake?

MAREK: Anyone who has studied the time will tell you: it's unthinkable to
            have a kid walking all around with such freedom of movement.
            Look at this map: the Ghetto wasn't a city; it was a cage. And
            once they began the deportations, any child was condemned to
            death. Only an angel could have moved around like that.

9

OLD MAN: Post office. Employment office. Aryan Sector Exchange Office.
            Factories: shoes, uniforms, ammunition. Each line stands for
            one hundred workers. Hospitals, dining halls, police, by groups:
            Jews, Polish, Ukrainians… Get it out of my sight. Let's just forget
            about it.

GIRL: ????

OLD MAN: It was stupid to think you would be able to manage something
            like this. Go play with your friends. And take that.

GIRL: But what did I do wrong?

OLD MAN: The bad mapmaker wants to put everything in. If you put every-
            thing in, no one will see anything. I've told you a hundred times:
            "Definitio…"

GIRL: "Definitio est negation."

OLD MAN: Sacrifice: that's the most important thing about mapmaking.
            What do I want to make visible? Once I know that, I will know
            what to exclude. "Definitio est negatio."

GIRL: I'm sorry.

OLD MAN: A map isn't a photograph. In a photo there are always answers to
            questions no one has asked. In a map, there are only answers to
            the mapmaker's questions. What are your questions?

GIRL: …

OLD MAN: Asking questions of oneself is much more difficult than measur-
            ing and drawing. What are yours?

GIRL: …

OLD MAN: This isn't just any old map. It can't look like any other map that
            you've seen. It's the map of a world in danger. An ark.

GIRL: ?? Noah?

OLD MAN: Open the cupboard. Bring me the other folder, the red one.
            You're going to see something I've never shown anyone, not even
            your grandmother. Do you know what this is?

GIRL: Looks like Warsaw. But it's really weird.

OLD MAN: It is the life of my mother. She never left this city. This is where
            she would buy her bread. This star here is the place where she
            died.

GIRL: !!!!

OLD MAN: This one is the map of my father. Every day for forty years, he'd
            take this route to work. My parents were born nearly 700 miles

apart, but their maps crossed at precisely the right time. This one is his brother Stefan, the one who emigrated to Argentina. Compare them: at the beginning they're almost identical, but little by little, they start separating and they never come back together again. And this map here, do you know who it is?

GIRL: ??

OLD MAN: Don't you know your father? There you are, your birth.

GIRL: !!! I'm also in this one!

OLD MAN: That one is a failed map. It took me years to create that symbol system. The road to my grandfather's house, where I first saw a map. My best friend's house, the house of the first woman I kissed, the park where I met your grandmother, the bed where she died, graves of men whose names no one remembers. Places where I was loved, places where they humiliated me. Lines of happiness and of misfortune, of fear and of hope. My wish was that, in just a glance, anyone could say: "I know this man." An image of my life, that's what I wanted to draw. Now I'll never finish it, who could think of himself during these days?

GIRL: Let me try it again. Let me try once more.

OLD MAN: What's more important, the police station or the brothel? The post office or the patio where the teacher Berman, despite everything, continues to teach children how to play the violin? What's important when there are four hundred thousand lives in danger? Go back out in the street and ask yourself what should be remembered? You will be the one who saves or condemns. I'm not going to help you with that.

10

BLANCA, GIRL, and DEBORAH, walking.

11

OLD MAN: I'll look like a clown.

GIRL: Would you rather be cold? Don't be stupid, put it on.

OLD MAN: … A clown.

GIRL: You look very handsome.

OLD MAN: How did you get it?

GIRL: In exchange for tobacco.

OLD MAN: Where did you get the tobacco?

GIRL: In exchange for soap.

OLD MAN: And where…? Never mind.

GIRL: … "Ta Da!"

OLD MAN: A LeFranc pencil!! When was the last time I saw a LeFranc…? Do you want to show me something?

GIRL: …

OLD MAN: Come on, let's see it.

GIRL: …

OLD MAN: … A wedding? This is where the reception was. This is where they made her the wedding dress, this means tailor. Ajcyk, the shoe-shiner, with his box between his legs, always at Café Europa. Szlengel wrote a sonnet this morning! Here they've started a mural about Job, here is where the young communists meet. This is where "God of Vengeance" premiered yesterday. Six cases of typhus in the orphanage. Sign of orphanage; sign of typhus. This is where the groom bought his suit… What is this mess?

GIRL: The price is difficult; it changes every hour.

OLD MAN: This is where the Kometa movie theater used to be.

GIRL: Now it's where they take those that they bring from Lodz. Those that arrive from Lublin, they take here.

OLD MAN: The first number is the people that live in the house; the second the children… Lines are better than dots… What is this?

GIRL: Leszel Cogehn. She tried to cross the wall.

OLD MAN: … And these gray spots?

GIRL: An informer lives here. Jews and Germans get together in this bar. This is the Germans' favorite barber shop.

OLD MAN: Erase these spots. Limit yourself to observing. Don't judge.

GIRL: It's part of the Ghetto.

OLD MAN: A man shaves another because he's afraid, because he's scared for his children. What right do you have to judge him?

GIRL: It's part of the Ghetto.

OLD MAN: … Why are you so dirty?

GIRL: The roofs are dirty. There are things you can only see from there.

OLD MAN: … What do you see on the other side?

GIRL: A merry-go-round.

OLD MAN: … Go play.

GIRL: I'm not going to go play.

OLD MAN: … Let's take a look at this zone. Let's go up this way until Twarda Street.

GIRL: It would be better to go this way. I've heard they've opened a slaughterhouse.

OLD MAN: … Ok, we'll go up this way… Wait. We don't want a map that the enemy could use, right? If they capture it, today or in 100 years, we don't want them to know how to read it. Let's encode the map. Distances, names, signs. We'll call the school the warehouse, the warehouse, the school. The synagogues we'll draw as churches. We won't call it Warsaw. That friend of yours, the one who stopped talking. What is his name?

GIRL: Hurbinek.

OLD MAN:	Hurbineka. We'll call it Hurbineka. Where is that music coming from?
GIRL:	From outside, in Hurbineka.
OLD MAN:	Shall we dance?

12

RAÚL:	See, it looks like it doesn't weigh a thing, right?
BLANCA:	It's very pretty.
RAÚL:	I saw it in the window, and I thought: Blanca would look lovely in this dress.
BLANCA:	Thank you.
RAÚL:	Aren't you going to try it on?
BLANCA:	…
RAÚL:	I was right. Red is your color. You can't wear it for the first time to just any old place. Don't you feel like dancing, dressed like this? The ambassador told me about a restaurant on the Vistula, with an orchestra. He told me what we have to order: Sazy Zabjane. I've made a reservation for our anniversary. And this weekend we'll go away to Krakow. The ambassador told me about this amazing hotel. You still haven't been to Krakow.
BLANCA:	I have to go somewhere on Saturday.
RAÚL:	??
BLANCA:	An antiques dealer. He only sees people on Saturdays.
RAÚL:	You're still on that.
BLANCA:	…
RAÚL:	Can I go with you to see that man?
BLANCA:	I prefer to go alone.
RAÚL:	Can I help you look for that map?
BLANCA:	I prefer to do it by myself.
RAÚL:	… And if you don't find it?
BLANCA:	…
RAÚL:	You're not going to find it, Blanca.
BLANCA:	…
RAÚL:	You should do something to keep busy. Study something. You spend too much time alone. What do you do while I'm at the embassy?
BLANCA:	I also make maps.
RAÚL:	?? What kind of maps?
BLANCA:	I hadn't made a map since elementary school.
RAÚL:	I see lots of maps, every day. I have one of Europe in my office that covers the whole wall. You must come see my office. What sort of maps are you making?
BLANCA:	A different one each day. It's like a diary.
RAÚL:	… Are you coming to bed?
BLANCA:	I have to make a map.

13

MAGNAR:	Can I help you?
BLANCA:	??
MAGNAR:	We met at the cocktail hour. I work for the embassy.
BLANCA:	… Sorry, I didn't recognize you. You work in the embassy?
MAGNAR:	I work *for* the embassy. Nothing permanent. I was your husband's interpreter at the European Constitution Conference. I give Polish lessons to the personnel. To your husband. Are you looking for something?
BLANCA:	This building.
MAGNAR:	But this map…
BLANCA:	From the war. The wall passed through there.
MAGNAR:	A boxing club, here? Now there are kids, not everything gets worse. Did you know that Chopin and Gombrowicz used to walk through this park?
BLANCA:	They must have drawn this from the outside. This map isn't made from within.
MAGNAR:	… A chocolate?
BLANCA:	Thank you… Yum!!!
MAGNAR:	Wedel, the oldest chocolate factory in Warsaw. The same recipe as a hundred years ago, the same flavor. A bite and you enter another time. Where did you get that map?
BLANCA:	In a flea market.
MAGNAR:	The market in the Kolo neighborhood? Lots of stalls with communist souvenirs.
BLANCA:	Yes… Is one of those kids yours?
MAGNAR:	The one in the red sweater. Tomek.
BLANCA:	Of course, he looks like you.
MAGNAR:	He doesn't look anything like me, he the spitting image of his mother. Could you look after these papers while I go push him on the swing? He'll get sick of it right away…
BLANCA:	So, you also translate German.
MAGNAR:	It's for a popular science magazine. This one is about a group that studies snow. Mathematicians. They're looking for a way to predict avalanches. Three euros per hundred words. But I learn a lot. They give me good articles, about all sorts of things. I learn. Before, they used to trigger avalanches with dynamite to study them, it was really dangerous. From a shelter, they would measure the velocity, the trajectory… Now all of that is done by a computer, they don't even have to touch the snow. They process tons of data, real or invented: humidity, temperature, time in the sun… Snow is tough. It seems simple, but at a microscopic level it's very complex. Put a handful of it in the fridge and come back after a while and you'll see how it's changed. It's in constant metamorphosis, it's difficult to study something that is transforming

all the time. They want to understand what factors determine the connections between the crystals, what makes a layer strong or weak. Snow is like a cake with many layers, some many feet thick, some as thin as paper. On the surface, the crystals are affected by wind, by the sun… While that's occurring on the outside, what's happening on the inside? And what happens if a storm leaves an even heavier layer there on the snowy surface? The most likely scenario for an avalanche is when a weak layer is covered by another stronger one. A little bit of pressure can fracture the weak layer and trigger a huge displacement. But, contrary to popular belief, sound does not cause avalanches.

BLANCA: Snow is tough.
MAGNAR: Very tough. What's your name?
BLANCA: Blanca.
MAGNAR: …
BLANCA: You teach to me?
MAGNAR: It's not a very useful language outside of Poland. Only those who are thinking of staying study it.
BLANCA: To understand people. To speak people.
MAGNAR: You speak very well.
BLANCA: Very badly.
MAGNAR: … Let's see if you can read this.
BLANCA: … "At Utopia everything begins at midnight."
MAGNAR: A guide to Warsaw's nightlife. By David Beckham.
BLANCA: Really?
MAGNAR: No. Do you like to dance?
BLANCA: I used to.
MAGNAR: In Polish.
BLANCA: I used to.
MAGNAR: Where did you meet your husband?
BLANCA: In college.
MAGNAR: Say the whole thing: "I met my husband in college."
BLANCA: I met my husband in college. I've never seen a frozen river. Where is that music coming from?
MAGNAR: From Utopia. If you don't dance anymore, what do you do?
BLANCA: Maps.

14

OLD MAN: … Children's Chess Tournament… A crazy lady is dancing in circles… They've finished the mural of Job!… Go rest.
GIRL: Are we going to Chlodna? They say there are many changes there.
OLD MAN: Tomorrow we'll go to Chlodna.
GIRL: See you tomorrow.
OLD MAN: Wait, come here… What are these scratches?

GIRL: I fell.

OLD MAN: You're going around almost barefoot. Doesn't your father see this, that you're going around barefoot? You're very skinny. What have you all eaten today?

GIRL: Meat.

OLD MAN: You ate meat and all you bring me is a bowl of soup? A bowl of watery soup. Look at me in the eyes. What's going on out there? Do you think I won't be able to handle it? Don't fool me, please. Don't you fool me too.

GIRL: Here, a girl steals bread from another, they chase her, she puts it in her mouth before they catch her, they hit her. A man kills for a bag of sugar here. From here to here, there's no electricity, from here to here, no water, there's no water to put out the burning houses. It's been weeks since any coal's gotten through, people are trying to heat one room where everyone sleeps. The doctors don't have anything to soothe the pain, in school we don't have chalk. People keep coming. One man who escaped from Lodz says that there...

OLD MAN: I don't want to hear stories. Just bring me what you see.

GIRL: My father says that things are going to get better from now on: Czerniakow has obtained permission to take trash out of the Ghetto and to make unleavened bread for Passover. My father heard on the radio that the Russians are going to get us out of here.

OLD MAN: I don't want stories. Was there really a children's chess tournament?

GIRL: I've never lied to you.

OLD MAN: If you're not going to tell me everything you see, don't come back.

GIRL: ... Alex Krunz, who worked on the other side, for smuggling a packet of lard. The Buczowscy brothers, the delivery guys from the shoe factory, for letting a horse die. Pawel Fink, for not understanding an order. Karen Brycik, for being on Ogrodowa Street, nobody knew that Ogrodowa was prohibited. Bert Wabeck, our own people killed him for being a snitch. Salomon Toplitz, I don't know why.

OLD MAN: Salomon Toplitz? My friend Salomon?

GIRL: Mr. Wolski, my teacher, for not wearing his arm band. They say he forgot it, but it wasn't forgotten. The cart that picks up the dead departs from here. People can't bury them and they leave them on the sidewalks.

OLD MAN: ... What have you eaten today?

GIRL: My father doesn't have anything left to exchange. My mom's sewing machine, but if he loses the machine, he'll lose his job in the uniform factory.

OLD MAN: Is old Sznapman still alive?

GIRL: The store is still open.

OLD MAN:	Take him the white folder. Get everything you can for it. No money, only food.
GIRL:	I'm not going to sell your maps.
OLD MAN:	They're not originals. I could never afford originals. I've been an irresponsible idiot. It's a miracle they haven't stopped you yet. We're not going to continue with this.
GIRL:	What would it matter if they stopped me? I have everything in my head.
OLD MAN:	The Ghetto is probably full of informants.
GIRL:	No one knows what I'm doing. No one looks at me.
OLD MAN:	I'm ashamed. How much death have you seen already? I was wrong about the map. The map we should have done was the one to get you out of here.
GIRL:	We have to go on.
OLD MAN:	If your father comes in and sees this, he won't let me see you anymore.
GIRL:	He won't come in.
OLD MAN:	It's over. Don't come back here.
GIRL:	Tomorrow we'll go to Chlodna.
OLD MAN:	Don't come back.

15

RAÚL:	The place is really beautiful, and the orchestra magnificent. I ordered Sazy Zabjane. The best table, right next to the river. It would have been beautiful. Happy anniversary, Blanca.
BLANCA:	Zrazy Zawjane. Your ambassador will be happy. You went to the place that he told you go to. You ordered what he told you to order.
RAÚL:	The ambassador is helping me. It's against protocol, I've only been here a short time, but, if I ask for a transfer, he'll support me.
BLANCA:	Request the transfer if you want. I can't leave Warsaw.
RAÚL:	I thought leaving London would help you. Everything's gotten worse since we've been here. You have to leave here. I'm going to get you out of here.
BLANCA:	I'm not leaving Warsaw.
RAÚL:	… It's raining.
BLANCA:	It's not rain. It's snow.

16

OLD MAN:	What are you doing here? Didn't I explain myself well? What do you smell like?
GIRL:	Like shit. They're taking people away. They say they're taking them to work out east. They took the prisoners from Pawiak jail,

but they are also taking old people and children, they took the children from Dr. Korczak's orphanage, the doctor got on the train with the children. I've seen the trains. I went out through a sewer and...

OLD MAN: You left the Ghetto! You should have stayed there. You have to go back there.

GIRL: Six thousand a day.

OLD MAN: What's the Council doing? What is Czerniakow doing?

GIRL: They gave him a paper to sign. A paper requesting them to take away all the people the Council can't feed. Czerniakow asked to be left alone to think about it. He had cyanide. Many people carry cyanide.

OLD MAN: You know how to get out. Use what you know to save your life and someone else's, whoever you want. A life is more important than all the maps in the world.

GIRL: Six thousand a day. They call it the Contingent. The diamond shapes show the raids. They carry out raids because there are never enough volunteers. If you hear the whistle you have to leave right away, so many sleep in their clothes in order to leave right away, they line them up facing the wall and they make the first selection. Some get spared showing their work certificate, people call them "Life Numbers." Today they were paying ten thousand for them. There are many fakes. Those who don't have a number only go out at night, but they also take people with a number. My father says he's safe in the uniform factory because the Germans will always need uniforms. There are three ways to escape. The first, blending in with those who are going to work on the other side, but if they discover you, you need to be carrying six hundred. The second, the death carts, and it costs ten thousand for the driver and thirty thousand for the German. The third, the sewers, the spirals are the sewers, if you get lost you can pass out from the gasses and drown. On the other side of the wall there are people who help the Jews, some for nothing, others make their living from it, hiding a Jew with blue eyes is worth two thousand a month, with black eyes five thousand, the Germans pay three thousand per Jew, hiding a Jew is punishable by death. The plaza. They call it the Loading Zone. Fifty by eighty. This black circle is the entrance, that is where they make the second selection, people always carry some money on them to try to free themselves, even inside you can free yourself if someone can round up ten thousand, at the door there are people that want to get someone out, or pass a message to someone, sending a message costs fifty. A German and a Jewish policeman go about counting. One hundred per wagon, sixty wagons. They don't take those that look the sickest, my father says it could be true

	then that they take them to go work, and that's why they don't want the sick. They give six pounds of bread and two of jam to those who volunteer. To those who don't, two pounds of bread and one of jam. The conductor is Polish... You're burning up.
OLD MAN:	I'm fine...
GIRL:	Here, four people tell jokes while they wait for the raid. María Traube, even though right now she's eating alone, continues to put out the entire table setting. A blue dot is a recent birth. Aunt Vera gave birth to a baby boy. Are you listening to me? Aunt Vera gave birth to a baby boy!
OLD MAN:	If the wall is only two men high, from the second floor they see what is happening on this side. They know what's happening. The world knows what is happening! Can they sleep, can they love one another knowing what's happening?
GIRL:	They're also scared.
OLD MAN:	Isn't that this house? What is that gray line?
GIRL:	My father's route. Every morning, at six, my father leaves the house. But once he gets here, instead of going this way, toward the uniform factory, he goes this way, until he gets to this building, and he enters an office with a great big map of the Ghetto hanging on the wall. They pass him papers and he draws on the map. He always returns with something. He brought those cookies and that soap from there. My father is going to move the big wardrobe against the wall. In the back of the wardrobe, he's going to make a hole that I can fit through. On this side we're going to put that fabric. When he leaves us food, he'll give a signal, this signal... We can't confuse the signals, this signal... We are going to cover the window, except for a little corner so we can know if its day or night. During the day we can't move or talk. At night, we can speak softly, but my father says it's best if we don't talk. At night we can move around, my father says we have to move around, but we have to wrap our feet. If we hear the whistle, we lie down. People come to take things after they empty a house, so we have to be patient. My father says if in three days we haven't heard the signal, this signal... If we haven't heard it, we have to leave. My father could bring you a doctor, but it's better if nobody comes in here. My father will bring us something for the fever.
OLD MAN:	What are you doing?
GIRL:	I'm going to wash you. Then you'll wash me.

17

TARWID:	How did you find us?
BLANCA:	Asking around. One person led me to another, that one to another...

TARWID: Asking what?

BLANCA: I'm interested in that time period. They told me you only receive visitors on Saturdays, I've come by a few Saturdays, but…

TARWID: Don't touch anything, sit over there. Here is the catalogue. If something interests you, jot down the number.

BLANCA: …

TARWID: 217. I'll go look for it. Don't touch anything… Here it is. 217: "In its apparent naiveté, this is an exceptional document. We witness the history of the Ghetto in just one image, exactly as it was seen from inside. But the most extraordinary thing is the perspective from which it was drawn. There are very crude elements, and others that are very stylized, as if the mapmaker grew up while making it. But childlike wonder always appears in response to what it is seeing. Look how it expresses how the space is reduced more and more. The artist is becoming aware that she is drawing herself being hunted. And that she is not making a map for her contemporaries, but for us." My sister writes the cards. There are more than 500 objects, I can't handle all of them.

BLANCA: Then, the mapmaker is… I thought the old man drew it from the girl's information.

TARWID: Look at the names. It's a kid's handwriting.

BLANCA: How is it that you have it? How did it get to be in your hands?

TARWID: Whoever put it in our hands knew what he was doing. We could sell it to a museum, to an American university, they offer us fortunes, but we don't sell. Although, if you wanted to give me something for this piece, I wouldn't refuse. Do you know what a teacher's pension is, after forty-one years of work? And what it costs to maintain a collection like this, do you know?

BLANCA: Who are you?

TARWID: … The first time we entered the Ghetto we didn't come with a plan to take anything. We were the first to set foot in it when the Germans retreated. They had destroyed everything that was still standing before they left. If steam was coming out of a hole, that meant there was still life inside, so they blew it up. When they left, the Ghetto was just a glow. At night we thought we heard voices, little by little we stopped hearing them. One day my sister saw something shiny amidst the rubble. She wouldn't dare get close, but I thought it was stupid not to grab it. Jump to today, and she still doesn't dare touch these things. It became a game, get out of school and come see what we could find. Later people started bringing things to us, they searched us out to bring us things they had found. I don't know what they've told you about us, but, before you judge us, think: What would have become of all of this if we hadn't protected it? It's thanks to us that this map wasn't devoured by light and moisture.

BLANCA: You only have photographs?
TARWID: We photographed each object to protect it.
BLANCA: Can I see the original map?
TARWID: No one can see the artifacts; we've made sure of that. Do you want to see anything else?
BLANCA: The girl and the old man, do you know if one of them survived?
TARWID: My sister and I argue about that often. 134: "Theodolite." A German brought this to me along with number 135: the compass. He was an army photographer. Out of obligation and for fun, he spent the day taking photos of the Ghetto. It was inevitable he and the girl would run in to each other. He told us he took these things from her and let her go. My sister doesn't believe him. "At the end of the day, he was a soldier," she says. Observe Pawiak Street. The line, doesn't it appear to stop abruptly? My sister says they got her while she was drawing this street. That that was the last thing she drew. Isn't it beautiful, that she drew until the very end?

18

GIRL: It's nighttime now.
OLD MAN: Today they were really close. Sooner or later, they'll get here.
GIRL: You have to stretch your legs. Lean on me.
OLD MAN: This park, do you remember it?
GIRL: Walk.
OLD MAN: Your father used to take you here to play. Continue this way, going along the edge of the gas factory, you have to get to here. Avoid Nowi Swit, elegant streets, you'll go more unnoticed on Mokotow. 7 Krakowski Street, don't get it wrong, there used to be a restaurant here, a stationery store here, it has another entrance on Mariensztat. Don't approach the house the same day you find it, observe who comes and who goes, the movement of the neighboring houses. When you're sure it's safe, never the first day, knock on the back door and ask for Mrs. Bogulova. Marta Bogulova. Give her this.
GIRL: ... No.
OLD MAN: You must go to the other side and make a copy of the map there. If not, all will be lost. It's in your head. You can reconstruct it, every detail.
GIRL: ... And you? What will become of you?
OLD MAN: Your father won't let me die. Walk carefully, but so that no one notices you're walking carefully. Don't trust anyone. If they stop you, you're... Mirka Wojtowicz
GIRL: Can I be Jadzia Wojtowicz? I don't like Mirka.
OLD MAN: Can you think of a way we can lighten your hair, Jadzia Wojtowicz?
GIRL: ...

OLD MAN:	What are you doing?
GIRL:	I'm going to sew something for you. Two thousand in each leg, don't forget.

19

MOLAK:	You disappoint me, Deborah. You're free to go, it's your career, a different plan for your future. Just yesterday, in this office, we were talking about your promotion. I'm going to act like I never read this letter, Deborah.
DEBORAH:	I appreciate your respect. I have learned a lot in this building. But I have always wanted to work for children, and I believe the moment has come to make that dream come true.
MOLAK:	Children. You don't have any, right?
DEBORAH:	No.
MOLAK:	You are… Thirty-six years old?
DEBORAH:	Thirty-seven.
MOLAK:	I'm asking you to reconsider your request, I'm afraid it won't be understood. Working here is an honor, the highest a Polish mapmaker could possibly aspire to. I share your concern for childhood but drawing school maps is not the most useful thing you could do for this country. Poland has invested a lot in your training. You had the privilege to be sent to Moscow to study with the best teachers. You can't just think of yourself, Deborah.
DEBORAH:	For a few months now, I've observed inaccuracies in the editions of my maps. I've alerted my superior about it, but no response. It doesn't just affect me, but the entire department. I don't mean the maps where we place elements of a, shall we say, propagandist nature, I'm referring to…
MOLAK:	Propagandist elements?
DEBORAH:	Avenues that are still only in the planning stage, parks that still…
MOLAK:	But you aren't referring to these types of inaccuracies. What sort of inaccuracies do you mean, Deborah?
DEBORAH:	Buildings are missing, or they've been moved. Streets are missing.
MOLAK:	You didn't strike me as naïve, Deborah. "Moved" buildings? "Erased" buildings? You know we're not talking about just any type of buildings. Streets are missing? You know what is on those streets.
DEBORAH:	Entire towns are missing.
MOLAK:	In our maps, towns are missing, and this place where we make them shows up as a theater. The first lesson, Deborah, that our teachers taught us, was to never make a map without considering that it might fall into enemy hands. The location of our factories, the coordinates of our leaders' houses, where we draw our maps, the enemy wants to know all of this, and we're not going to tell him. Not before he removes his own mask.

DEBORAH: The map for the fast train to Krakow. This is what I drew, this is what they've hung in the train cars. The route, distances, everything has been falsified. People don't know where they're going, they don't know where they are. I've come to imagine I don't work in Cartographic Services but in the Department of Disorientation. I wonder if, to know where I live, I should just consult a foreign map. I cannot accept that a map of mine is falsified. I can't.

MOLAK: So now I understand what you think of us. Now I am sure that you need to reconsider your decision. The delicate nature of this work makes the State observe each one of our movements. No one is going to stop you from working with children if that's what interests you. But know that from the moment you leave this building, everything you do and everything you've done will be scrutinized, same for your family and friends. Don't forget that your last name, today as ever, makes you suspicious, Deborah Mawult. As soon as you think it over, you will decide to stay with us. We'll take care of you. Outside of here, who will protect you?

20

DUBOWSKY: "Deborah Mawult. Forty-nine years old."
DEBORAH: Fifty.
DUBOWSKY: "Deborah Mawult. Fifty years old. Geographer."
DEBORAH: Cartographer.
DUBOWSKY: "Deborah Mawult. Fifty years old. Cartographer." What sort of maps?
DEBORAH: Scholastic maps. Textbooks, atlases. I also work for the press, especially for the Cronos seminar.
DUBOWSKY: Did you make this map for Cronos? It doesn't look scholastic.
DEBORAH: I made that one for fun. I've been making a personal guide to Warsaw for years.
DUBOWSKY: For a foreign publication?
DEBORAH: It's a private guide. For me and my friends.
DUBOWSKY: Is Adam Rybak a friend of yours?
DEBORAH: … We were friends.
DUBOWSKY: You probably know Rybak fled to the West.
DEBORAH: Yes.
DUBOWSKY: You know? Who told you?
DEBORAH: I don't remember who mentioned it.
DUBOWSKY: Maybe you tried to contact Rybak, and, when he didn't answer the phone, didn't open the door, you thought he'd left?
DEBORAH: I didn't call him or go to his house.
DUBOWSKY: Someone told you: "Rybak has fled to the West." You don't remember who. Do you remember if they said it like this: "Rybak has fled to the West?"

DEBORAH: I don't remember what words they used to tell me.

DUBOWSKY: We found this map in Rybak's house.

DEBORAH: Maybe I gave it to him, I don't remember. Or he could have gotten it from a mutual friend.

DUBOWSKY: Do you share a lot of friends with Rybak?

DEBORAH: I don't know what to tell you.

DUBOWSKY: You said: "Or he could have gotten it from a mutual friend." Who were you thinking of?

DEBORAH: Nobody in particular.

DUBOWSKY: Do you think Rybak could have taken your maps abroad?

DEBORAH: I don't think they're that important to him.

DUBOWSKY: Have you received any money from the West for this map?

DEBORAH: I didn't get any money for this map.

DUBOWSKY: This copy was found in Holland. How do you get your maps abroad?

DEBORAH: I don't send my maps abroad.

DUBOWSKY: I'm of the camp that thinks making maps is work that should be reserved for the State. What would happen if everyone decided to make their own map? We've spent all morning looking at this map. What does it represent?

DEBORAH: It says it right there.

DUBOWSKY: Here it says, "Chopin's Warsaw."

DEBORAH: It shows present-day places that were important in the life of the composer: where he thought of a particular work, where he met a particular person… The idea is to make an atlas of biographical maps. It's amazing to compare those maps. People separated by centuries chose the same haunts.

DUBOWSKY: The opposite can also happen. That two people live at the same time in the same place, but in different worlds.

DEBORAH: Indeed.

DUBOWSKY: Our cartographers suspect that you're not working on any biographical atlas, but toward some other end. You know this city like no one else does. We think this map shows the positions one would need to take to conquer Warsaw.

DEBORAH: You really see that in my map?

DUBOWSKY: A plan to seize hold of Warsaw's key communication and transport lines.

DEBORAH: You're accusing me of…? What are you accusing me of?

DUBOWSKY: "Deborah Mawult. Aged fifty. Between 1951 and 1968 she worked in the National Cartographic Service, where she was let go per her own request. She makes maps for schools and for the press, especially for Cronos. She also makes them for her friends, including Adam Rybak." What are we accusing you of? Sabotage? High treason? Terrorism? We don't know what we're accusing you of yet. I'll tell you when you explain what this other map means.

DEBORAH: Gombrowicz's Warsaw.

DUBOWSKY: I know how to read. What does it represent?

DEBORAH: ??

DUBOWSKY: Did you know, I'm sure you know, that they put a bomb under a table full of maps to get at Hitler? Can you imagine? The little happy guy, leaning over his pretty maps, and all of a sudden, boom! Are you tired?

DEBORAH: I'm fine.

DUBOWSKY: You're tired. You'll be able to rest soon. But before that, I want you to see two photographs. Jana Zablocki before and after January 20th. January 20th, when she was on her way to fly a kite, at this point on Krakowskie Street, she was caught off guard by an explosion. The target of the bomb wasn't the poor Jana, of course, but someone who lived at 22 Krakowskie Street. The people that placed the bomb have been arrested. On them we found "Gombrowicz's Warsaw."

DEBORAH: I haven't heard anything about any explosion.

DUBOWSKY: Before the war, my grandfather had a stationery shop on Krakowskie. He taught me everything about paper. How to cut it, how to protect it from humidity... I can distinguish the quality by the smell. Before the war there was a quality of paper that hasn't been seen again in Warsaw. On what type of foundation do you make your maps, Deborah?

DEBORAH: Szondi 75.

DUBOWSKY: Pencils... Let me guess. Tindall?

DEBORAH: LeFranc.

DUBOWSKY: Do you draw the maps directly or do you draw a smaller sketch first?

DEBORAH: I haven't heard anything about any explosion in Warsaw.

DUBOWSKY: Maps are the work of the devil. Is the mapmaker responsible for how others use her maps? I don't think so. I think you made this map without knowing what they would use it for. I also think that you're going to write down, on this pretty paper, Szondi 75, the names of the people you give your maps to and the places where I can find them. If you prefer, make me a map. A chocolate? Take a bite, trust me. It's a Wedel, inimitable.

21

DARKO: Mawult, Mawult ... I'm sorry, denied, we can't help you get to Sarajevo. Please understand, our priority is health care personnel. Except for doctors and nurses, we don't accept anyone older than fifty. You are sixty.

DEBORAH: Sixty-one. I've studied this map that the newspapers published, the one they found on that sniper. Someone made it who knows the city like their own body. He's grown up there, knows what is behind every door, the shooting positions that would do the most damage. I can make another map, sewers, tunnels, the blind spots underneath the bridges, the hours when the shadows cover each street ... The besieged has to look with the eyes of the besieger, only that way will he discover what he can't see.

DARKO: A map like that would be useful, of course. We'll call you.

DEBORAH: You don't take me seriously, young man, you take me for a crazy old lady. Look at this, I've spent my whole life drawing. My map will save lives. It's urgent.

DARKO: We'll give you the information you need for your map.

DEBORAH: I can't do it without being there. I have to go there.

22

RAÚL: Once you left the house you stood there, like you didn't know which direction to take. You started to walk to the left. Soon it was easy to guess what you would choose at each crossroads: always the narrowest street. You entered the plaza through that arch and you walked slowly to here. In the dirt you drew a map with your fingers.

BLANCA: ... Shouldn't you be at the embassy?

RAÚL: You never ask me what I do at the embassy.

BLANCA: What do you do at the embassy?

RAÚL: I read reports. From those reports I write more reports. I want to believe that the ambassador reads them, or someone in Madrid, I want to believe that someone reads my reports, in order to write more reports. On Mondays, Wednesdays and Fridays, I have Polish class. My Polish teacher, to make me speak, asks me all these simple questions. "What are you going to do this afternoon?" "Where did you meet her?" "Is she pretty?" "What color are her eyes?" I wanted to ask him a question, but I lack the words: "How do you win the love of a woman who once loved you?" Because I know you loved me once. I lack the words.

BLANCA: ... Shall we go home?

RAÚL: ...

BLANCA: ... Can you help me?

RAÚL: What do you want me to do?

BLANCA: I'm going to lie down over there. Naked. I want you to draw my silhouette. Without touching me. Don't touch me, please ...

RAÚL: ... What are you going to make with it?

BLANCA: A map.

RAÚL: … Can we talk? Can you at least look at me? Blanca, I'm going to call your family. You're going back to Madrid. They'll take care of you there.

BLANCA: No. I have to make the map. You look at your body and things appear. People, animals, words. Colors, sounds, dates. Places. Madrid. Warsaw. London. Separated things appear together. Forgotten things return. You when I met you. Alba the day she was born. Alba the first day of school.

RAÚL: Blanca …

BLANCA: Alba walking alone through London.

RAÚL: Blanca …

BLANCA: Why don't we ever talk about her?

RAÚL: Because it hurts us to talk about her.

BLANCA: She was alone. Where were we while she was sinking?

RAÚL: She didn't even seem sad.

BLANCA: We didn't even see she was sad.

RAÚL: …

BLANCA: It could be done the other way. You could go around the world leaving bits of your body.

RAÚL: Will you let me see how you do it? Let me stay, please.

BLANCA: … Her empty room. At five she is still here, I enter her room at five, she has her eyes closed, but she isn't sleeping, now I know she wasn't sleeping, I wish I would have kissed her, my legs were heavy from so much dancing, my head hurt from drinking and laughing, I just wanted to get in bed, every night I dream that it's that Sunday again, and I wake her up with a kiss "Get up, Alba, it's a beautiful day, don't waste it," I should have kissed her. I heard her footsteps, she left without kissing us, trying not to make noise, if only she would have slammed the door, if only she would have left shouting at us, if only she would have insulted us. If only she would have hit me. At six I return to her room and she's not here anymore. The closet open, she wondered if she should wear the red shirt, she put it on, it was thrown on the floor, in the end she chose the white one. She cut her hair after getting dressed, there weren't any hairs on the red shirt, we didn't find the scissors, only her hair on top of the bed. Sometimes I think I saw her leave, she has very short hair and she turns her head, smiling at us, but it's not true, I must have dreamt it later, or I dreamt it before, I had to have dreamt that smile. She doesn't take the fastest route, they see her pass by here and here, she doesn't know where she is heading, seeing a girl barefoot on such a cold morning stood out to the guy from the bar, her hair badly cut, the white shirt, here's where the guy from the bar saw her, the newsstand woman here, she walks always choosing the narrowest street, she doesn't know where she is, she's never stepped foot on those streets, she's not far from home, we would see her if we could look in a straight line, you know, as the crow flies. If anyone approaches her, she crosses the street and speeds up, she can't go back now, she would stop to sleep on the sidewalk, she's afraid of falling asleep, she hasn't slept for days, she'd give anything to close her eyes and sleep, no one will hurt her here, between the swings, nobody is in the park, she's cold, that dog isn't going to hurt her, stray dog between the swings, the last thing she sees is that stray dog, she closes her eyes, finally she's at peace, finally she smiles.

23

OLD MAN:	...!! How do I know that you aren't a dream?
GIRL:	The air smells good. There are birds, children ... Theaters, store windows ... Wedel, where you used to buy me chocolate, is still open. I saw our house. I saw the people that now live in our house.
OLD MAN:	How is Marta?
GIRL:	She must have been very pretty.
OLD MAN:	What did she do when you gave her my drawing?
GIRL:	...
OLD MAN:	Did she really say that?
GIRL:	There was another girl in the house. I hadn't realized what I looked like, I realized it by how the other girl was looking at me. But Mrs. Bogulova kissed me without disgust. She told me that she could register me as her granddaughter.
OLD MAN:	If you aren't a dream, you should have stayed there. You have to go back there.
GIRL:	Don't you hear the shots? The Ghetto has risen up.
OLD MAN:	!!
GIRL:	I've brought you this. It has one bullet; I can't give you more.
OLD MAN:	How many are you?
GIRL:	I don't know.
OLD MAN:	Can you win?
GIRL:	No.
OLD MAN:	And, nevertheless, it's important to fight, of course it is. But so is finishing our work, and only you can do it.
GIRL:	The map is there. There's no longer another map to do. Ruins and fire, that is the Ghetto.
OLD MAN:	You need to to save yourself. Not for yourself, for each one of them. No one knows what you know. If you can live, your duty is to do it and tell the world what you've seen.

24

DEBORAH: Please, have a seat. I'll do the best I can, but I warn you my English isn't very good. We said ten minutes, right? How did you get my number?

BLANCA: Your editor gave it to me.

DEBORAH: That brave scoundrel, do you know how much that bastard owes me? Well, how can I help you?

BLANCA: You are a mapmaker.

DEBORAH: Retired. And you? Editor?

BLANCA: My husband is stationed at the Spanish Embassy.

DEBORAH: Spain. I've never been there.

BLANCA: You were born in 1931.

DEBORAH: Are you visiting mapmakers born in 1931?

BLANCA: I didn't know much about the Ghetto. Just what I'd seen in the movies, some documentary … If it upsets you to talk about it …

DEBORAH: I don't like talking about it, but I do when talking about it serves for something.

BLANCA: I was at the Cartographers' Association. There are only three mapmakers alive who were children at the time. And only one woman. I thought I might be in luck. Your editor told me you're a surv…

DEBORAH: "Survivor." I hate that word.

BLANCA: You grew up in the Ghetto.

DEBORAH: I hadn't yet turned ten when they gave us the order to relocate to the "Jewish District." Three days we were given to move. My father exchanged our house at 17 Odynca Street for a much smaller one at 40 Karmelicka Street.

BLANCA: They say that a mapmaker and his granddaughter…

DEBORAH: That's what this is about! I've spent all my life hearing that story. Even back then they spoke of them. Over time, the legend has been embellished. I heard they were thinking about making a film. The versions all differ the most in the endings. One puts the girl in Treblinka. Another one saves her and takes her to New York, to turn her in to a world authority on cartography. In the third version, my favorite, the girl abandons the map to join the uprising: she stops watching the catastrophe to fight against it.

BLANCA: Her map was also a form of combat.

DEBORAH: It's true, assuming there was such a map. I'm sorry to disappoint you, I wouldn't have minded being her, but I'm not that girl. Look around you, if you're not oppressed by so many maps. This is the kind of thing I look at: unemployment levels, divorce rates, shrines to the Virgin Mary … Nothing too exciting. I never had the occasion to draw those maps that scare people, about the progression of whatever sickness or about the reach of a new terrible missile.

BLANCA: You're very modest. Your editor told me you spent years in prison during Communism.

DEBORAH: It's nothing special, it was easy to end up there.

BLANCA: I've seen your book, *Cartography of Erasure*: map of the Spanish Republican exile, map of ethnic cleansing in Yugoslavia … It's a cartography of disappearance.

DEBORAH: I'm not that girl. My vocation came late in life. I did all kinds of jobs before getting into maps. I wanted to be a painter. The maps thing was only a way to make a living.

BLANCA: Your grandfather was also a mapmaker: Jakub Mawult.

DEBORAH: You know a lot, huh? All I have left of him is there. *Puss in Boots.* He used to tell me a story and I had to make him a map of it. I made a lot of them. *Little Red Riding Hood, The Pied Piper.* A terrible story, that Piper one. He takes the children away! I don't think they'll make that movie. The idea, the mapmaker of a world in danger, is too difficult. It would be better as a play, in the theater everything responds to a question someone has asked, just like maps. The map shouldn't show up, it would always fall short, the play should be the map. So, Spain, huh? Look, that is the Europe that they taught me about in school. One day they hung up that other one and I knew my life had changed. Maybe you'll also see it one day, the borders of your country are erased and new ones appear, places change names, look how that place changes names.

BLANCA: Chernovtsy … Cernauti … Czernowitz … Czerniowce … "European Train System in 1939" … Whoever made it, didn't know what they there drawing … "Fittko Route."

DEBORAH: With that map in hand, some were able to cross the Pyrenees.

BLANCA: "Sarajevo" and "Sarajevo." There are maps that kill and maps that save. "Map of Europe for Africans!"

DEBORAH: Ever since I retired, I only make useful maps, maps for people who are fleeing.

BLANCA: You see the world through the perspective of the Ghetto …??

DEBORAH: "Warsaw Today if That Thing Hadn't Happened."

BLANCA: … Can I show you some photographs?

DEBORAH: What are you waiting for?

BLANCA: …

DEBORAH: Where have I seen these photos before? In the Nozik synagogue? Yes, in the exhibit.

BLANCA: Did you know them?

DEBORAH: No.

BLANCA: I understand, you're not that girl. Can you take a look at this?

DEBORAH: … How much did you pay for this?

BLANCA: Nothing.

DEBORAH: Even so, it's a fake.

BLANCA: How can you form such a judgment just from a photograph?

DEBORAH: Because it's a bad map. If this were the map, it wouldn't deserve to have survived. A bad mapmaker wants to put everything in. "Definitio est negatio." It would be horrible if this were the map. Besides, they would have made sure that not just anyone could use it. Even if you had it in front of your eyes, you wouldn't recognize it. Likewise, if they had the intelligence and the courage to make the map, they would have looked for a way to preserve it. They wouldn't have made it on paper. They wouldn't have used wood either, anticipating that even the last splinter of the Ghetto would be devoured by fire.

BLANCA: So?

DEBORAH: A few years ago, walking along Chlodna Street, do you know it?

BLANCA: Yes.

DEBORAH: A house made me remember that time. From a window, an old woman invited me to approach, or that's what I wanted to believe. I went up a dark staircase, really, really narrow. At the end there was a closed door, I could sense the old woman on the other side, finally she opened the door. I followed her down an empty hallway, the whole house seemed empty, until we got to a wall covered with a sheet. She removed the sheet. There was nothing there. That's what it seemed to me at first. At first, I didn't realize that the wall was filled with marks, like incisions made with a punch. Drawings, words. Names. A map sculpted on the wall!

BLANCA: !!

DEBORAH: I looked into it. That house had been built after the war. I was sorry, believe me, I like the story about the girl mapmaker. We all liked it. The legend was born from the people, from those of us who were going to die, we wanted to believe that we weren't going to be forgotten. Old wives' tale. But I have nothing against stories if they help to remember. What does it matter if the girl existed or not? She could have existed. But you want more, you want to save the girl. Or at least, save the map.

BLANCA: It can't be that all of it was in vain. It can't be.

DEBORAH: It's time for my walk. Want to join me?

BLANCA: Please.

DEBORAH: Pass me those tennis shoes, I'm always barefoot at home. The doctor has ordered me to walk an hour a day, but I'm lazy, every day my legs are heavier. To convince myself, I say to myself: "We're going to this place, Deborah, let's see if it's still there" and I go out to check if it still exists or what they have changed it into. But as soon as I'm out there, I let myself be pulled by a sign I've never noticed before, the gleam of a store window, the racket of a street, or its silence. Every day I find a corner where I've never been, every day I lose myself in my city. If you want to get to know a place, get lost in it. If you want to see the border between the city of the wealthy and that of those who only have their body, you have to get lost. I walk committing it all to memory, as if I had to tell what I saw to someone who was waiting for me. People look at me strangely, someone who walks slowly while looking around is suspicious. I have time, all the time in the world, I could have died at ten years old. I never go directly, I walk all around it in circles, I look at the place at different times of the day, I try to remember what used to be there. Don't trust your eyes, what your eyes see hides things. Stay still while everything else moves, move to one side, move back. It's not enough to observe, you must actively remember, the most difficult thing to see is time. If you focus, you'll see scars about to be lost. Chopin and Gombrowicz liked to walk through that park, the old prostitutes of the Ghetto met up at that entrance, there used to be a boxing club here, my father liked boxing, I think I remember he liked it. It's all going to be erased, the mind is a map surrounded by water, a piece of paper that wants to dissolve. The last thing to be erased is what no one can draw. The shine of his boots, the filthiness of our bare feet. The moans of the Ghetto, the silence of the Ghetto. From here it took 1,200 steps to get to school, we formed the soup line there, our house was here, that's where my father's room was, my room there, the map table there. The wall went by here. A few inches, the wall is the width of a child's step. Here is the Loading Zone, from here is where the trains leave, here is where I see my grandfather for the last time.

25

BLANCA: Aren't you going to the embassy?
RAÚL: Can you help me?
BLANCA: What can I help you with?
RAÚL: I'm going to lay down there. Naked. I want you to draw my silhouette.

26

GIRL chooses a tile from the floor; she picks it up; on the back side of the tile there are marks. GIRL makes another mark. If we turned over all the tiles, we would see them as a grid of a map.

5 *Reykjavik*

Translated by Jerelyn Johnson

Translator's Note

As of this writing, Russia is again mounting an aggressive attack upon one of its neighbors, Ukraine, and by extension, the collective West, and perhaps this play has a renewed relevance now as dramatization of the dynamics of the Cold War, a story about two human beings used as pawns in a political power struggle. *Reykjavik* revolves around the retelling of the meeting between the Russian Boris Spassky and the American Bobby Fischer at the World Chess Championship in the summer of 1972 in Reykjavik, Iceland. When Spassky resigned on September 1 after twenty-one games, Bobby Fischer was crowned champion, thereby ending years of Soviet dominance of the World Chess Championship.

Our play is set in a park. While the characters in the dramatic space remain within a park where they meet to play chess, the imagined world represented in the play spans the globe, from New York, to Moscow, to Reykjavik, and from the present back to the Cold War period. Mayorga weaves this historical event, the chess series, into an intricate game of imagination with Waterloo and Baylen (or Bailén in Spanish) interpreting the roles of Bobby and Boris, and a young boy acting as their necessary interlocutor. The Boy eventually takes on other roles and voices, ending as the heir to Waterloo's position. While the characters re-enact exact chess moves from the Reykjavik match, the characters represented in this play are not limited to the two chess opponents. A symphony of voices surrounding this Icelandic, Cold War spectacle are heard through Waterloo and Bailén: Bobby's mother in Brooklyn, the U.S. Secretary of State Henry Kissinger, an Irish bodyguard, psychoanalysts, Boris's wife, among others. With only shifts in the dialogue to signal changes in characters and time and space, Mayorga complicates the distinction between past and present, historical fact and imagined encounters, using multiple historical figures, settings, and moments in time.

The character's names, save for the Boy, are all the name of battles where Napoleon was defeated: Waterloo, Baylen, and, finally, Leipzig. Also, the text uses the metaphor of a "Napoleonic defeat" perhaps referring to one side or the other meeting their "Waterloo," that is, ultimate defeat. What can we take

DOI: 10.4324/9781003228301-7

from this? Is it a reference to the balance of power shifting from a bipolar one to a multipolar one, similar to that of post-Napoleonic Europe? All of this speaks to the emerging multipolar world of today. What will happen now that Russia is being shunned by most of Europe? Will the United States and Europe, along with the other member states of NATO, continue to work as a combined force in the conflict with Russia? Can we even talk now about Russia as a center of power given the invasion of Ukraine and the West's response? Certainly, the game of wills between Russia and the West has been re-engaged. How can this play help us to understand the political and psychological dynamics of this tension?

Of all the translations, the work on this text may have been simultaneously the most challenging and rewarding. Because I do not play chess, this particular translation required study of the game as well as the events surrounding the 1972 World Chess Championship. I read *Fischer/Spassky: The New York Times Report on the Chess Match of the Century* for details surrounding the final matches, and I re-watched the 2020 television series *The Queen's Gambit* with the subtitles in Spanish to ensure I wasn't missing anything – an approach referred to as the study of parallel texts in translation courses. Everything from the names of the chess pieces to the annotation of their movements differs between Spanish and English. For example, the piece known in English as the knight, is in Spanish called horse ("caballo") while the rook is a tower ("torre"). Therefore, when Mayorga notates certain moves in chess, "Cf6," for example, the translation also needs to consider that the "C" stands for "Caballo" which in English is "knight". However, in English chess annotation, one does not use the "K" for that is already assigned to the "King". Therefore an "N" is used. These details compound to make this a tricky translation, one I enjoyed, and I hope you do as well.

First published in 2014 as part of Mayorga's collection of works titled *Teatro. 1989–2014* (Theater. 1989–2014), *Reykjavik* premiered on March 27, 2015, at the Teatro Palacio Valdés in Avilés, Spain, under Mayorga's direction. This translation is based on the most recent changes to the text sent to me by the playwright in the summer of 2019. I have changed all measurements from metric to imperial, and all currency to dollars.

Characters (in order of appearance):

Boy
Waterloo
Baylen

The BOY stops before a chess board, on which there is an abandoned game.

WATERLOO: Blacks play and win in four moves.

The BOY hadn't seen WATERLOO. He's a stranger, one shouldn't talk to strangers. The BOY is about to continue on, but he stops when he sees WATERLOO move a black piece. The BOY ends up moving closer to observe the new layout of the board. He moves a white piece. WATERLOO and the BOY carry on playing until WATERLOO says:

Checkmate.

The BOY confirms that it is, indeed, a checkmate.

Should we go again?

Without waiting for an answer, WATERLOO places the pieces as at the beginning. They play; the BOY tries to do it a different way.

Mate.

BOY: (*Resuming his walk*). You play well.
WATERLOO: It wasn't me. It was Fischer. It is the fifth of Reykjavik. You have no idea what I'm talking about, right? Bobby Fischer, Boris Spassky… Do those names mean anything to you? What do they teach you in school? Whatever it is they teach you there, it's shit compared to what you could learn here. In just a little time here, you will learn more than in a lifetime at school. About Reykjavik and about any place.
BOY: I get out at two. At two-thirty I could be back here.
WATERLOO: I don't know where I'll be at two-thirty. I don't know if I will be alive at two-thirty.

Silence.

BOY: In second period I have a final exam. Comprehensive. My grade depends on it. Oral.
WATERLOO: A comprehensive final oral exam! Comprehensive oral final! No wonder you are so tense. A stroll through Reykjavik will do you some good. What do you know about Reykjavik?
BOY: Capital of Iceland.
WATERLOO: Very good. Palm trees? Girls in bikinis?
BOY: Cold. Rain. Wind.

WATERLOO acts out the cold, rain, and wind of Reykjavik.

WATERLOO: Cold, rain, wind…and chess. If it weren't for chess, they would go crazy, without fail. Imagine the waves hitting the island during a winter's night. Do you hear the waves? Do you hear them?

BOY: Yes

WATERLOO: I can't hear you. I can't hear you over the wind!!

BOY: Yes!!!!!!

WATERLOO: Chess protects them from the wind, from the cold, from the rain, from life. The Final Battle had to be held here. In any other place, it all would have been more civilized, more human, smaller. When Fischer set foot here, little did he know he would die here. Little did he know…

BAYLEN: You're cheating, Waterloo.

The BOY hadn't seen BAYLEN.

You're trying to prejudice him in favor of Fischer.

WATERLOO: You're not welcome here, Baylen.

BAYLEN: Fischer would die here, but many years later. He's trying to turn you against Spassky.

WATERLOO: He doesn't need your version. He doesn't need you.

BAYLEN: Don't let him confuse you: Fischer's death…

WATERLOO: He doesn't have time. In his second period, comprehensive final oral exam. Complete. Total. He can't get held up comparing versions of the story. His grade depends on it!

BAYLEN sits in front of the board.

You aren't staying here.

BAYLEN: Oh, so it's yours, this "here?"

WATERLOO decides to act as if BAYLEN weren't "here."

WATERLOO: When he sets foot on Icelandic soil, it doesn't make him think of death. When…

He turns toward BAYLEN.

What are you doing?

BAYLEN: What are *you* doing? Who is that kid?

WATERLOO: You said you weren't coming back.

BAYLEN: I always say, "I'm not coming back." I always come back.

WATERLOO: Too late.

BAYLEN: I needed that time. Were you looking for my replacement? How many have there been apart from that guy? Will you tell him to get lost or do I throw him out?

WATERLOO: I am looking for a replacement. But not for you.

BAYLEN: ??

WATERLOO:	I'm looking for an heir. I'm sick.
BAYLEN:	What do you mean "sick?"
WATERLOO:	Like the black bishop in the first of Reykjavik.

Silence.

BAYLEN: If you are looking for a successor, I should be involved. Whoever ends up being your heir concerns me as much as you. It concerns me more than you.

He takes a white pawn with one hand, a black one with the other, he hides them behind his back. He offers WATERLOO his two closed fists.

WATERLOO: Don't you think that, considering it could be the last game, we could skip the lottery? Seeing it could be the last one, I would like to be Fischer.

Silence.

BAYLEN: Considering it could be the last one, I would like to be Spassky. And I think Spassky prefers it too.

WATERLOO: You really think that I have something against Spassky. You offend me.

BAYLEN: I haven't slept a wink thinking of the opportunities that I wasted. I've been studying. I've discovered variations.

WATERLOO: Baylen's bringing variations! Scary!!

BAYLEN: I finally understand what happened in Reykjavik. I finally understand who Boris Spassky is. I know him better than he knew himself.

WATERLOO: There you have it: improved Spassky. Ask him anything you want to know. He will answer any question, as Spassky, in first person.

BAYLEN: Go on then, don't be scared.

Silence.

BOY: Mr. Spassky… Can you tell me…your age?

WATERLOO: Can't you think of a harder question?

BOY: Who taught you to play, Mr. Spassky?

WATERLOO: Better. That is hard. Chess is a "father" thing.

BAYLEN: I learned at this place in Saint Petersburg, watching soldiers play. Chess got me out of Saint Petersburg. Moscow sent talent scouts around the country. They were looking for smart boys and ballerinas.

BOY: But did your dad teach you?

WATERLOO: I can't speak for Fischer with the same certainty with which he speaks for Spassky. I don't "know him better than he knew himself."

BOY:	Do you prefer I ask you your age, Fisser?
WATERLOO:	Fischer, with s-c-h. German last name.
BAYLEN:	Jewish German.
WATERLOO:	I taught myself, with a little instruction sheet. When I understood how the knight moves, I realized I'd be World Champion.
BAYLEN:	Fischer, I forbid you to bring the chess board to class! If I see this board again, I'll throw the both of you out the window.
WATERLOO:	Thanks to my teacher, I discovered I don't need a board.
BAYLEN:	Son, we've been in the car three hours, and you haven't looked out the window once. You only talk about moves. You go to sleep, and you wake up talking about moves. Are you listening to me?
WATERLOO:	Yes, Mom.
BAYLEN:	Do you listen to me when I speak to you or are you thinking about moves?
WATERLOO:	Both, Mom.
BAYLEN:	I'm going to do whatever I can to get you away from chess.
WATERLOO:	She takes me to the psychiatrist.
BAYLEN:	Is your mother important to you, Bobby? Is there anyone you feel affection for? When you see a piece in danger, what do you feel for it?
WATERLOO:	I would have gone crazy if it weren't for chess. I visit a sick uncle, not because he's sick, but because he plays chess. We play on the bed, it smells of piss, he dies, and I'm left with no one to play chess with. I look for rivals in Central Park, at a dollar a lightning round, ten-minute games, what I win I hide in my chess set, so that my mom doesn't take it from me, I buy books on chess, books full of dead champions' moves, I play with dead champions, I play simultaneous games against dead champions.
BAYLEN:	If only you would play with kids your own age… I am going to put out an ad looking for boys to play with you, let's see if you make friends with other boys.
WATERLOO:	A dollar a game, in one hour I make a hundred bucks. I spend six for a ticket to see the Russian selection on tour in America. There I see them together for the first time: the stars and stripes and the sickle and the hammer. The Russians are killing us.
BAYLEN:	What are you doing in the dark, Bobby? Don't you notice it's nighttime? Can you turn down that radio? That preacher makes me sick.
WATERLOO:	The Lord is preparing an exemplary punishment for humankind.
BAYLEN:	Have you done your chores? No matter how well you play, it's not a job, you must get a real job.
WATERLOO:	At 13 I win the U.S. Junior Championship and the Russians start to talk about me. At 15 they invite me to Russia, but they only let me play with kids. At 16 I finally get to compete against

the Russian masters, in the Mar del Plata Tournament. They see me as a threat.

BAYLEN: What we see is how peculiar you are. Nikolai, look at this odd guy. He doesn't know how to tie his shoes. Or relate to people. He doesn't look at you, he only looks at that pocket chess set that he always carries with him.

WATERLOO: It's a myth, my pocket chess set. You don't need a chess set to play chess.

BAYLEN: I beat him with the bishop's gambit, and he starts to cry. Between Mar del Plata and Reykjavik, we play in four different countries, three times we draw, the other I win again. Then he disappears, they say he's given up chess. Where is Fischer? He reappears in the Candidates Tournament. Quarterfinals: Fischer–Taimanov.

WATERLOO: 6–0.

BAYLEN: Semifinals: Fischer–Larsen

WATERLOO: 6–0.

BAYLEN: Final: Fischer–Petrosian.

WATERLOO: 6.5–2.5.

BAYLEN: Who the hell is he? What does he read? What kind of women does he like? (*Sweeping*). He doesn't have a girlfriend. As he was leaving a brothel, he was overheard saying:

WATERLOO: Chess is better.

BAYLEN: (*Sweeping*). *Playboy*, Superman comics, and books about chess. His father didn't teach him, he doesn't know his father. (*Stops sweeping*). Son, doesn't that sweeper seem weird to you? He's spent three hours cleaning the same sidewalk. (*Sweeping*) Jewish woman. Compulsive protestor for the rights of women, blacks, Indians…

WATERLOO: …the Vietnamese, whales…

BAYLEN: They were about to remove custody: her, protesting, and the son alone with the radio.

WATERLOO: The nuclear catastrophe will turn the world into a frozen purgatory…

BAYLEN: Religion on the radio and chess, that was Fischer's childhood. He gives a third of his winnings to that preacher, he never plays on Saturday, and he isn't circumcised. Fidel invited him to play in Cuba, they wouldn't let him, so he played by phone. It was his mother's idea. She won't hesitate to use her son against national interests.

WATERLOO: Boris, check out that sweeper, he doesn't know how to hold the broom. (*Sweeping*). Larissa, ex-ballerina from the Bolshoi, second wife of the champion. Boris Spassky has Jewish blood on his mother's side, his father abandoned him when he was a child. He's refused to join the Party three times. Politically immature, they heard him say.

BAYLEN:	Stalin was syphilitic. (He was seven years old; not Stalin, him.) (*And he points at himself*).
WATERLOO:	He doesn't say Leningrad, he says Saint Petersburg. He reads Bulgákov. He made an inappropriate comment about Lithuania.
BOY:	(*Sweeping*) What comment?
BAYLEN:	"Poor Estonia." (*Sweeping*). No known friends in the resistance. He's known as "honorable anti-Semite." Stalin used to read Bulgákov.
WATERLOO:	(*Sweeping*). You always defend him, are you his lawyer? It was a mistake to make him World Champion. He thinks he won the title alone. He should be accompanied at all times. The Americans intend to use him, taking advantage of his delusions of grandeur and his weakness for women. He likes blondes, and he reads Tolstoy.
BAYLEN:	I like brunettes and I read Dostoevsky. I play like Dostoevsky: strong in defense and imaginative in the attack. Don't believe what you hear about me, Fischer. Ask me directly. What interests you about me?
WATERLOO:	Nothing.
BAYLEN:	I've beat you twice, you haven't gotten past a draw. Do you really not want to know anything about me?
WATERLOO:	Why do you communists like chess so much?
BAYLEN:	Chess is communist. Concentration, patience, and will. Chess is as communist as the circus and the ballet. But don't get confused: I'm not a communist. The Party didn't teach me how to play.
WATERLOO:	I heard that you got married twice. We chess players shouldn't get married.
BAYLEN:	I heard your mother took you to the psychiatrist.
WATERLOO:	To three psychiatrists.
BAYLEN:	The war taught me. I learned in Saint Petersburg, surrounded by death. That is my strength, that is what has made me World Champion.
WATERLOO:	The corruption of world chess is what's made you Champion, you Russians have rigged world chess, I should have been champion ten years ago, it's all organized so a Russian will always be champion, you guys singled me out because if I have to choose between two tournaments, I choose the one that pays more, "Fischer plays for money," of course I play for money, I'm not a prince like you guys, in America there's no respect for chess, I'll beat any Russian you put in front of me.
BAYLEN:	Let's play once and for all. Fifteen cities want the Championship. Choose four and order them as you like.
WATERLOO:	1. Belgrade. 2. Sarajevo. 3. Buenos Aires. 4. Montreal.
BAYLEN:	1. Reykjavik. 2. Amsterdam. 3. Dortmund. 4. Paris.

WATERLOO:	Reykjavik? Why would the Russians want Reykjavik, Father?
BAYLEN:	Look at the map. It's in the middle, between Washington and Moscow.
WATERLOO:	Why Reykjavik, Father?
BAYLEN:	The silence. There you'll find a silence of chess.

Silence.

WATERLOO:	Why Reykjavik?
BAYLEN:	They all play chess there and they bet everything on chess: the wife, the kids... Their bodies have atrophied from playing so much chess, they are only heads and hands. They're putting up more cash than anyone to get the Championship.
WATERLOO:	How much?
BAYLEN:	Twenty times the last championship.
WATERLOO:	They have that much money?
BAYLEN:	They believe they'll earn it all selling the matches to the television stations.
WATERLOO:	Televised chess? Who is going to sit in front of the TV to watch two guys playing chess?
BAYLEN:	This is much more than chess. In the Moscow airport, as I get out of the official car, I see that thousands have come to send me off. The President of the Committee. The Minister of Physical Education and Sports. One hundred children with red scarves around their necks singing the national anthem in my honor.

He encourages the BOY to sing. The BOY sings – The Internationale? – BAYLEN interrupts him.

That's not what they're singing. They all want to shake my hand: the Minister of Industry, the President of the Ice Hockey Federation, another hundred kids...

The BOY sings another song. BAYLEN interrupts him: It's not that one either.

Now I don't know whose hand I'm shaking. The Soviet Supreme? Lenin's mummy? Marx's ghost? It hurts like all the Soviet people had squeezed my hand, all the pariahs of the land, the whole famished crowd. Do they shake my hand to wish me luck? They shake it to warn me that I can't lose. You can't lose, comrade Spassky. They send me off like they send off the troops. There hasn't been a champion that wasn't Russian for twenty-five years.

WATERLOO:	There hasn't been an American champion for eighty years. And that guy, Steinitz, wasn't born in America. American heroes: Joe DiMaggio (*baseball player pose*), Jesse Owens (*track star pose*), Joe Louis (*boxer pose*). From Boston to San Francisco, go ask

about Steinitz on any street… How many Americans know how to move a knight? I'm not going to Reykjavik to fight for them. Victory will be only mine. You can't lose Boris.

BAYLEN: Larissa tells me, kissing me on the lips. I'm afraid of her lips.

WATERLOO: Are you getting it? The game begins way before we sit down in front of each other in Reykjavik.

BAYLEN: I can't lose. What will happen if I lose, Nikolai?

WATERLOO: You can't lose for three reasons. Because you've always beat him. Because for 25 years world champions have spoken Russian. And because that guy has no sense of humor.

BAYLEN: They treat Taimanov like an outcast since he lost to Fischer in the Candidates Tournament.

WATERLOO: Taimanov was condemned because they found imperialist literature in his suitcase.

BAYLEN: Only for that?

WATERLOO: He lost 6–0.

BAYLEN: He was condemned publicly.

WATERLOO: Condemnation must be public for it to be of use to all.

BAYLEN: They took him in front of the Committee to explain himself, they had expelled him from the national team, they had prohibited him from going abroad. He was a model citizen, now he is a traitor.

WATERLOO: He wasn't even able to draw.

BAYLEN: Look at the London bets. Two to one that Spitz wins six gold medals in Munich; five to one that Franco dies before Christmas; three to two that Fischer is crowned before July 20th.

WATERLOO: What do the English know about chess? Look out the window, Boris, we're arriving – doesn't it look like the moon? The Americans bring their astronauts here to train. The whole island is ice and volcanos, the ocean is also full of volcanos. Did you see those horses? The city, look, it's surrounded by lava – now do you understand why Reykjavik means "smoky bay?" That building in the shape of a mushroom? That's where we're going to play. We have ten days before the first match, ten days to get used to sleeping although it's sunny, it never sets, we will see it crawl across the horizon, check out our shadows, we must get used to all of this as soon as possible: elongated shadows, that gray brightness, that gray rain, this marsh smell, that strange language,

BAYLEN: this silence.

WATERLOO: Your photos in all the storefront windows, fans from all over the world will invade Reykjavik. Close your eyes, Boris, you can open them, go out on the balcony and look at the lake. You have me right next door for whatever you need, day or night. In the next room, Botvinik, who knows everything about all the

	matches Fischer has played since he was eleven years old. In the next, Bondarevsky: Defense Analysis. In the next: Geller: Openings. In the next, Brodsky: Physical Preparation. In the next, Laitis: Psychological Assistance. In the next, Kovacs: Translator. In the next, Pavlov: Doctor. In the next, Sasha: Chef. Nei is...
BOY:	in the next one.
WATERLOO:	We've reserved the whole floor.
BAYLEN:	Why is my room at the end of the hall?
WATERLOO:	It is the best suite in the best hotel in Reykjavik. Moscow didn't want Nei to come, it is a concession to you.
BAYLEN:	I'm glad Nei is here so I can have someone to talk to. Who is in the next one?
WATERLOO:	The *Pravda* correspondent.
BAYLEN:	I don't want a translator. I don't want a KGB man following me everywhere.
WATERLOO:	Kovacs isn't KGB.
BAYLEN:	If it's not him, then who is the KGB man in the team?
WATERLOO:	It's honorable to work with the KGB, we all have the duty of vigilance. You should be protected, Boris, it's in your interest more than anyone else's that there aren't any leaks. Let the KGB do its work so that we can concentrate on our own thing.
BAYLEN:	I didn't come to win the war, Nikolai, I came to a chess party. Chess isn't Russian or American. I am not a member of any party, nor do I play from a Marxist-Leninist perspective.
WATERLOO:	I'm not a Party member either, it's important some aren't Party members. Reception, remove the TV from room 313. It doesn't matter what we are if we have good memory. Apart from playing, they also taught us how to tie our shoes. We are the best paid players in the Soviet Union, no other country dedicates so many resources to a game. The Federation has produced all the finalists since '48. Our triumph is based on solidarity. Exactly who is competing in the championship is irrelevant. The one who is in the best theoretical, physical, and moral shape is the one who plays. It's not personal, Soviet chess cannot be defeated. We will be victorious, and they will receive us in Red Square just like the cosmonauts.
BAYLEN:	Three days until the opening ceremonies. Nikolai, when will Fischer arrive?
WATERLOO:	His lawyer – a Hollywood lawyer – says he wants more money for playing.
BAYLEN:	What he wants is a pretext for not playing. 24 hours until the opening ceremonies – where is Fischer?
WATERLOO:	No, Mom, really, I don't want you to come with me to Reykjavik.
BAYLEN:	(*Sweeping*). In the New York airport, surrounded by journalists. Today he's entered six times with his lawyer and he's left six

times with his lawyer. In addition to the set amount of thirty-five thousand dollars and a third of the television rights, he wants a third of the ticket sales.

WATERLOO: And a pool for just me, I don't want to swim with anyone.

BAYLEN: He'll ask for more and more until he forces them to cancel the championship. I've beat him twice. He's scared of me; he's not going to show up.

WATERLOO: He's on the plane… He has gotten off the plane…he's afraid we'll sabotage him.

BAYLEN: Can we sabotage him?

BOY: Twenty bucks says he'll show up.

Silence.

BAYLEN: (*Challenging the BOY*). Opening ceremony. American anthem.

The BOY attempts it.

Soviet anthem.

The BOY attempts it.

The President of Iceland's speech.

The BOY attempts it.

He says that in Iceland there no pollution or crime because everyone plays chess, at any hour there's someone playing chess. He gives me the book *History of Iceland*. The auditorium looks like a large cavern or cathedral. White speakers hang from the ceiling. They remind me of angels, the white speakers. Something about the arbiter makes me think about God.

He challenges the BOY to do God. The BOY attempts it and fails.

WATERLOO: Twenty-four matches, a win is one point, a draw is a half; if the series ends in a draw, the champion will retain the title; two and a half hours for every forty moves; once five hours have passed, it will be postponed until the next day; you will play Tuesday, Thursday, and Sunday. You will never play on Saturday.

BAYLEN: Is it his voice? The way he moves his hands? Or is it his smell that makes me think of God? He speaks from behind the board as if it were an altar. I sit to his left, to his right, an empty chair. Where is Fischer?

BOY: Twenty bucks says he doesn't show.

BAYLEN: I look at the door hoping he appears. They say they have seen him in Reykjavik, they say that he arrived last night in a submarine. You aren't going to show up, Robert Fischer, you're scared of me, here your story ends.

WATERLOO:	In light of his failure to appear, we request the disqualification of the challenger.
BAYLEN:	(*On the phone*) We request a postponement in light of this medical certificate.
WATERLOO:	We request that the challenger be examined in Reykjavik by a neutral doctor. We rule that, if he doesn't appear within twenty-four hours, the Champion will retain the title. We denounce the partial attitude of the German arbiter who is trying to protect the American player. Twenty-four hours have passed. Boris, let's return to Moscow.
BAYLEN:	Let's wait one more day.
WATERLOO:	Moscow wants us to return with the title. We have the right, legally and morally.
BAYLEN:	One more day, Nikolai. Riiiing.
WATERLOO:	Who is this?
BAYLEN:	It that you, Robert Fischer?
WATERLOO:	If it were, with whom would Robert Fischer be speaking?
BAYLEN:	Speaking is… Can you turn off that radio, kid?
WATERLOO:	The Lord is preparing a storm of steel…
BAYLEN:	Thank you. Kissinger speaking.
WATERLOO:	Your accent is like Kissinger on TV. Who are you really?
BAYLEN:	I want to communicate the affection that the President, and with him all the American people, feel towards you.
WATERLOO:	It could be that I'm Fischer. You most certainly are not Kissinger. The National Security Adviser wouldn't waste his time with a chess player.
BAYLEN:	If I could be a chess player, I wouldn't be National Security Adviser. There's nothing like sitting in front of another man that wants to show you he's stronger than you, that he has more imagination and balls than you. I look at the Washington sky and I say to myself: "See those blue stars that sparkle far away? Well, there are more moves on the chessboard than…"
WATERLOO:	You'll forgive me, but I'm going to put on the radio.
BAYLEN:	My office is filled with chessboards. Cuba, China, Israel: there are many possible moves and sometimes none of them are good. Know what I most like about you? That you never opt for a draw. It's what I most like about us: we have courage.
WATERLOO:	Who are you really? Don't you realize that the future Secretary of State wouldn't waste a second with a chess champion?
BAYLEN:	You wouldn't be speaking with the future Secretary of State and future Nobel Peace Prize winner if it had to do with chess. The last American champion was a century ago and he was born in Europe.
WATERLOO:	What's wrong with being born in Europe? Hitchcock was born in Europe. Chaplin was born in Europe.

BAYLEN:	All this hard bargaining – now I ask for this, now this other thing – it's to shake off the pressure and put it on them. We know how to manage the Russians, right Bobby?
WATERLOO:	My mother was born in Europe. You were born in Europe. Even Cary Grant was born in Europe.
BAYLEN:	You haven't been to Vietnam. The doctors certified four reasons why you shouldn't be permitted to put on a uniform.
WATERLOO:	I play alone, I don't represent anyone. Why do I have to fight for my country? Does my country fight for me? In Russia, they take care of their players like heroes, I have to drag myself from tournament to tournament just to put together a few dollars. I'm considering requesting Soviet nationality.
BAYLEN:	The Soviet Union is a chess player's heaven; chess is religion there. From one Jew to another, do you think that chess is a Russian sport?
WATERLOO:	No.
BAYLEN:	You can make it so there's a chessboard in every house in America, all you have to do is beat that Russian. He wants to lose. He knows that if he wins, his government will say that their system is better than ours.
WATERLOO:	Isn't it?
BAYLEN:	It isn't between you and that man; it is between the free world and tyranny. You are going to do it for them: to free those Russians from tyranny. I have your medical report on my desk, and it doesn't have anything that would prevent you from going to Vietnam. Look at me in the eyes when I talk to you. We are going to lose sixty thousand boys in that war – do you want to know why you weren't drafted?
WATERLOO:	The world wants this Championship. I won't play if they don't pay me what I ask for. I must win all that I can before the nuclear holocaust.
BAYLEN:	Do you know that your mom is one of the six million Americans that I have under surveillance?
WATERLOO:	You can't force me to go. Launch your missiles over Moscow, throw my mother in jail, but you won't get me mixed up in your stuff.
BAYLEN:	I know you'll do your job, Bobby, as I will do mine. If we fail, the American people will not forgive us. We can't lose. And now, if you excuse me, I must deal with Chile.
BOY:	Was it really like that? Did that Bassinger call him?
BAYLEN:	What do you mean by "really"?
WATERLOO:	"Bassinger"!!!! We will have to try that variation.
BAYLEN:	Sometimes the Englishman really calls him. Sometimes they both do. Sometimes neither one does.
BOY:	What Englishman?

BAYLEN: Riiiing
WATERLOO: Won't you leave me alone, Kiss…
BAYLEN: Slater
WATERLOO: That accent…you were born in Europe, Slater. Who are you really?
BAYLEN: I'll double your winnings if you play that Russian. I'm not doing it for you, I just don't want to lose some good bets I have going on. And I want to know if the money is the problem or if the problem is that you're a coward.
WATERLOO: No, Father, I am not going to greet them, nobody touches me, get me out of here.
BAYLEN: (*Sweeping*). He is in Reykjavik, he arrived on the night flight. (*Stopping sweeping*) That one that you pushed is the President of Iceland. He just wanted to give you the book *History of Iceland*.
BOY: Fuck.
WATERLOO: This incomprehensible language is so beautiful.
BAYLEN: Where is he staying? Has he come alone?
WATERLOO: He registered at the Excelsior. He sent someone there, dressed like him. He is in that blue house in that neighborhood under construction on the other side of the lake. The houses around him are empty. That guy shutting the curtains is called "Socks," he never takes them off at night, not even in bed, he plays chess as if he were playing poker, ranked number 30.
BAYLEN: I see a priest.
WATERLOO: Number 37, a Jesuit.
BAYLEN: And that bald guy?
WATERLOO: From *Life* magazine. He doesn't have permission to address Fischer directly or to take his photograph. The rest are lawyers. Father, I want to see where I am going to play.
BAYLEN: Patience, Bobby, do you know what time it is?
WATERLOO: It's daytime, let's go.
BAYLEN: It's always daytime in July in Reykjavik. You must rest. There are only eight hours until the first game.
WATERLOO: I want to see it now, Father. Nooooow. Tell them to open it for us, explain who I am. Tell them to turn on the lights. How many people are they thinking of fitting in here?
BAYLEN: It fits 3,000. That zone is reserved: Soviet delegation, American delegation, press, authorities, celebrities, former champions…
WATERLOO: What former champions?
BAYLEN: Larsen, Bourbaki, Kavalek…
WATERLOO: Can we stop Bourbaki from attending? What's that noise?
BAYLEN: They're finishing construction. Tomorrow there won't be any noise.
WATERLOO: Tell the guard to sit where the audience will sit.

At BAYLEN's signal, the BOY does it.

Get up. Sit down. Get up. That chair and that one make noise. Walk. Come in and go out. Tell the Icelanders that they must get rid of those chairs and fix that door and put thick rugs down, I am not going to play with 3,000 guys causing a racket. I don't want any noise outside.

BAYLEN: We'll make them block off the street.

WATERLOO: Tell him to sit there, as if he were the Russian.

The BOY sits. WATERLOO sits facing him.

I want the swivel chair that I used in Buenos Aires. This table must be lowered a centimeter. More light, but not blinding, and not bouncing off the board. Less light, I don't want to feel the light. The board, not so shiny and not so matte. The pieces are too big for these squares, I want the bigger squares, those are a good size, but they feel horrible, this rook is too heavy, the whites aren't white enough, there has to be more contrast between the white squares and the black ones, I want a Staunton of London board, I don't want any camera in front of me, or at my right, I don't want spectators in the first seven rows, more light, less light. They have offered him three chairs, they are making him a replica of the one he used in Buenos Aires, they have offered him eight different boards, they are making the pieces by hand. We aren't going to tolerate his whims.

BAYLEN: We will play with the board he wants, with the pieces he wants, with the light he wants. I won't give him any excuse to leave Reykjavik.

WATERLOO: If a spectator whispers or unwraps a candy or chews a candy, he should be thrown out. I don't want any kids in here. I will sign three autographs a day for the people who can prove they know how to play. I don't like the arbiter; I don't want an ex-player arbiter. Is there anywhere on this island where you can eat a real hamburger? Why didn't anyone tell me that there isn't even one bowling alley in Iceland? The bread tastes weird.

BAYLEN: It doesn't taste weird to me. We can't change the arbiter or ban kids from attending.

WATERLOO: The Russians are going to try to kill me. Each time we get in a car, I want them to check the brakes. I want you to squeeze oranges for me during the matches, they are going to try to give me something to read my mind. I will not play Friday afternoon.

BAYLEN: There are no afternoons in July in Reyk... (*His phone rings; he moves to the side to deal with it − "I'm sorry, sweetheart, I am overwhelmed..." − He comes back, pointing to the phone.*) The

Russians. They request that you forfeit the first match as punishment for your delay. Maybe we can avoid it if you write an apology letter.

WATERLOO: Ask the Russians for forgiveness? Never.

BAYLEN: Do you want to start a point behind? You aren't going to write the Russians, you'll write Boris Spassky.

WATERLOO: I'll kill myself before I'll ask a Russian for forgiveness.

BAYLEN: I'll write it for you. We'll send it first to the press, so that the Russians can't reject it.

WATERLOO: "...My admiration for you is so great..."

BAYLEN: "...My admiration for you is so great..."

WATERLOO: They sent it to the press first so we can't reject it. Look, Father, the Russian is on TV!

BAYLEN: (*Spassky*) A press conference at this hour? (*Father*) A press conference at this hour?

WATERLOO: This championship will be remembered for one unbelievable image: the champion waiting for the challenger. What is he saying? Translator! Someone translate what that Russian is saying! Bobby Fischer, who missed the opening ceremonies, has apologized to Boris Spassky in writing. But at the same time, he is trying to distract him with absurd demands, continuing in his unsportsmanlike behavior. We don't blame the challenger; he's being used to insult the Soviet people. The Champion has more than enough reasons to demand victory in the first match or leave with the title. But out of respect for the fans and to not offend the Icelandic hospitality, he has decided to play, and he will play as long as the challenger plays fair. "He has apologized in writing"!!! It was a private letter! I'm going back to New York. Let me go, Father.

BAYLEN: Don't you see they are trying to provoke you? If you go, you will give them what they're looking for.

WATERLOO: What is that guy doing sweeping at this hour? I want the whole team to sign a document swearing they will not speak with anybody while we're in Reykjavik, I don't see your signature, Father, wake me up at twelve, no one get up before twelve. You should be sleeping Boris. Tolstoy or Dostoevsky?

BAYLEN: Fischer: *My Sixty Memorable Games*. He includes three losses. He lost them, but he includes them here among his triumphs. Because of a move, or an idea, although he ultimately fails. If he thinks "No one's dared try that," he will try it. It's not enough for him to win, he wants to make history. He wants to make history with every move. He isn't playing against me; he's playing against History. That is what's going to defeat him. He'll defeat himself.

WATERLOO: We've been studying him since he was eleven years old. We have discovered patterns to his game. We know he will sacrifice the bishop before the knight, the mother before himself. We know all about the player and about the man. You can rest easy.

BAYLEN:	We haven't been able to stop him from coming here.
WATERLOO:	He shouldn't have gotten here, neither Taimanov nor Petrosian did their job, nor did their teams. We won't fail, there are three champions in this team. You're not alone, Boris.
BAYLEN:	Do you hear that?
WATERLOO:	??
BAYLEN:	The silence. I haven't heard a silence like this in any other place in the world.

Silence.

WATERLOO:	What are you doing there? Who are you?
BAYLEN:	Your bodyguard, sir. My name is Ari.
WATERLOO:	If you're Icelandic, you'll know how to play. Let's play a game.
BAYLEN:	They didn't choose me because I knew how to play. They chose me because I know English and I walk fast. I won't lose sight of you for a second.
WATERLOO:	That woman, is she a prostitute? What did she say to you?
BAYLEN:	She said: "The Russian is more handsome." She isn't a prostitute.
WATERLOO:	Do people want the Russian to win?
BAYLEN:	We've worked hard to organize the championship. You don't help us, you offend us. People say, "The Russian is a gentleman."
WATERLOO:	You know what, Ari? If there is a man who can beat me, it's Boris Spassky. I should be sleeping, but my nerves won't let me. I'll teach you. We don't need a board, it's a pain, the Cossacks played while riding. You only need memory and imagination. e4
BAYLEN:	e5
WATERLOO:	Bc4
BAYLEN:	Nc6
WATERLOO:	Qh5
BAYLEN:	Nf6
WATERLOO:	Qxf7. It's the second fastest mate. It's called the Scholar's Mate.
BAYLEN:	What are you doing there? You should be sleeping.
WATERLOO:	I'm teaching my bodyguard to play. Did you know that the Icelanders are comparing us? They say he's a gentleman and I'm a barbarian.
BAYLEN:	He is a gentleman; you are a barbarian. Go to bed, Bobby. Tomorrow is going to be a hard day, the first of many hard days.
WATERLOO:	Spassky isn't better than Petrosian. I'll be champion before July 20th.
BAYLEN:	Spassky is better than Petrosian, Larsen, and Taimanov combined, and you know it. I've seen the files you keep under your pillow: "Spassky whites," "Spassky blacks." You have hundreds of his games full of notes, you put exclamation marks by the plays that impress you, question marks by the ones you don't understand. Go to sleep, Bobby.
WATERLOO:	To sleep, Boris.

0–0: They try to sleep. In vain.

BOY: How do you know if they slept well or not? How do you know that they didn't sleep like logs?

WATERLOO: It's the night before the battle. Haven't you read *The Iliad*? What do they teach you now in school?

BAYLEN: The night before the battle, warriors toss and turn in their beds. The lake is an eye that wants to devour them, their eyes find each other over the lake. They fall asleep at the same time and dream the same dream: an infinite board. In the audience I recognize great masters: Ólafsson, Najdorf, Bourbaki. Everywhere, signs asking for silence, "Silence" they say "Zoegn." On the table, the two flags. The arbiter looks at his watch, it's time, where is Fischer? He signals that I should move, where is Fischer? I hear a great silence before the first move. d4 and Fischer's clock starts, tick-tock, tick-tock, where is Fischer? tick-tock, tick-tock. He arrives fifteen minutes late and his suit wrinkled.

WATERLOO: I never leave the house without wrinkling my clothes.

BAYLEN: He walks in without looking at me. He approaches a spectator.

WATERLOO: How much did you pay to be here?

BAYLEN: He is still the boy I met at Mar del Plata. I extend my hand over the board, he accepts it without looking at me, which of the sixty-four squares is he looking at? Finally, he looks at me.

WATERLOO: If only it were in Moscow. I am not only going to beat you, I am going to make it so you never play again. I'm going to eat your heart.

BAYLEN: I am going to beat you because you don't love life, because you're a monster, because you only see in me someone you want to beat. I can't lose because if I lose, you'll eat my heart.

WATERLOO: d4

They box. It is a segmented combat in which each physical movement is accompanied by a statement by one of the chess players: Nf6, e4, e6… Afraid that they'll hurt each other, the BOY tries to separate them.

BOY: Don't you play chess?

WATERLOO: I don't know.

BOY: What do you mean? You beat me a while ago, twice.

WATERLOO: It was Fischer. A move taken from memory.

BOY: ??

WATERLOO: It's too violent of a game for me.

BAYLEN: I do know, but I'm not good enough. If you aren't good enough doing something, it's better that you do it from memory.

He takes out a book. He lets the BOY read the title.

BOY: "The Final Battle: Reykjavik Games Explained."

WATERLOO takes out an identical book and lets the BOY read.

BOY:	"When the first game was finished, Fischer shut himself in to watch TV. For his part, Spassky…"

WATERLOO:	I found it here. I waited to see if anyone would return for it, I didn't steal it. I opened it just to open it, I never gave a shit about chess. After reading it for the third time, I realized that I heard waves. Then, all of a sudden, I saw another guy reading a book like mine.

BAYLEN:	I also heard the waves.

Carried by the waves, they resume the combat. WATERLOO falls. 1–0.

I'm exhausted, but I can't get to sleep. It was so easy, that bishop, you made a rookie mistake. Impatience got the best of you, your anxiety to begin with a big blow.

WATERLOO:	Incomprehensible. Icelandic TV is very good if you don't know Icelandic. (I have a variation where I destroy the room in a rage, another where I leave to scream in the rain.)

BAYLEN:	Finally, I fall asleep and dream of Stalin dressed like a white queen, and I wake up feeling guilty. The lake is beautiful, it makes you want to walk along the shore, it's what I want to do on my rest day, stroll along the shore, but I keep to the program: breakfast with the team, one hour in the pool with the team, analysis of the first game, we take it apart, play by play like in an autopsy, openings with Vladimir, lunch with the team, defenses with Dimitri, tennis with Nei, the whole team sits to watch us play, dinner with the team. I read *The Brothers Karamazov* in bed, my eyes close, but I can't sleep, and if it wasn't an error? And if your loss was a trick?

WATERLOO:	Who is it?

BAYLEN:	It's me, Bobby.

WATERLOO:	What's up, Father?

BAYLEN:	What do you mean what's up? The second game… Can you turn down that TV? The second game starts within the hour.

WATERLOO:	Who is that guy that was on the TV with him? They left together when the game was over. Is he his friend?

BAYLEN:	Nikolai Kropius, number five in the ranking. He isn't his friend, his friend is Nei, who he plays tennis with. You should have been there.

WATERLOO:	I've been thinking. I know why I lost. There was a noise. I managed to pinpoint it. The cameras. I don't want cameras. That Kropius, I don't want him to sit where he can look me in the eyes.

BAYLEN:	We can't change the agreed upon conditions nor can we stop them from sitting where they want.

WATERLOO: They know they can't beat me on the board, and they are trying to create a situation where I'll have to leave. I won't play with cameras.

BAYLEN: The Russians haven't brought the cameras, you signed a contract, you've been paid for it, the arbiter has started your clock, article 5 of the rules: a player loses if he does not appear one hour after his clock has started. They've agreed to get rid of the cameras, hurry Bobby, the clock is running.

WATERLOO: Call the embassy, Father, they must protect me, I am here because I've put the interests of our country before mine, they have to stop that clock, no, they have to put it back to zero.

BAYLEN: Kissinger on the phone, he left a summit with the Soviet Minister of Foreign Affairs, he is very angry with you, at the door you have a police car running, and all the traffic lights are green, am I going to have to bust the door down? You're scared of him, you fucked it up by sacrificing that bishop, the Russians are pissing themselves, go and show them that you know how to play. Now you don't have to leave, you have two days to keep jerking off.

2–0.

BOY: I don't think the priest would talk to him like that. Fischer would have fired him with a kick to the butt.

BAYLEN: You have all your life to keep jerking off, not even your fucking mother bets a dollar on you. "The championship is finished," the whole world is saying. It is finished, you're finished, should we pack our bags?

WATERLOO: I didn't fuck it up by sacrificing the bishop. Where I fucked it up was in the thirty-first move, but nobody realized it.

BAYLEN: *The New York Times* is asking you to continue. Following Kissinger's instructions, the astronauts are letting you play in their bowling alley.

WATERLOO bowls; BAYLEN plays tennis.

WATERLOO: Riiiing, John Wayne, riiing, Frank Sinatra, "Don't give up, Bobby," "Resist, Bobby," suddenly the Americans care about chess, riiing, Francisco Franco? Father, do you know if Walt Disney has called?

BAYLEN: Riiing, the Minister of Industry, riiing, the cosmonaut Gagarin, riiing, Fidel, "We can't lose, comrade Spassky," riiing, one hundred children (*He sings like one hundred children*).

WATERLOO: What's going on with you? What are you thinking? Is anything missing?

BOY: Women. And if Spassky finds an American female astronaut who's gone astray? Or Fischer's Mom and Kissinger travel incognito to Reykjavik. Bobby doesn't want to meet them, but they get in dressed up like cleaning people. Or it's Bobby who asks her to come: "I can't sleep, Mom. Come and read me chess stories like when I was little." They end up arguing over what to do with the prize money and Bobby asks Kissinger to take her away from Reyk…

BAYLEN: One hundred girls (*He sings like one hundred girls*). I see my reflection in the lake, a face of a dead man. Has Fischer fooled me again? There's a personal matter that I want to talk to you about, Nikolai.

WATERLOO: You and I don't talk about personal matters, Boris. It's improper for well-mannered people.

BAYLEN: I would like Larissa to be here.

WATERLOO: The Committee already took a position on that matter.

BAYLEN: It would help me to have her here.

WATERLOO: It is not going to be necessary. The Championship is about to end. Fischer demands to play the third game in a different location.

BAYLEN: "Demands"?

WATERLOO: He says that he won't play with an audience. He proposes to play in the basement of the auditorium. We've answered no.

BAYLEN: "We"?

WATERLOO: Moscow thinks we have been too patient with the Americans. If Fischer doesn't show up, we will demand more than the 3–0. We will demand the title.

BAYLEN: Let Fischer know that I'll play wherever he wants. Without an audience, only the arbiter and a witness chosen by each player.

WATERLOO: Fischer is desperate and he's trying to divide us. We must stay united against him. Boris, try to think politically. Accepting a change of venue would be a tactical-political error.

BAYLEN: He's looking for an excuse to run out of here. I won't give it to him.

WATERLOO: I will ask Moscow, when you've won the third game, to authorize Larissa to visit you.

BAYLEN: I appreciate what you do for me, Nikolai.

WATERLOO: I don't do it for you. I enter the basement with a wrinkled blue suit and seven minutes late. What's that?

BAYLEN: It's not for the TV, it's for the spectators in the auditorium that have paid an entrance fee.

WATERLOO: I said no cameras.

BAYLEN: You won't even notice they're filming you.

WATERLOO: The arbiter stood up to the Russians. You, German, have stood up to the Russians! Let's go to New York.

BAYLEN: (*God*) Iceland will sue you and you will only play to pay the lawyers. No country will ever invite you to a tournament again.

The world will hate you; you have an obligation to chess. You spent your whole life dreaming of sitting in front of a Russian in a World Championship, and you finally have the chance to show them you are better than them, you won't get another.

BOY: (*God*) He's beat you four times. Are you scared of him? Are you a coward?

WATERLOO: Just one noise and I'm leaving Reykjavik.

BAYLEN: I take fifteen minutes for the first ten moves.

WATERLOO: Me, thirteen.

BAYLEN: At the twentieth, I've taken 100 minutes.

WATERLOO: Me, forty-two. I need a minute for my thirty-fifth move.

BAYLEN: I spend twenty minutes in my response, I only have two minutes left for the move, a smile starts on your face, you're about to beat me for the first time in your life, for the first time I see something in your face that looks like happiness, it makes you happy to see me fall. I pity you, Robert Fischer, you're the loneliest man in the world.

1–2.

WATERLOO: Boris, a call from Moscow.

BAYLEN: You answer it, Nikolai.

WATERLOO: It's you they want to talk to.

BAYLEN: Sir.

WATERLOO: It's three degrees in Moscow, Boris. What's the temperature in Reykjavik?

BAYLEN: Three degrees, sir.

WATERLOO: Where's the problem, then?

BAYLEN: I don't have any complaint, sir. I'm enjoying the championship.

WATERLOO: We haven't slept a wink. It surprised us that you used the Settembrini variation, whose inconsistency was proven by Naphta in his study "The Kingside Castling and the Swiss Defense." But that's not what's made us lose sleep. What worries us is discovering antisocial features in a member of the team. We are looking at the fresco "Lenin playing with Gorky." Gorky didn't know how to play, and yet this painting expresses a great truth. Lenin said, "There is no revolutionary theory without revolutionary practice, nor revolutionary practice without revolutionary theory."

BAYLEN: He also said: "In politics one learns from the enemy."

WATERLOO: Lenin said: "Apart from power, everything is illusion."

BAYLEN: He also said: "We dream, but under the condition that we believe in our dreams."

WATERLOO: Lenin said that?

BAYLEN: Yes, sir.

WATERLOO: The Soviet people haven't been informed of your loss in the third game. We ask ourselves if there is something political in your defeat. If there is something inside you that wants him to win. Look at us in the eyes when I speak to you, Boris, look at me in the eyes when we speak to you. We have studied the film of that particular game. Your hands, your face. You don't control your emotions; you lower your eyes as soon as you see him. We don't understand what your relationship is with him?

BAYLEN: Playing against him pleases me. It also pains me.

WATERLOO: Before the Committee, Taimanov spoke of a "demonic magnetism." He makes everyone believe that he is a wizard. You don't think that, right? You aren't going to let yourself be hypnotized.

BAYLEN: He isn't a wizard, he's a cheat. He plays all the time and from everything he tries to get an advantage. His rivals commit errors that they wouldn't against another. His talent consists of making his rivals sick. He never beats healthy men because he makes them sick. I am not going to get sick.

WATERLOO: You accept everything he asks you as if you were his serf. You compromise Soviet society with your humiliated behavior.

BAYLEN: I want to beat him on the board.

WATERLOO: That is idealism, I mean, vanity. You like to say you learned to play in Leningrad while the city was being bombed.

BAYLEN: That's what happened.

WATERLOO: We evacuated you once the war broke out and you didn't return until it was over. The Soviet man is not vain, Boris, the Soviet man knows he is imperfect, he looks for his faults and he pulls them out at the root. We don't like what you read, but we won't mind what you read when you return to Moscow with the title. You will win if you see the confrontation from an elevated perspective. Others have had to fill in for you so you could be here in Reykjavik. In a steel mill, in a nuclear submarine, in a tank on the streets of Prague. None of those people can travel so you can be in Reykjavik, all those people are with you in Reykjavik. Lenin said, "The interests of humanity have to bend to the interests of the proletariat." There won't be any more selfish decisions. If you lose, we will dedicate twelve lines in the bottom part of a left page of *Pravda*. We will demand that the board have smaller squares. From here on out, our chair will also swivel. The fourth game, as with all the rest until the final victory, will be played in the auditorium. As soon as you win one more game, Larissa will travel to Reykjavik.

2 ½–1 ½; 2 ½–2 ½; 2 ½–3 ½; 3–4; 3–5; 3 ½–5 ½; 3 ½–6 ½

Can we speak with you, Boris?

BAYLEN: Come in, Nikolai. Vladimir…Dimitri…Mijaíl, Vasili… Wouldn't we all be more comfortable in the living room?

WATERLOO: We are all together in this, Boris. What a great start there in the fourth, we had the game in our hands, the lead with the rook was infantile, it was the knight that was opening a winning line. Nothing to reproach you for in the fifth, none of us could foresee that the exchange of queens would be fatal. In the sixth, when the audience applauded, why did you join in on the applause? Why that gesture? At the half of the eighth, you sat there staring at the black bishop like a brain-damaged boxer, your gaze is still there. In the tenth, you deviated from the line tactic. We are all together in this. Since he lost the Candidates Tournament, they've been treating Taimanov's team like they are pariahs. We've asked Moscow to send Larissa as soon as possible.

BAYLEN: They found *The Master and Margarita* in Taimanov's suitcase. I don't know why I lead with the rook, I'm sorry. In the tenth, his responses were so fast that I thought that there had to have been a leak, it was as if he knew everything that I was going to do, that's why I improvised. In the sixth, I applauded the beauty of the game.

WATERLOO: You applauded your defeat.

BAYLEN: I also applauded myself. It was a work of art made by two.

WATERLOO: How big is this room, Boris?

BAYLEN: I don't know, Vasili. 500 square feet?

WATERLOO: Where does your brother Sergei live?

BAYLEN: I would like to say on Petrova Avenue, Mijaíl.

WATERLOO: It's 17 Petrova Avenue. How long has it been since you've been there?

BAYLEN: I've never been, Dimitri.

WATERLOO: You would love it. It's one of those precious bourgeoise houses with parquet flooring and high ceilings decorated in plaster. The Revolution chopped it up according to Lenin's calculation that 100 square feet is the necessary space for a person. The room where your brother Sergei, your sister-in-law Neva, and your nephews Iosif and Dunia live is only 300 square feet. The rest, up to the 400 square feet, is made up by counting a fraction of the shared spaces. Hallway, bathroom, and telephone have to be shared, just like the kitchen, where there could just as easily be a birthday celebration or a brawl. To live at 17 Petrova, one has to get used to clothes hanging everywhere, furniture piled up, smoke from the kitchen, drunks, and informers. If you ever visited your brother Sergei, you would realize that he now only knows how to express himself in whispers. Do you really want to live in the 100 square feet that would be allotted to you? Seven minutes late, wrinkled purple suit. The Russian opens with the king's pawn. And me with the queen's bishop.

BAYLEN: Second time in your career that you open with the queen's bishop. The other time was against the guy ranked 50th. I haven't managed to make you respect me. You keep looking at me like a pawn, "the Russian," any old Russian, for you Tolstoy and Dostoevsky are the same. You touch the pieces – do you touch them? – like you're playing a piano, I can measure the strength of a man by the way he touches the pieces, knight for bishop, rook for knight, I look for some trembling in you, a change in the color of your lips, something that expresses that you have an idea, if you covet a certain zone of the board, if you realize you've made a mistake, I make a mistake, you conquer the center, five columns for the blacks, you offer me a knight for two pawns, that's it, you've seen something, you move the queen forward to provoke me, you know I am collapsing, you wait for my eyes to signal the moment to strike, you cover yours so I don't see the piece that you're looking at, there's a weakness in my left flank, have you discovered it?, I have a frenzy of black bishops threatening from afar, two bishops in a line, where have I seen those two bishops in a line before?, I have to think quickly, I know that your memory is also working, my head is a depository of thousands of games that others played, all the games that I've feared, all that I've dreamed, two bishops in a column, now I know, Finney/Amundsen, Genoa, 1832, I compare three variations, I am going to punish you for your lack of respect of human beings, I return the knight to its original position.

WATERLOO: He's returned his knight to its original position? You've returned your knight to its original position! Good, Boris Spassky, the stronger you are, the stronger you force me to be. The better you play, the more I will enjoy it.

BAYLEN: Whatever you do, I will capture your queen. You feel like her: alone, abandoned. I feel the tension in your forehead, the bitterness in your heart, you look at the board like at an abyss, you look at me like at an abyss. You respect me. And this night, and all the nights of your life, you will remember what you should have done and didn't, and there won't be any consolation for you, nor will you be able to blame anyone but yourself. The king dies and you are the one who dies.

4 ½–6 ½

BOY: Two to one for Spassky! Ten to one for Spassky!

WATERLOO moans.

BAYLEN: I'm going to take you to the hospital, Waterloo.
WATERLOO: Let's go to the evening adjournment, please. Please, Baylen.

BAYLEN gives in.

BAYLEN: Let's jump to the 5–7.

             5–7.

             The clocks say four hours, I have to hold out for one more hour.
WATERLOO: I have to avoid the adjournment; I have to create an opening to
             put together a good strike.
BAYLEN: I sacrifice the forty minutes left of the five hours allowed, I write
             my secret play, I put it in an envelope, the arbiter seals it. The
             game is adjourned until tomorrow. Do you understand, kid, the
             thing with the secret move? It's so no one has an advantage. If
             you don't understand it, don't act like you understand it.
WATERLOO: If I were stupid, I wouldn't be here. The lights turn off and the
             pieces are left alone, in the dark, together with the sealed enve-
             lope. Fischer has the whole night to think about what Spassky
             put in that envelope.
BAYLEN: Spassky has the whole night to think about what Fischer is
             thinking.
WATERLOO: Tonight, they won't be alone, they will be facing each other in
             their thoughts.
BAYLEN: Life stops, and others help them think about how to continue
             living.
WATERLOO: Socks, your socks against Father's collar that you can't guess
             what the Russian put in the envelope.
BAYLEN: His objective is to make you get the bishop out of the way. He
             wrote Rd7.
WATERLOO: What does your God say, Father?
BAYLEN: Spassky is in his room with four of the best players in the world.
             He has four telephones on the table and at the other end of
             every phone is another team of four grand masters. Under the
             table there is a fifth phone that connects with the Party's Central
             Committee. When he forced the adjournment, Spassky had all
             those phones in mind. I don't think he'll settle for just getting
             rid of your bishop. Nei, I want you to leave this room.
WATERLOO: What do you mean, Boris?
BAYLEN: You can go play tennis with your American friend.
WATERLOO: ??
BAYLEN: They've seen you with an American. You are trying to stay in the
             West.
WATERLOO: I'm not going to leave Russia, Boris. You offend me.
BAYLEN: What have the Americans offered you?
WATERLOO: I don't have any American friend. I ran into that priest in the
             elevator, we've only spoken two times. I am your friend, Boris.
BAYLEN: I don't want you on the team, not even to play tennis. I don't
             want you in Reykjavik. If you were Fischer, what would you
             play, Dimitri?
WATERLOO: If I were blacks, I would move Bg3.

BAYLEN:	I'm not asking you what you would do if you were blacks, I'm asking you what you would do if you were Fischer.
WATERLOO:	Fischer could respond with h7 like he did in a similar situation in the Junior Championship of '61. How would we respond, Boris?
BAYLEN:	I would like to meet Larissa at the airport, Nikolai.
WATERLOO:	Vladimir is going to deal with Larissa so that you can work.
BAYLEN:	I bet a sock that they expect h7.
WATERLOO:	That's what I did at the Junior Championship of '61. They know it. They know that I know that they know.
BAYLEN:	What are you looking for, Bobby? If they wanted to plant microphones, do you think they would put them there?
WATERLOO:	Let's suppose the Russians have planted microphones. What move would be in my best interest? What would you do, Ari?
BAYLEN:	I would move the rook to open space for the pawn.
WATERLOO:	When I win, I am going to take you to America with me to meet the President. Larissa arrived, Boris, can you concentrate on this? Riiing, Moscow has found a variation with a bishop and two pawns.
BAYLEN:	Riiiing, Kissinger has found a variation. My head is burning, Nikolai, I need to sleep a couple of hours. Shouldn't you rest a little, Bobby?
WATERLOO:	You're right, Father. I will watch some TV.
BAYLEN:	You aren't going to tell me what you think you'll move?
WATERLOO:	No. What are you doing, Father?
BAYLEN:	Packing. I'm going to New York. Fuck you, Bobby.
WATERLOO:	Moscow says we can go to bed, the most that Fischer can wrench from us is a draw. I want everyone to go to bed without talking to anyone, not even yourselves, not even on the phone. Sleep well, Boris.
BAYLEN:	Sleep well, Bobby.
WATERLOO:	Look how skinny you are, Boris. You look younger.
BAYLEN:	I want you to return to Moscow, Larissa, before the game.
WATERLOO:	This match is killing you. This game kills.

Larissa and Boris make love. Until WATERLOO interrupts the game.

	Look at those eyes. He's leaving us, he's going.
BAYLEN:	He's never been in Reykjavik. He isn't brave. What you see in those eyes is fear.
BOY:	Fear of what?
BAYLEN:	You have nothing to fear. I don't think there is a Napoleonic Defeat available.
BOY:	Napoleonic Defeat?
WATERLOO:	What are they teaching you in school nowadays?
BOY:	Are there more like you?
BAYLEN:	Probably.
BOY:	Who put this chessboard here?

BAYLEN:	Probably the city, same as those monkey bars you see other there. That has the look of the mayor.
BOY:	Did you know I was going to stop here?
WATERLOO:	Not many pass through here. It's not a logical way to get to any class or anywhere.
BOY:	You were also waiting for me. You are conspiring together.
BAYLEN:	I don't even know what this guy's name is outside of here.
BOY:	Then, you're not always here.
BAYLEN:	Of course not. There is a world outside of this.
WATERLOO:	Whatever you do outside doesn't count here. If you have a profession, if you live with people, if you talk to them about me, I don't know any of that. You can tell whatever you want about yourself, we don't believe you.
BOY:	Do you do this often?
WATERLOO:	When we meet. We meet up for this. Months can go by without doing it, or we could do it days in a row. There are days when we've done it three times. No more than that, it's very tiring.
BOY:	And if the book had been about poker or parchisi?
BAYLEN:	We were lucky with the book. Chess is difficult.
WATERLOO:	There's a lot of death. It's a game about death.
BOY:	I don't understand why you do this.
WATERLOO:	Outside of here I haven't been world champion of anything.
BAYLEN:	It's what the whole world does, live the lives of others, but here you know that you're doing it. They have chess and we have them. If it weren't for Reykjavik, I would have gone crazy. Outside of here there are no rules. Well, there are a lot of rules, but they aren't obeyed.
BOY:	Is it always the same? Spassky and Fischer all the time?
BAYLEN:	It's not "always the same." It is always with the same rules, but each time is different. We can't contradict the book: the games, the footnotes, the photos… It has eight photos (*he shows them to him*). We have limits, just like the knight or the queen. Sixty-four squares, thirty-two pieces: that you can't change, nor how the bishop moves. The rook can do a lot, but it can't move diagonally. There are rules, and if you ignore them, if you cheat, it's stops being worth it. You can't exchange Reykjavik for Jerusalem. The cold, the rain, the 1–0, the 2–0, there's no changing that. But the last time I was Fischer, it was very different, and the last time I was Spassky, it was different. You change the order of two words, and you change everything, a gesture changes everything. You try to guess what the other will do, but the other changes your plans. And there's time, the pressure of time. When you are Fischer, you must defend it to death; when you're Spassky, to death. The arbiter who thinks he's God, one hundred kids with their fists raised, absent parents, dead champions, the black knight that threatens the white bishop, naked Larissa, you

can be any of those. You can also be yourself, but that is the most difficult of them all. There are infinite versions of Spassky, infinite Fischers, infinite versions of you. There is a version that is taking an oral exam. There are positions where you'll always lose. Who will win and who will lose, that you can't change, but you can make it so your character, the one you get, is up to his victory or his defeat. The important thing is the king's safety.

Silence.

BOY: I have to go. I am very grateful to you, but I have to go.

He leaves.

WATERLOO: "I am very grateful to you?" Did you see what you did?
BAYLEN: So, it's my fault.
WATERLOO: Of course it's your fault. You rushed into it.
BAYLEN: I didn't rush into it.
WATERLOO: You didn't rush into it, it's what you were looking for since the beginning. And to top it off, this little sentence: "The important thing is the king's safety." Now what?
BAYLEN: Another one will show up.
WATERLOO: I don't have time.
BAYLEN: Another one will show up in time.
WATERLOO: That boy is special.
BAYLEN: What do you mean, special?
WATERLOO: Like the precocious pawn in the tenth.
BAYLEN: I don't know what you see in him.
WATERLOO: And what will become of him, after what he's seen?
BAYLEN: No one ordered him to come.
WATERLOO: He was looking for it, you mean? You're terrible.
BAYLEN: Me or Spassky?
WATERLOO: Both of you.
BAYLEN: If he's as good as you say, he'll know how to take advantage of it. Shall we continue?
WATERLOO: That's what it's about, continuing.
BAYLEN: I am not going to continue without you. I want you to return to Moscow, Larissa, before the game.
WATERLOO: That was my favorite part: the nocturnal adjournment.
BAYLEN: Next winter I'll make you a snowwoman, Waterloo.
WATERLOO: You say that every year, Baylen.

Silence. Until the BOY returns.

BOY: And what about me?
BAYLEN: You tell us. What's waiting for you out there? Who waits for you out there? If we have one wish, it is not for you to miss a morning of school. If you leave here, you'll think you've imagined us. If you leave here.

BOY:	Can I talk to you alone?
BAYLEN:	It's not possible to talk to me alone. There are always others.
BOY:	We don't get along. Don't worry, I will leave when I know how this ends.
BAYLEN:	I want you to return to Moscow, Larissa, before the game.
WATERLOO:	This game is killing you, Boris, this game kills. Let's make love. I will return to Moscow before the game.
BAYLEN:	The arbiter opens the envelope: Bg7.
WATERLOO:	Rd5
BAYLEN:	Did you really make that move? My eyes search for Nikolai, who observes the board, incredulous. Nobody in the auditorium believes that you could have done that, nor those who are watching on the TV. Those who are following it on the radio believe that the announcer has gone crazy, tick-tock, tick-tock, I have to find a response, I hear players all over the world looking for a response, the dead champions look for a response.

5–8.

Have you seen the front page of *The New York Times*? A baseball stadium? A chessboard! We've done it, Bobby: we've changed America.

WATERLOO:	Why did you lock the door, Boris?
BAYLEN:	I'm studying a variation.
WATERLOO:	Very good, let's analyze it.
BAYLEN:	I am not going to expose myself to any more leaks.
WATERLOO:	If you don't open this door, I will have to knock it down. *Pravda* has stopped reporting. Moscow wants us to ask for a break for medical reasons so that you have time to reflect, but Fischer demands that a neutral doctor examine you. Are we going to have to really make you sick, so that you can reflect?
BOY:	Come on, Boris! Bobby could just look for a draw, but he'll be shooting for victory in each game, he'll make more errors and this time you'll know how to take advantage of them. The medication will help you.

5 ½–8 ½; 6–9; 6 ½–9 ½; 7–10; 7 ½–10 ½; 8–11; 8 ½–11 ½.

WATERLOO:	The champion is committing errors never before seen during his career. We suspect the challenger is using hypnotic methods. We demand that no one outside of our delegation come into contact with our orange juice and that the challenger's seat be scanned.

He looks for a page in the book and gives it to the BOY to read.

BOY:	"...they examined Fischer's chair with X-rays, and in it they found a dead fly, which was then analyzed..."
BAYLEN:	Now we must let this character have a say. The fly sees things that no one else sees, hears what no one else hears...

BOY:	But it's dead!!!
WATERLOO:	There are still four games to go! There are only four games left! Red wrinkled suit, twenty minutes late, where is Spassky? Boris, Fischer is waiting for you in the auditorium. You must fight until the end. At least have the courage to lay down your king in front of him. Riiiing. The arbiter on the phone.
BAYLEN:	(*To the phone*) I won't continue to play. I've been defeated. Robert Fischer is the new World Champion.

BAYLEN and WATERLOO start to put away everything they've used in their game.

BOY:	And??
WATERLOO:	Isn't that enough?
BAYLEN:	The book stops there, with those three sentences. "I won't continue to play.
WATERLOO:	I've been defeated.
BAYLEN:	Robert Fischer is the new World Champion."
WATERLOO:	Period.
BOY:	What happened later?
WATERLOO:	Later? The book doesn't speak of it. I think the war didn't happen. Or did it?
BOY:	Them, what happened to them?
WATERLOO:	The book doesn't say. I imagine that I flipped out on learning that he had forfeited, there are three games left! I arrive two hours late to the awards ceremony. The President of Iceland gives me the envelope, I count the money in front of him, I give a third to my church, I break it off with my church upon seeing that their prophesies did not come to fruition.
BAYLEN:	I imagine I weighed twenty pounds less when I landed in Moscow than when I left for Reykjavik.
WATERLOO:	Hey, you, where do you think you're going?
BAYLEN:	Home. I'm Boris Spassky. I've just arrived from Reykjavik.
WATERLOO:	You must get in line and show your passport like everyone else. Don't forget to fill out the forms. Open that suitcase.
BAYLEN:	I haven't filled out a form in years. The police paw through my books, they find the title funny *Crime and Punishment*. When I finally get through customs, only Larissa is waiting for me. No official car, I imagine. Let's take a bus.
WATERLOO:	A limousine, the mayor's limousine is waiting for me at the New York airport, they take me from network to network in the limousine. When you have seen Icelandic television, the American one seems insipid. I miss Reykjavik. I miss Spassky.
BAYLEN:	They call me in to the Committee, I imagine. Topic: "The Agony of Soviet Chess." General Dermontov defends me saying it's a problem of nutrition. They treat me with kindness the whole time. With kindness they tell me "You should have never

played in that basement." They never tell me "You have been punished." Three street sweepers sweep my sidewalk day and night. The first year after the defeat I read *The Grand Inquisitor* three times and Bulgakov's clandestine translation of *Don Quixote* three times.

WATERLOO: I spend my day studying. Not chess, religions. I compare them, I compare variations. The time comes to defend my championship, I make one hundred thirty-six conditions, they only accept one hundred thirty-five, they rob me of my title, they give my title to…a Russian! All around my house there are sweepers from the KGB, the FBI, and Mossad. I yank my name off my mailbox, I sleep in hotels under false names, each night in a different city, a policeman stops me.

BAYLEN: What do you have there?

WATERLOO: A juicer and religion books.

BAYLEN: Where do you live?

WATERLOO: I can't remember, I have so many addresses… Finally, I say: "Reykjavik!" I'm tortured for three days, where am I? Help!! Can anyone hear me? They tell me they confused me for someone else and they let me go. I keep the trophies, the letter from Fidel, and the notes about religion in sixty-four boxes and I go to live with my mother. She asks me to leave, she doesn't like my opinions about the Jews (I don't like them either, I don't say "them"), I sleep on the beach, I don't have the money to go to the dentist, I hear they have operated on my face and now I play under a different identity, I would go back to playing if they made an adequate offer.

BAYLEN: I like knowing that he hasn't played since Reykjavik. Larissa never asks me about Reykjavik.

WATERLOO: What really happened in Reykjavik, Boris?

BAYLEN: The pronunciation of your name annoys me.

WATERLOO: "Bobby Fischer:" I don't want to hear that name again. Don't you think you've had enough to drink for today?

BAYLEN: We divorce the third year after the defeat. Five years after the defeat, do they let me emigrate or do they invite me to do so? Wherever I am – Paris, Lima, Cairo –, I dream about Stalin every night.

WATERLOO: Stop crying over your mistakes, learn from them for the future.

BAYLEN: Is there a future for me, Comrade?

WATERLOO: Don't be vain, the world is not going to collapse because you've lost a few games.

BAYLEN: The Soviet Union and the Soviet Chess Federation collapse. I get his mother's name in the black market. I've sent Bobby a thousand letters, Ma'am, don't you think I deserve a response? My son doesn't open his mail, due to the explosives. Could you pass along a message from Boris Spassky? They want to organize a rematch.

WATERLOO:	I won't play against a Russian again if they don't give him a bishop advantage. In Reykjavik?
BAYLEN:	I don't play under the Russian flag anymore. They want it in Belgrade. I already told them that it can't be in Belgrade.
WATERLOO:	Well said, we'll only play in Reykjavik. We must save chess, Boris. Those new Russians – Karpov, Kasparov – they are destroying it with their immoral play.
BAYLEN:	Turn on the TV: they are bombing Sarajevo. Kissinger is prohibiting you from doing business with the Serbs.
WATERLOO:	I've heard good things about Serbian TV.
BAYLEN:	Open the mailbox, a letter from Kissinger. He warns you that if you play in Belgrade, jail awaits you in America.
WATERLOO:	You deserve an opportunity, look what I do with that weakling's letter.

They square off like boxers whose bodies don't know how to fight anymore.

The bombs don't let us hear the waves. I am not going to go back to America, so they put me in jail. When my mother dies, I won't be able to attend her funeral.

He can't go on, due to fatigue or emotion. BAYLEN takes over.

BAYLEN:	When my mother dies, I attend her funeral dressed up like a street sweeper, the casket is monitored by sweepers, America sends out an international arrest warrant against me, the man who brought down Communism, where is Fischer? Japanese policemen – or are they Korean? – throw me to the ground with my arms handcuffed behind my back.
WATERLOO:	Arrest me too, put us in the same cell, these two men without a country, and give us a chessboard!
BAYLEN:	I'm embarrassed I never had a girlfriend at my age, and I marry a woman that visits me in jail, but what I want is a young woman to reproduce myself and preserve my ideas. America is asking for extradition; the Icelanders give me asylum. Ari reminds me of my promise to take him to the White House, he took it seriously! Kissinger is going around saying that he told me the moves to make, they put me in the Encyclopedia of Famous Jews. I walk because I can't leave the island, I walk going over all the games in history looking for tricks, History is full of tricks, I have a radio show "Bobby Fischer Here, Disclosing the Russian, American, and Jewish Tricks." I sleep in the street, I play for food, I don't stop thinking about the eleventh, How did it not occur to me to protect the queen with the rook? Look, he looks like a bum. I lost with him.
WATERLOO:	Who are you?

BAYLEN:	My name isn't important. All the games I won, the victory over Bourbaki with bishop and queen, the mate against Korchnoy with two rooks, none of it matters. I will always be the man who lost to Fischer. Ask anyone about me. "Spassky? The one who lost to Fischer." I tell my kids: "Take your mothers' last names." I am condemned to my life being only Reykjavik, all the rest is either prologue or epilogue to the defeat.
WATERLOO:	Too much Dostoyevsky, Spassky. I am more Tolstoy.
BAYLEN:	Going back to the island to die, that is more Dostoyevsky than Tolstoy.

WATERLOO lies face up

WATERLOO:	To die with so many games in my head, what a waste!
BAYLEN:	To die with so many lives in my head, what a waste. Isn't it strange, Robert? Your name and mine are going to be united forever – Fischerandspassky, Spasskyandfischer – and, nevertheless, we never exchanged more than a pair of sentences separated by a chess board before millions of eyes that impatiently observed our hands. I would have liked to have had a conversation with you, alone. I would have liked to have told you that I'm the winner. I won at Reykjavik.

He acts like he's burying WATERLOO. BAYLEN and the BOY meditate or pray. Until WATERLOO stands up, shaking himself off.

WATERLOO:	You didn't need to really throw dirt on me. You don't need to really throw dirt on me.
BAYLEN:	If it doesn't contradict the book, it's not prohibited.
WATERLOO:	It's not prohibited, but it's better without dirt.
BOY:	I have a variation.

Silence.

WATERLOO:	Go ahead, Leipzig.
BAYLEN:	"Leipzig?" He just got here, who does he think he is?
BOY:	The night before I surrender, I go out on the balcony with *Crime and Punishment*. I look up to see someone walking along the shore. I can't see his face, but I recognize that way of walking. I also see him, looking at me up on the balcony. We walk along the shore until we meet up, we walk together guided by the sound of the waves, on the cliff we trace out a board with pebbles. Surrounded by ferocious winds, extremely high waves, we play the game of our lives.

Silence. WATERLOO gives the BOY his book, he says goodbye to BAYLEN, and he moves away until he disappears. LEIPZIG and BAYLEN act out the cold, the rain, the wind of Reykjavik.

6 The Collection

Translated by David Johnston

Translator's Note

This intricately written and carefully designed play is (or is among other things, as is often the case with Juan Mayorga) a multi-layered exploration of the implications of *ars long, vita brevis*, the Latin aphorism whose surface translation suggests the idea that art outlives human beings, while its origins in the Greek of Hippocrates insist that, for the vast majority of us at least, it takes more than a lifetime to acquire and hone any real (in the sense of transcendental) skill or talent. Around the aphorism, typically in the case of Juan Mayorga's theatre, the play dramatises a set of almost obsessively posed core questions: in this case, what does art do? Are there transcendental realities or goals in life that are worth sacrificing everything else for? What talents do human beings need in order to extend the meaning of the individual life beyond the terminating limitations of time and space? These are questions deeply rooted in the philosophical – and the play obliquely references the work of a range of thinkers from across time and space to weave a suggestive intellectual backdrop for the action: Heraclitus's method of creative conflict, Aristotle's cave, Kant's theory of the artistic sublime, Benjamin's exploration of the life and afterlives of the work of art, Santayana's examination of the rival claims of art and morality, and of course Malraux's imaginary museum.

But these sources of the philosophical are also shadows of questions deeply embedded in the everyday living of life, where we are confronted with their mundane counterparts of what we do with our time, how we spend surplus money, how we identify what is really important to us, and the final question facing us all, of how we try to ensure that what matters to us is afforded some measure of continuation. Mayorga, like Benjamin, characteristically depicts worlds caught between the desire for the unattainable transcendental and the omni-threat of barbaric destruction, and *The Collection* offers a complex human situation that, in spite of its physical contiguity to a collection of artefacts that straddle the whole range of human creation across oceans and across centuries, is communicated to the spectator through an effortlessly controlled and eminently recognisable everyday discourse of desire, possession, ambition and sacrifice. Yet it is within this discourse, set against the interlocking

DOI: 10.4324/9781003228301-8

patterns of verbal parallelisms and repetitions that bring a haunted sense of recurrence to character motivation and action, that the real task of translating this play lies.

One of the great achievements of Mayorga's theatre is the way in which philosophical conundrums are set within the contours of recognisable human experience. Admittedly, these are contours whose roots, we get the sense, go back for centuries (again the presence of Benjamin lingers here) but, for all that, they are no less urgent in the immediate context of the lives we lead today. In order to achieve what we might call this conflictive balance between aspiration and recurrence, Mayorga writes with an extraordinary economy of language, effectively creating, in terms of interwoven echoes of key vocabulary and repeated phrases, the grammar of a world threatening to spin out of control in spite of our attempts to fix it to the force of our desire and the structuring elements of our language.

Translators, schooled in the ethics of cultural and linguistic difference, tend to immediately bring their powers of interpretation to bear on words in the source language, looking for equivalences that are invariably more conceptual than linguistic. In the case of this play, in terms of, for example, the rhythmical patterns of the interlocking discourses of how Hector and Berna talk about the world of art from the perspective of their ownership of the collection, the Spanish word *cosa* ("thing") assumes a key importance. This is so often a catch-all term that translators will seek to interpret and, always aware of the pied beauty of stylistic variation, will extend into a range of translations that are each appropriate to their shifting contexts. Here Hector uses it as an invariant term to refer to the individual work of art (Berna, with equally invariable, but no less conflictive, linguistic clarity refers to the same item as the "piece").

Now it would seem paltry to point to the terminological recurrence of *cosa*/thing and *pieza*/piece as a translational challenge (although it is true that every occurrence needs to be negotiated into recognisable English rhythm and usage). But the two terms function on stage as part of the carefully contrived machinery of a concentrated, boiled down and intensely resonant stage language. It is a language configured by the interlocking discourses of the transcendental and the immanent, of the core actions of acquiring, loving, sacrificing and testing, and the series of interleaving verbal echoes and repetitions, all of which together make this play an extraordinarily tightly written work of theatre. Within this tightness, the distinct elements of language assume the force of a mantra. To keep the fear, the threat of barbarism, at bay? Perhaps. But the fact remains that the process of translating a play that manages to be both resonant and verbally honed requires the translator to treat it in part as a technical document and in part as a piece of concrete poetry. In my experience, that is unique.

Written in 2020 during the COVID-19 lockdown, *The Collection* premiered in 2024, at the Abadía Theatre in Madrid, directed by Juan Mayorga himself, and was published shortly afterwards by La uÑa RoTa.

Characters (in order of appearance):

Berna
Susana
Carlos
Hector

1

Dusk. Emptiness. SUSANA and CARLOS enter. CARLOS is carrying a suit-case, which he puts down, and leaves through a different door. SUSANA looks at the room. There is a hole in the roof. BERNA and HECTOR enter by the door through which CARLOS has just left. He follows immediately behind. BERNA and HECTOR are old; SUSANA is young, as is CARLOS, who stands at a discreet distance from them.

BERNA: Mrs Gelman.
SUSANA: Mrs Pereira. Mr. Pereira.
BERNA: Berna, please. And Hector.
SUSANA: Susana.
BERNA: Please sit down, Susana. Perhaps here where we can see you better. A drink? Wine – red, white? Juice?
SUSANA: Water, thank you.

> *CARLOS serves the drinks, red wine for BERNA, juice for HECTOR and water for SUSANA. Every so often BERNA exercises her hand to stimulate the circulation.*

BERNA: How was your journey?
SUSANA: Very easy, thank you.
BERNA: It's us who're grateful to you. We know you have many other responsibilities. And to be truthful, our invitation could have been clearer.
SUSANA: It was clear enough. I didn't think twice.
BERNA: The label tells you which piece the box corresponds to. Hector doesn't call them pieces. He calls them things. And he calls this place the cave because he says that it contains all the shadows of the things. I call it the ring because it's where we do our fighting. If you take a walk round the area and have look at some of the buildings of the same period, you'll see that … All right, Hector, I'm coming to that. Do you want to? You go ahead.

> *Silence.*

HECTOR: We're old. We have no children. People wonder what will happen to our collection. Logically.

Silence.

I think this is all very premature. If I'd had my way, we wouldn't have invited you here. Not yet.

BERNA: You know perfectly well why we did.

HECTOR: I had an episode, that's what Berna means. I blanked out. Just for a few moments. Just three times.

BERNA: We've been imagining this moment for years. Hector was the first to say it out loud, but both of us have been thinking it for years. "What happens to the collection when we're gone?"

HECTOR: "When we're gone." But we're still here. And might be for a long time to come.

BERNA: Before we wrote to you we discussed a range of possibilities. In the first place, some sort of agreement with the State.

HECTOR: We don't trust the State. We don't trust any state.

BERNA: We've been approached by various states.

HECTOR: What if some politician or civil servant or jobsworth should take it into their head one day that a thing is immoral or that its maker is, and order it to be dumped in the basement? We don't trust them.

BERNA: We've talked through the possibilities. None of them meets our basic requirement. Which is the unity of the collection. That it shouldn't be split up or merged into something else. The collection is much more than the sum of its pieces, it's the relationship between them. They simply cannot be allowed to be separated or dispersed among other pieces, no matter how valuable those other ones may be. The collection is the thing.

HECTOR: You have a family.

SUSANA: Yes.

HECTOR: A husband and a small daughter. What's going on out there? Is it some sort of celebration?

BERNA: They must have something to celebrate. I realise this is the first time we've actually spoken, Susana, but we've been aware of you. Observing you. We noticed you, even though we've never been in direct competition.

HECTOR: We recognised something in you. An affinity.

BERNA: The first time was in Berlin. You were a collector without money. But there was something in your eyes that went beyond money. The items you stopped in front of, how you looked at them, that glint in your eyes, looking at a piece you were already beginning to covet.

HECTOR: You bought something in Berlin that no one else had noticed. But it showed ambition. And vision.

BERNA: Drink?

HECTOR: Conviction. Passion.

SUSANA: Water, please.

CARLOS pours water for SUSANA, red wine for BERNA and juice for HECTOR.

BERNA: You could have had that piece for half of what you paid for it. We can teach you the tricks of the trade. Tomorrow, after you've rested, you'll visit the collection.

SUSANA: I thought the visit would be today.

HECTOR: We suggested you pack for several days.

SUSANA: I assume there's an important reason why the visit can't be today.

BERNA: You're impatient. Are you an impatient person?

SUSANA: I have an appointment tomorrow I can't get out of. I didn't mention it because I've only just found out.

HECTOR: Did we send the wrong letter? We drafted it three times. Do you have it there?

SUSANA: Yes.

HECTOR: Would you read it?

BERNA: Hector …

SUSANA takes out the letter. She reads.

SUSANA: "Dear Mrs Gelman. We would be honoured to receive you. We suggest, if convenient, the 14th March. We will cover your expenses. If you wish to travel by train or air, let us know your arrival time, and we will send a driver to meet you. Should you wish to come by car, we attach a map. There is space to park in the yard in front of the house. Please pack for several days. Sincerely Berna and Hector Pereira."

HECTOR: Second draft. "Pack for several days"

BERNA: This can't be rushed, Susana. We won't take a second less than what is necessary. But we need to get to know each other, you, Hector and I.

SUSANA: I can be back the day after tomorrow.

BERNA: We can't wait for you to come back from the appointment you can't get out of, and you can't visit the collection today. You need to rest first. We want you to see the collection with fresh eyes, free from preconceptions. There are a lot of rumours about the collection, As there are about us. And our state of mind.

HECTOR: People have said the collection doesn't exist. That we don't exist.

BERNA: Some have said we only have forgeries. Copies and copies of copies. Or that that we buy pieces just to destroy them. "To get rid of them once and for all," someone said.

HECTOR: Or the collection is a front for something else. Perhaps for another collection. And that we just work here. Perhaps for another collector.

BERNA: There are people who write about the collection. obsessively as if their sole mission was to discredit it, whether they've seen what's in it or not. Very few have been invited to see it.

HECTOR: The collection can't be shown to just anyone. We don't want tourists.

BERNA: We discussed it and we decided to keep tourists out.

HECTOR: We don't want people who see the collection just to kill time. Kill time!

BERNA: Some people open their collections because they feel guilty. Embarrassed about being collectors. We don't feel that guilt. We don't lend our pieces out either. And people hate us for that, but we can live with their hatred. Anyway, collectors are always hated, it's logical.

HECTOR: Our collection instructs the world. But the world doesn't have to see it.

BERNA: Any photographs or recordings of pieces you may have seen are from before they entered the collection.

HECTOR: What do you know about the collection?

BERNA: Don't look so innocent. Ever since you got our letter, even before that, you've been doing your research.

HECTOR: A long time ago, you recognised something in us too. An affinity.

BERNA: We know you've spoken to people who claim to know us. And all of them you've asked about us and the collection.

SUSANA: I've talked to three people who say they've visited it. It was like they were talking about three different collections. One talked about medieval icons, another about machines, another about children's stories from the interwar years. Perhaps each of them only spoke about what had impressed them most. Or maybe there really are various collections. As for the place, one said it was like a labyrinth, another a garden, another a scrapyard. Two of them described a mosaic in the form of an ellipse, which they had to view from a metal platform not to walk on it. And I once met a van driver who said he'd delivered pieces of wood here, burnt around the edges, some mechanical figures – he couldn't be more precise – and a large colourless sculpture. "But not like it'd been made without colour," he said, "like it'd lost it."

Silence.

HECTOR: You should rest.

BERNA: Rest first, then visit the collection, and we might make you an offer.

HECTOR: You should rest.

BERNA: Have dinner any time. We don't have dinner any more.

HECTOR: You should rest. I still have a few rounds to do. Fifteen a night.

BERNA: Carlos will show you to your room. Anything you need, just ask Carlos. We'll meet tomorrow at dawn. The collection has to be viewed in different lights and from different states of mind.

HECTOR looks up at the hole in the roof.

HECTOR: Sunrise tomorrow is at seven thirty-three.

HECTOR walks towards the same door through which he entered with BERNA.

SUSANA: An offer? You mean a job?

HECTOR: We might offer you the collection.

Silence.

SUSANA: I couldn't even afford the least valuable of your pieces. Not even the cheapest thing.

HECTOR: Afford? If you pass the test – yes, Berna, it is a test, let's not beat about the bush – we will give you the collection.

BERNA: It is a test. No, we won't beat about the bush. We need to be sure that whoever the collection goes to feels the same about it as we do. That they'll treat it with the same respect and the same determination.

HECTOR: Whatever you've heard about us, put it to one side. Our only concern has been to do justice to the things. And at the end now, still that: to do justice to the things.

BERNA: We'll do what we must. We're under no obligation to justify ourselves to anyone. Of course, if we do reach an agreement – if you pass the test – we would draw up a contract. Not to protect us, because no contract can ever give us security. Not to protect us. To protect you.

HECTOR: She means because of our age; people will think you've taken advantage of us.

He moves towards the door.

We're not looking for a buyer. We're looking for an heir.

He moves and stops again.

This isn't the first time, is it? Was there not something like this years ago?

BERNA: What do you remember?

HECTOR: I remember you or me saying to someone: "It's logical, when people hear we're going to separate they wonder what will happen to the collection. We've talked through the possibilities. We need to find someone who feels the same about it as we do." Something like that. Years ago.

BERNA: We never thought about separating. What would have happened to the collection?

HECTOR turns to go out. BERNA goes to whisper something in his ear. HECTOR replies in similar fashion. They argue into each other's ear, increasingly heatedly. Silence.

Don't be alarmed, Susana. Conflict is our method. Fighting, that's how we've made the collection. At the start we don't agree on anything. We fight and keep fighting until it becomes clear we should either go for a piece or forget it, either pay the asking price or keep haggling. It's the only way we know how. Sometimes one of us starts fighting again where the other left it off, hours or days or years later. Sometimes we hurt each other, sometimes we love it. Sometimes we hurt each other and we love it. Fighting helps you think. We've fought a lot about whether this is the right moment to leave the collection. When we agreed it was, we fought about the people we should test to see who we could leave it to. It's only fair to tell you we're considering other candidates. Hector believes you could be the ideal person, but that the time isn't right; I think the time is right, but that you're not the ideal person. Ring or cave, this is where we plan our activities, where we think the collection, where we dream it. Open any of the boxes. I call them the "Catalogue," Hector the "Atlas." There's a box for each piece, in order of acquisition. Each box contains descriptions of the piece, which don't always coincide, as well as where and when it was made if we've been able to find that out, a proof of ownership, a list of previous owners, an account of how we came by the piece, whether in one go or after years of pursuit. Hector calls it the "Atlas" because each box has a map tracking the piece from the moment it was made to its arrival here. Each piece is a history.

They turn to leave again.

You'll find a non-disclosure agreement on your bed. It sets out what you can and cannot say about you might see and hear in this house.

HECTOR: From your window, just as it's getting dark, to the right, you'll see the shadow of two boxers fighting.

They leave. Silence. CARLOS picks up SUSANA's suitcase.

SUSANA: No, it's ok.

Silence.

No need. I'm not staying.

CARLOS puts down the case and steps aside. Silence. SUSANA goes over to the Catalogue or Atlas. She takes the first box and opens it. Fade.

2

The same place, later. SUSANA has just finished examining the contents of the first box of the Catalogue or Atlas. Like the other boxes, it may well contain a recording of the younger voices of HECTOR and BERNA describing their acquisition of the piece, which may be the final thing SUSANA listens to before she closes it. Silence.

SUSANA: Have you known them long?
CARLOS: Not very.
SUSANA: You're like their confidant?
CARLOS: I think they trust me, yes.
SUSANA: Do you mind talking?
CARLOS: No.
SUSANA: You don't mind me asking you questions? Or am I wasting my time?
CARLOS: I don't mind, no.

Silence.

SUSANA: Is it easy living cheek by jowl with such rich people?
CARLOS: They never make me feel they are rich.
SUSANA: Do you dress that way because that's what they expect?
CARLOS: I choose my own clothes.
SUSANA: And what are you officially? Secretary? Servant? Drinks pourer?
CARLOS: We're not all equal.
SUSANA: And what are you to the collection? That is, if you have anything to do with the collection.
CARLOS: Everything here has to do with the collection.
SUSANA: The people I know who've been here never mentioned you.
CARLOS: That's part of my job, not to be mentioned.
SUSANA: But you have hidden qualities?
CARLOS: Whatever they need, I do my best.

Silence.

SUSANA: Can I have a whiskey?

Pause. CARLOS pours her a whiskey.

          Why did you come here, Carlos?
CARLOS: I was lucky.
SUSANA: Sorry?
CARLOS: Berna said I reminded her of a figure in a painting. Hector argued with her. No point in trying to identify the painting. I've changed a lot since then.
SUSANA: When?
CARLOS: It wasn't a child.
SUSANA: You go where they go. You take them places.
CARLOS: They don't need me to take them. Berna manages very well. She's a good driver.
SUSANA: Sometimes you go to places for them, don't you? I saw you in Venice, I think.
CARLOS: I have one of those faces.
SUSANA: Do they have many people who go to places for them?
CARLOS: If it gets out they're interested in anything, the price goes through the roof. They have people who buy for them.

SUSANA: Actors?
CARLOS: Representatives.

Silence.

SUSANA: Are they as capable as they pretend?
CARLOS: People laughed at them when they sold Buenos Aires 11.7.92 and said they were mad when they bought Madrid 23.2.81. But everyone copies them now. What others were throwing away, they turned into objects of beauty, and time proved they were right to ignore what it took others years to recognise as worthless. The collector is measured by the quality of their bets, and time has proved them right. But it's always too early to know what's a success and what's a failure. It's always too early to know the value of anything.

Silence.

SUSANA: Is this chair part of the collection?
CARLOS: Sorry?
SUSANA: I was thinking that perhaps the collection extended through the whole house. Perhaps the bed they had made up for me, that might be part of the collection too. Perhaps you're part of the collection.
CARLOS: Perhaps you are.

Silence. SUSANA takes another box from the Atlas or Catalogue. She opens it and begins to examine its contents.

SUSANA: What do you collect?
CARLOS: I don't.
SUSANA: Nothing?
CARLOS: I don't think they would like it.
SUSANA: Everybody collects something. We're all collectors.
CARLOS: I've never felt the need.
SUSANA: You collect something. You must.

Silence.

CARLOS: Gestures – the body, the face. Body language.

He makes some gestures that we have seen already in BERNA, HECTOR, and SUSANA.

But I don't think that really counts as collecting.

Silence. SUSANA imitates some of the gestures CARLOS has made.

SUSANA: So your collection's in here.

She touches her forehead.

CARLOS: It's not collecting.
SUSANA: You must have met a lot of collectors. All sorts.
CARLOS: Not so many. Hector and Berna don't like them.

SUSANA:	You don't like us much either, eh?
CARLOS:	Collectors … wherever you go, you're always on the make. Like wild animals on the prowl for more meat: you haven't finished chewing one piece before you turn your greedy eyes on the next. Anything you can't have becomes irresistible. You sicken for what you can't have, and as there's always something you can't have, you're always sick. I don't understand you. We can all love something, of course, but that doesn't mean you have to possess it. You have nightmares about fires and floods and you die with your catalogue under the pillow. You could die for a single piece. You could kill for a single piece. You could get even married for a single piece. I understand loving something … but to have to possess it. I pity you.
SUSANA:	You have no idea. Collectors are the happiest people in the world.
CARLOS:	I pity your happiness.

Silence.

SUSANA:	They've done this before, haven't they? Tested other people.
CARLOS:	I don't know.
SUSANA:	You don't know?
CARLOS:	I don't know if they are testing you.

Silence.

SUSANA:	What do you suppose the test is?
CARLOS:	They'll set you tasks. They'll ask you to acquire some new piece for their collection. A painting by Velazquez. They say they need one.
SUSANA:	Berna said she has others in mind. Did she ever mention anyone by name?
CARLOS:	They wouldn't like me repeating their private conversations.
SUSANA:	Is there another candidate in the house?
CARLOS:	Sorry?
SUSANA:	It occurred to me they might have brought two potential heirs to the house to compare them. They compare people like they compare pieces. They go off to sleep and leave the candidates to their own devices. By sunrise, one's killed the other. At seven thirty-three. Perhaps that's the test, to see who's willing to kill.

She asks for another whiskey, which CARLOS pours.

I like watching gestures too. I was watching you, while the two of them were explaining their plan to me. You had an opinion about what you were watching. Not a good one.

Silence.

CARLOS:	I understand why they're worried. If you have something that you think's valuable, of course you wonder what will happen to it when you're gone. If you don't have children, it's a problem.
SUSANA:	No. It's their solution you don't like.

CARLOS: I don't think a collection can be inherited. Whenever they talk about a piece, they light up remembering how they acquired it. They see something in each piece that nobody else can inherit.

Silence.

SUSANA: Do you think they should sell it and leave the money to the poor?
CARLOS: They could help a lot of people.
SUSANA: They don't want to break up the collection. And they don't trust the State, or any state.
CARLOS: I'm surprised they're considering another collector. You have your own sickness.

Silence.

SUSANA: The fact I'm a collector, you think that's a problem. Just as well, you're not the one who's testing me. Or are you?
CARLOS: Me?
SUSANA: What do my gestures tell you, Carlos?
CARLOS: What?
SUSANA: Is it not part of your job, to observe whoever they're dealing with and report back? So what does my body language tell you?
CARLOS: You work hard to seem so confident.

Silence.

SUSANA: You want me to leave without seeing the collection.
CARLOS: Yes.
SUSANA: In case I damage something? In case something damages me?
CARLOS: I don't know what's in there.
SUSANA: Really? They don't let you in?
CARLOS: They've never invited me.
SUSANA: You don't know what's in the collection?
CARLOS: I've only seen pieces on their way in. Always in packing. And when they come out, they're in packing too.

Silence. SUSANA opens her case and takes out a briefcase containing car keys, an envelope with money, and a tightly sealed bag.

SUSANA: "Anything you need, just ask Carlos." That's what Berna said. I need you to go to this address.

She takes out a sheet of paper and writes an address. CARLOS takes it, reads it and gives it back to her.

CARLOS: It's too far.

SUSANA takes the piece of paper.

SUSANA: "Anything you need, just ask Carlos." Berna was absolutely clear. This is the name of the person who lives there.

She writes down the name.

He's agreed to see me at nine in the morning. That's the only time he'll see me. He'll open the door to you when you tell him you're Jaime, my husband. I've told him about you. And about my daughter, Lorena.

She writes both names.

The reason why you, Jaime, have gone instead of me is because I've had to stay to look after Lorena. Nothing serious, just a touch of asthma. When Alberto opens the door, ask about his leg, be friendly, don't rush him, don't say why you're there until he raises the subject. You're there for a letter. Are you following me? You're there for a letter. You speak the language it's written in, but you're not going to read it, I don't want you to read it. You're the husband of a writer– me – who's doing some research into his wife. She died some years ago. Since then, the man you're going to see, and I've never met, became a recluse. I hope you can read his body language and not frighten him off. Win him over. Don't let him see you're anxious, take your time. He might deny its existence, he might swear, as he did when he told me about the letter, that he had made it all up. All that matters is you don't leave there without it. Handle it as little as possible. Put it in this bag. You'll find the amount I'm prepared to pay in this envelope. I'd be very grateful if you didn't use it all. If you don't like driving in the dark, you should leave now. If you hurry up, you can sleep for a while in this hotel – I booked a room for myself.

She writes down the name of the hotel. She holds out the bag, the envelope, the keys and the sheet of paper. CARLOS doesn't take them.

Believe me, I'm not comfortable asking you to do this. I'd rather go myself.

CARLOS: Why don't you send your husband? Your real husband.
SUSANA: My husband, the real one, might feel sorry for him. Jaime has a heart.

Silence.

CARLOS: I can't go without telling them. They like knowing where I am.
SUSANA: If you lost this job, how easy would it be to find another one?
CARLOS: I've got savings. I wouldn't need to rush.
SUSANA: If I pass the test, if I inherit the collection, you'll be part of it. I won't forget what you did for me. Or what you didn't do.
CARLOS: You're offering me a job? I can't imagine being here without them, Mrs Gelman.

Silence.

SUSANA: "Anything you need, just ask Carlos." I'm not going to tell you again what I need. If they call to ask where you are, tell them I asked you to go for medicine.

She writes down the name of the medicine.

I have asthma. Like my daughter. That's the truth. You won't find the medicine. They took it off the market ages ago.

Silence.

What are you waiting for? Did Berna tell you to watch me? Are you worried I'll do something to them? You're fond of them? If you work for me, you don't even have to like me.

CARLOS: I don't have to like them. What is it you're interested in? The stamps? The paper? The person who wrote the letter? Are you really interested in the man's wife? Does he have any idea of what the letter's worth?

SUSANA closes the suitcase.

SUSANA: Before you go, if it's part of your job, would you take it to my room. But only if it's part of your job.

CARLOS: If they ask me where I am, I won't lie. I never lie to them. Your room is at the end of the corridor.

He lifts her suitcase and leaves through the same door as HECTOR and BERNA did earlier. SUSANA is alone. She takes out her phone and dials. She talks to someone she can see on the screen.

SUSANA: Tired. How are you? ... What did you have for dinner? ... Put her on ... Are you still not in your pyjamas? Come on, Lorena, get ready for bed ... Tomorrow evening. Are you helping daddy? ... What did you do in school today? ... You need new pyjamas! You can see your tummy ... No, Lorena, time to sleep. My eyes are closing and you have to close yours. Yes, stop pretending! ... Tonight's is called "The Magic Shoes." There are two little girls, the same age as you. They decide to go out. One of them is a princess and she rides in her gold coach. The other one is poor, and she goes in her bare feet. When the little princess sees the poor girl, she takes her shoes off and lets them fall through the window of the coach. The little poor girl watches the coach drive away and looks at the shoes. They're so beautiful. She puts them on and thinks how lovely she looks in them. But after a while her feet begin to feel a bit strange. She realises the shoes are taking her towards the woods and once she's in the woods towards a house that she's always been too frightened of to go into. She gets to the door of the house. And the door opens.

Fade.

3

The same place, that night. SUSANA is surrounded by empty boxes from the Catalogue or Atlas. She is examining the contents of one of them, perhaps listening to a recording of the voices of HECTOR and BERNA. Wearing night clothes, HECTOR comes in through the same door he left by earlier.

HECTOR: Can you not sleep? Neither can I. I can't stop wondering about you.

Silence.

You should leave tonight. Go back to your husband and your little girl, get away from the collection as soon as you can. And if it's not too late, do something else with your life. Not collecting. Berna would scold me if she heard that, but I have to tell you the truth. Berna and I used to be a normal couple ... hard to believe. Then one day, walking hand in hand down some street or other, I saw something in a shop window that I thought would be the perfect memento of a perfect afternoon. Berna didn't want to go in, but I insisted. We had no idea we were beginning a collection. We kept buying works – that's what we called them then, "works" – we kept buying works until one day we realised that the collection had become a work in its own right, it had become our work. That we lived for it. That, without ever talking about it, we'd decided not to have children. Berna hates talking about this, she gets angry when I ask her "What do you think our life would have been like without the collection? Would we have been parents? Would we have separated?"

Silence.

We were saving for a second-hand car to go to Morocco. When eventually we did go it was twenty years later. To buy.

He goes to leave through the same door. He stops when he hears SUSANA.

SUSANA: Why are there empty boxes?

Silence.

HECTOR: For things we don't have yet. Because we haven't been able to buy them. Because we don't know yet if they exist. Because they still don't exist. If you visit the collection tomorrow, you'll see that there are gaps that correspond to the empty boxes.

SUSANA: Like in the periodical table? It had gaps while they waited for new elements to be discovered. Or like a dinosaur skeleton that they finish bone by bone.

Silence. HECTOR is about to leave. He turns round.

HECTOR: You're wondering about my relationship with her. if there's anything between us apart from the collection. If there's any love.

Silence. He looks up at the hole in the roof.

We looked at a lot of places. It was the hole that decided us. Berna said, "It's an eye." We've always left it open. When it rains, the water gathers there.

He points to a spot.

When I can't sleep, I sit underneath. More and more now. Looking at the sky is calming. At the clouds, if there are clouds. At the moon, if there is a moon. The different colours. Berna is a good sleeper.

He punches the air, and again.

This isn't a house for living in. We didn't make it to live in; we made it for the collection. A lot of people start collecting to decorate their house, and they end up collecting to decorate themselves. Nearly everyone does it, you know that, but without good reason. Just to make themselves look beautiful or seem intelligent, and they end up believing that's what they are, beautiful and intelligent, because what they buy is. Or to hide something. Or to get to know the artists, they buy art because it's the artist they really want to buy. Or to meet unusual people, or to meet anyone so as not to be alone. Or to have an excuse to travel or "lead a more fulfilling life" or to "be part of civilisation." I'm not saying it's necessarily bad, but these are worthless reasons. Or to have some excitement in your life, that was part of it for us: the frenzy of the auctions, the pleasure of haggling, the pride you take in discovering a genius. Or to live with something easier to manage than people. Or to live surrounded by expensive things or to cover a wall or fill a gap or be on the list of the people who've owned whatever it is … do you mind, that light … it's shining in my eyes … or because they have no religion and this becomes their religion, their immortality … immortality! And then there are those who see it as an investment, but they're less contemptible than the pedants, because at least they're honest about why they do it. We compete with very rich people. They can afford much more expensive things, but they don't know how to put together a collection like ours. Any ragbag of things, bought without rhyme or reason, that's what they call a collection. Some of them do have an idea, they're tired of the world and they want to live inside that idea, but no idea is as powerful as ours, They start off with that idea, they want to show it's true. We're not trying to prove anything, the idea reveals itself. You think you choose things, that you put them into some sort of order, but it's the things that choose us and find their own order and make the idea visible. That first thing, it took us years to work out what it was that had attracted us to it. But the first one led to the second, some always lead to others. One day we had to move them all out and put them on the other side. This isn't a house for living in.

Silence.

SUSANA: Are you all right?

Silence.

Should I call Berna? Are you ok?

HECTOR: Where's Carlos?

SUSANA: I asked him to go and get me some medicine.

Silence.

HECTOR: I'm sure you think about death a lot. The things we collect always remind us of death. What medicine?

SUSANA: For asthma. He didn't want to go. He doesn't trust me. He's afraid I might do something to you.

HECTOR: He's right. A collector can become a criminal in a heartbeat.

SUSANA: Carlos thinks that a collection can't be inherited.

HECTOR: If there's one thing that can be inherited, it's a collection. It's made for that. An inheritance isn't a gift. There are conditions.

He produces a pen and paper and holds them out to SUSANA.

Do you mind? I don't have the hands any more, and Carlos isn't here.

SUSANA takes the paper and pen without knowing why. Pause. HECTOR indicates that she should write down what he says.

Today's date. I declare this to be my last will and testament. Colon.

SUSANA writes it down. She waits for HECTOR to continue, but he is distracted.

The celebration's over.

Silence.

We have no friends. Artists, dealers, other collectors, everyone else, Berna deals with them. She knows everyone has a price, and she knows how to find it. I haven't spoken to anyone for years. We would talk to people like us if there still were people like us. Nobody cares about the truth any more. We get sent lots of publications, but I only look at the photos of things. Not the interviews. Artists never speak the truth. When I look at something I try to forget who made it so that my judgment isn't clouded by what I think of the person.

Most so-called artists only know vocabulary, crude jargon. I have no interest in hearing what they think about their work, or what they set out to do. The only thing that counts is what the work does, not the intentions that lay behind it. If a thing is important, it knows things that its creator doesn't. Artists think they make things, but things are made by time. Goya said, "Time paints too." The truth is it's only time that paints. The collector is time.

Time passes.

When I look at something, I try to imagine how it will resonate with other things, its relationship with other things. Each new thing brings out something new in the things that are already here. Each thing is a new beginning just like each thing is reborn in the collection. It's different from the periodical table or like a dinosaur skeleton because the collection will never be complete. Sometimes we think "There's nothing to be added or taken away." Vanity. Just change the order of two things and everything changes. It must be the same for a writer. You change a word round or add one in or take one out. Sometimes the writer has to delete their best writing. The collection is a text written with other people's words – or words they think they've written. Over the last few years what we've done, more than anything, is take things out. It's too big. Less is better. At the start we bought a lot, you need to listen to a lot of voices in a language before you understand the grammar. It's more difficult not to buy, when you're offered the most marvellous things on a daily basis. A collection is a map. Too much detail and you don't see it. An ark. You need to create the collection as if the world was coming to an end and you can only save the things that matter. A marvellous work might not be for the collection, while something lesser might be crucial. Less is better. Your husband, does he like you being a collector?

SUSANA: He's a normal person. There are other things about me he likes.

HECTOR: What does he think about what you collect? Is he interested?

SUSANA: In a different way. He's not interested in possessing it. Because that's what matters to us, isn't it, possession.

HECTOR: Possession, yes, But not things. Possessing the world. If you didn't go home, would he come for you?

SUSANA: I don't know if he would.

Silence. HECTOR looks through the window.

HECTOR: If you didn't go home … Am I speaking very loudly? Sometimes, when Berna's not here to tell me, I don't notice how loud I am. When Berna gets cross, rub her hand. This one. It soothes her.

SUSANA: Speak louder if you want. Speak as loud as you want to me.

HECTOR: We'd seen each other a few times, but she never even looked at me. Until one day I turned up with a black eye. For some reason I told her I'd come from a fight, that I was a boxer. That seemed to catch her attention so I started going to a boxing club.

He punches the air, again, attacks an imaginary opponent and ducks and dives as he is punched in return.

I took some beatings. Beautiful punches. I think – Berna disagrees – that these episodes stem from those punches. They were worth it. Compared to Berna, everything else was dark. I couldn't bear it if she died first.

He signals to her to take the pen. SUSANA writes down what HECTOR dictates.

"On this day, I declare this to be my last will and testament: in the event of my death, with no heir designate, I request that my wife should destroy the collection, as I will do in the event of hers. It is to be destroyed in a manner in keeping with the safety of all concerned." 14th March and whatever the year is.

HECTOR reads the document and signs it with difficulty. He puts it away. He is about to leave.

Berna doesn't know. I have another collection. Just mine. It's a secret. I have another collection.

SUSANA: Our secret.

She takes HECTOR's hands.

I have two collections as well. One, the small one, is waiting for me at home. The other, the big one is in my head. That's where I keep the things I could never have any other way. Things from the great museums. Things destroyed by time. Things I've imagined. I'd love you to see them with me and to see your collections with you. Just you and me. Tonight. And for you to tell me each thing's story. Geneva 3.3.74. Tel Aviv 20.9.82. Guimaraes 5.8.1.

She caresses his hands. She lifts them to her lips. Silence.

HECTOR: Guimaraes 5.8.1. was the most difficult one. The greatest sacrifice. We had to do it. It chose us and we had to do it. You buy it but it possesses you. You feel that inferiority, that's the real discovery. But you, you've never made any sacrifice. You don't sell. You've never sold.

SUSANA: I never sell. It would be like selling a piece of myself, a piece of my life.

Silence.

HECTOR: You've never sacrificed anything you love for something you love more.

SUSANA: No.

HECTOR: Sometimes you discover you could have had something for a lot less than you did. But that's not important. Do you know what is? Discovering that a thing has deceived you. I don't mean forgeries, I mean lies.

He moves away from SUSANA and punches his imaginary opponent.

Sometimes when I'm on this side, more frequently now and angrier and angrier, I curse our luck. Then I go to the other side and I think how ungrateful I am about Berna, about life. The collections gives me much more than it's ever taken. The collection saves me from a world given over to money, speed, mirrors, that's what obsesses everyone, what everyone aspires to. These are not times for the wise but for the astute, for the practical people with only one talent that raises them a bare inch above the herd. The collection is a protest against the times. The ark and the rainbow over a flood of noise. I saw how you were looking at us. Asking yourself if there's anything between us other than the collection. If we matter to each other. Neither of us matters. Only the images matter. Some are from caves, others haven't become visible yet, but they all precede us. They precede us, which is why when they do appear to us, we tremble. When I walk among them, I tremble. In there I say to myself this is bigger than me, this is real, this is, at long last, true. I say to myself I know something about myself. Berna and I have always longed to know who we are. Perhaps we're the last people who want to know who they are. Outside the collection, there are only ghosts. That's why, once you've gone into the collection, it's impossible to come out. Because everything outside becomes insignificant. You don't come back from the collection. Go home tonight.

He is about to go, but appears not to know which door to take. Finally, he goes out through the one by which he entered. Time passes. SUSANA takes out her phone and dials.

SUSANA: I know it's late. I just wanted to hear your voice. Turn on your camera. I want to see you … say things … No, I'm not in my room, it's a sort of archive … I don't think they can hear me, I don't care … The other side of those doors, I suppose … I don't know how many people there are here … I've only seen the two of them and some sort of employee … No, I haven't seen any security, although there must be … I feel strange … Like I was inside the collection … I don't know what I mean … Let me see the little girl … She's lovely … Give her a kiss from me but don't wake her … Do you have plans for tomorrow? … The day after … Lots of love.

Fade.

4

Later, the same place. Rain outside. SUSANA, surrounded by boxes from the Catalogue or Atlas, perhaps set out in the form of a map of the collection, is listening to recordings of BERNA and HECTOR. BERNA, in night clothes, enters through the door through which she left earlier.

BERNA: If you're not comfortable in your room, you can have a smaller one. You might be better there.

SUSANA: I haven't been to my room yet, I'm sure it's perfect, thank you.

BERNA: Your bed, the rug in your room, lots of things you'll see round the house …we found them while we were looking for other pieces for the collection. Some were part of the collection. Not this though, it was here already, and we kept it on a whim. I apologise for Hector. I want you to leave with good memories.

She points to the boxes.

Does all of this say something to you?

Silence. To explain SUSANA makes use of the boxes.

SUSANA: Sometimes you need to decide on the spur of the moment; other times you need to know when to wait. You waited thirty-two years to get Tokyo 3.8.18. It's hardly ever all about the money, there's always something else to strengthen your hand. Warsaw 15.1.15, no amount of money could ever buy it, but you invited the owner to come and visit you. You knew how much he loved the piece and that he would realise this was the best place for it, so he gave it to you. Market intelligence opens doors: a death, a divorce, and people often sell. To get San Francisco 14.7.99 you waited until the owner had to deal with both. The price you paid for Belgrade 21.8.92 was to guarantee no one would ever know it's here. The creator of Bordeaux 14.7.83 offered it to you on the condition that you would exhibit it once a year, which you very politely refused to do. In the end he gave it to you anyway because he was desperate for it to be part of the collection. Box Guimaraes 5.8.1 is different from all the rest. All that's inside is ash.

Silence.

BERNA: A lot of artists want to give us their work. There are collections that demean reputation; ours assures it. Money can be important. It's a sore point for some collectors, that connection between collecting and cash. We are not ostentatious because it's easier not to be; the way we live suits the collection. We would help the poor if that helped the collection. We're hunters, Susana. Hector calls us image hunters. I'm going to miss all of that.

She pours herself a whiskey.

We fought like cat and dog about whether we should have somewhere specially built for the collection, or give it a place that would form part of it. We interviewed architects, who set out the most beautiful visions, but that was we wanted to avoid at all costs: visions. Then we started looking at places that had their own history and had contained other things – factories, barracks, brothels ... It was that hole that decided it for us. People accuse us of copying the Pantheon, but that eye was always part of this building. You keep your collection at home, don't you? You share your space with it.

SUSANA: It's all I can afford.

BERNA: Don't play the oh I'm so poor card with me, Susana. When Hector and I were starting out, we couldn't even afford a second-hand car. We re-mortgaged to buy our second piece, and then another loan not for the third piece, but for one we bought to sell on, which we did. And with the profits we were able to buy the third piece and the fourth. We've bought a lot of pieces to sell on. It's like gambling, I'm good at it, I have a nose for anticipating what you call the market. We could have made make a lot of money, but it was all for the collection. We could still make a lot of money, people offer us fortunes, our pieces shoot up in value by the mere fact they're part of the collection. We haven't just sold pieces that we bought to sell. We've also sold pieces that we had bought thinking they had some sort of light ... and then that light went out, pieces that ended up disappointing us. And there were some that we still miss. That's the worst of all, to turn your back on pieces you love and that might fall into indifferent hands. At any moment a new piece might appear, a piece that would enrich the collection, and that new piece might mean that another piece, even one we love, has to go. To turn your back on something you love: whoever succeeds us will have to do that too. It's not enough to conserve what there is; if it were, you wouldn't be here. Whoever inherits the collection will have to search for an heir one day, and explain all of this again. Explain that they are not important. I saw how you were looking at us when you came. You wondered if there's anything between us apart from the collection. If we matter to each other.

We're not important. Neither will our heir be. There's something else – Hector calls it Time – that keeps pieces or culls them. Only idiots boast they never sell: I never sell, they say. It would be like selling a piece of myself, a piece of my life. As though any piece can ever be theirs. As though their life had any importance.

She is about to leave. SUSANA stops her by taking her by the hand HECTOR mentioned to her.

SUSANA: I've never sold anything. But I will to take my collection to a higher level. The collection is more important than any of its pieces.

Silence.

BERNA: And would you stoop to conquer? Would you take advantage of someone weaker than you, for example? Or accept a piece acquired dishonestly?

SUSANA: Everything I say and how I say it matters. That's the test.

BERNA: And what you don't say. That matters too.

SUSANA: You're not looking for a good person, although you don't mind if they are, as long as it doesn't affect the collection. The collection is the only thing that matters. Frankly, Berna, I don't think I'm the right person for you, although I probably am for Hector. Let's assume the test finishes here. I have no time to waste, and I'm surprised you're wasting what little time you have left with me. If I had your problem, I wouldn't be looking among collectors. You create a collection, no matter how modest, and no other collection is as important as yours, it doesn't matter how great that other one is. I have my own dream.

She lifts her suitcase to leave. BERNA pours two whiskies.

BERNA: Hector and I have fought it out over this: if the heir having two collections would be a problem. If both collections needed a single piece, how could that not be a problem? But that situation would never arise, Susana. As far as we know, you have a good collection. A dream, you call it. You're right to exaggerate, if you want something to be treated with respect you need to talk about it with enthusiasm. But when you visit our collection, yours will seem irrelevant. Hector says – take this as a compliment – that your collection is like ours in miniature. So it began as a collection of love letters?

She offers her a whiskey.

SUSANA: In miniature! I will take that as a compliment. It began as a collection of love letters, but it's very rarely easy to know what's love, or something else.

She puts down her case and accepts the whiskey. They drink.

BERNA: I woke up dreaming about water. Hector dreams more about fire. We both dream about thieves, sometimes in the same night. The nightmares of the collector, you must know them all. How did it begin, Susana? Did you look at things and think one day you'll be mine?

SUSANA: It began with stickers.

Silence.

I bought the first letter when I was fourteen, the day after my father died. At first I only bought letters that were written after he was born, but that changed. Like everything else.

BERNA: You've done a lot of different jobs. I can't imagine you in any of them.

SUSANA: I've done all sorts of shitty jobs for the money. I don't particularly like the one I've got at the moment, but it's not particularly demanding either. I can keep my mind on what really matters.

BERNA: Hector and I can't agree about that, about what really does matter to you. But what's certainly true is that if you want something, you don't let anything get in your way. You had problems with the police.

Silence.

SUSANA: I was very young. I discovered a piece that ... I couldn't accept the fact that I couldn't afford it. And when I met the owner I was even more convinced that the piece would be better off with me.

BERNA: You wanted to save it.

SUSANA: I rushed in and I paid a different price. I've learned how to be patient.

Long silence. BERNA pours two whiskies.

BERNA: When we were young, and even quite recently, we used to lie here watching how the sky changed. We could spend hours here, just looking up, in silence, until one of us said something and then there'd be a fight that could go on for hours. We've done this together. We listen to anyone who can help us to look, and we have people looking for us all over the world, but in the final analysis we only trust each other. Some people have misled us, deliberately or not, but even that, all the losses and the deceits, we went through them together, they're part of the collection, the mistakes are part of the collection – although as Carlos says who can really know what a mistake is, it's always too early to know anything. We've discussed whether or not one person could manage all of this ... Your husband ... what's he called again?

SUSANA: He's called Jaime.

BERNA: Jaime.

She tries to memorise the forgotten name: "Jaime."

When I first met Hector he had a black eye, it was the first thing I noticed about him. He has his own collection. He keeps it secret. Old boxing photos. Boxers just as they're falling. Photos of defeat. He keeps it there. Jaime, does he help you with the collection?

SUSANA: If you're worried I have no one to fight with, don't worry. I have enough fights with myself. Carlos, I don't know what he's doing here, I would get rid of him, unless he's part of the collection. I sent him out for something. If he does it well, should I give him a tip?

BERNA: I don't know what Carlos is doing here either. Some people say he's the owner and that Hector and I work for him. And what are you doing here, Susana? Do you not like being with your daughter?

SUSANA: We like being together, all three of us.

BERNA: Is she a healthy child?

SUSANA: She's a happy child. She has asthma, like me. She likes having a story at bedtime, and she won't sleep unless I tell her one. Do you care about my daughter?

BERNA: No. I don't.

She makes a call on her phone.

What I do care about is you wondering if you should be here or with your child or what your husband might think if he could see you now.

Into the phone.

Two point four.

To SUSANA.

Hector asks me, more frequently now, what might it have been like if we'd had a child before buying that first piece.

Into the phone.

Two point six.

To SUSANA.

Our sole responsibility has been to the collection. Nothing or nobody has distracted us.

Into the phone.

No, Up to two point eight.

She finishes the call. To SUSANA.

We share the work, I look after the finances and the people. At one time we were constantly surrounded by people. We spent entire days in the galleries on 57th Street, and when we weren't there, we were in Basel or Venice, always with people. The sort of people who know that 63 is Warhol's most expensive year. Dealers who would set nine horrible pieces down in front of us, and one of the sort they thought we were looking for. Hector was driven to despair by auctions. I loved them.

She calls again and speaks into the phone.

Put in an offer for the house and contents.

She finishes the call.

It's been a while now since we were able to go anywhere near one. When the word spreads that we're interested in a piece or an artist or a period or a theme, anyone with anything even remotely like it goes crazy. What I like about auctions is all you have to do is come last. It's simple: two people want the same thing, who's capable of the greater sacrifice? I used to love reading the signs ... a quiver on the lips, anything can tell you your rival has reached their limit. Then suddenly, bang, the gavel comes down.

She knocks hard, like a gavel.

Susana, for you your collection is personal, you always want to beat somebody else to whatever it is. Of course there are times when we have to fight to stop someone who doesn't deserve to get it, but even then we have to remember what really matters. In Barcelona, last autumn, there was one person bidding against you every time, and you fell into the trap and paid too much for that one piece so you couldn't afford the next one and you must still regret that. Not only thieves, floods and fires, you still dream about some faceless rival who snatched what you wanted right from under your nose.

She takes out two files and opens them in front of SUSANA.

This piece is being auctioned in London tomorrow, this one in New York. We want them both. The New York auction begins five hours after the London one. We might be able to afford both pieces. But if we pay too much for this one, we might not have enough for this one. But if we pass on this one, we might end up with neither. Sometimes you have to leap before you look. What's your method?

Silence.

SUSANA: A piece gets inside my head, and I buy it, that's my method. I never know what I'm looking for. I wasn't born into a cultured family. The time came when I had to work out why some pieces gave me so much joy and others caused so much damage and why I was desperate to possess them, and I began to read and to study and to listen – I listen to as many different people as I can – but what really matters, nobody was able to teach me that. What matters is I don't need anyone's approval and that I have to distrust reputation and price and all that chitchat and listen to myself to work out which piece among so many is going to keep me awake at night. And that each buy has to be a huge step towards something I'm running away from. Something I have to obey that's much greater than taste, something that makes me feel I'm still alive.

BERNA: That something that goes beyond taste, is that what made you try to buy that piece in San Miniato?

Silence.

SUSANA: I nearly got it.
BERNA: A Japanese buyer got it.

Silence.

SUSANA: Yes. A Japanese buyer.
BERNA: Who bought it for us. You won't see it tomorrow, the pieces we buy to sell on we keep them somewhere else, we don't want them anywhere near the collection. Are you surprised? We left you clues to say it was us.

Silence. SUSANA takes the London and New York files. She uses them to illustrate her ideas, as she did before with the boxes.

SUSANA: The London auction begins five hours before the New York one. Five hours is a lot of time. I would buy the London piece to put it opposite Seoul 20.6.9, thereby rendering both Glasgow 22.7.85 and Santiago 8.6.3 expendable. They can be sold in the time available – five hours is a lot of time – enough to place a winning bid for the New York piece. There is only one piece in the collection that is indispensable: Guimaraes 5.8.1. You would never consider selling that under any circumstances. When you're standing in front of it, do you not feel the price you paid for it was too high?

Silence.

BERNA: Can I touch your hands?

Silence. SUSANA holds out her hands. BERNA takes them. She caresses them.

Are they always so cold? Are you in good health?
SUSANA: I'd like to see the collection with you. On our own. Tonight. I want you to tell me the story of each piece. Guimaraes 5.8.1.

Silence.

BERNA: Guimaraes 5.8.1. We made countless bids until we realised that no amount of money would ever secure it.

BERNA raises SUSANA's hands to her lips.

Patience, Susana. One night might not be enough. Maybe we need more time, more days and more nights, before you visit the collection. If so, because time is pressing, we would test other possible heirs in the meantime. You might meet them in the house, which could be uncomfortable for you. Hector and I have talked it over, about whether your husband and daughter could be here too. We concluded that they could not. This is no place for a child. So we would compensate you for any additional expenses you incur while your husband is looking after the child on his own. I could talk to him and explain.

Silence. SUSANA moves away from BERNA, takes out her phone, calls, and speaks into it.

SUSANA: Yes, I know it's late. I wanted to tell you I've just discovered they're not going to show me the collection. They'll invent some excuse. They'll talk endlessly and then find some excuse to get me out of here, knowing that what I imagine will serve the legend. The collection is a story, that's why they bring people here. To spread the story, and to push up the money. "Our pieces shoot up in value by the mere fact they're part of the collection." A money machine, that's what the collection is. And these two old crooks, just a pair of speculators.

She finishes the call. Silence.

BERNA: Our bags are packed. One very light suitcase. We won't take a single piece with us, not even the smallest of them. But we won't go until we're sure the collection is in the hands of someone who will love it more than themselves. Someone who will have to look after the legend that protects it. The collection is a story as well, it has to be. It doesn't matter who tells the story as long as it's told well. I don't think we're going to give to you. After you visit it, that would break your heart. You should leave tonight.

She leaves through the same door by which she entered. Silence. A drop falls through the hole. Another. Another. SUSANA lets the water fall on her face, even as the rain gets heavier. Fade.

5

The same place, just before dawn. Nobody. The rain has stopped. BERNA and HECTOR, elegantly dressed, enter through the same door through which they exited. They wait in silence.

BERNA:	You slept well.
HECTOR:	No, you slept well.
BERNA:	You were so peaceful. Not like you at all. You frightened me.
HECTOR:	I felt you covering me with the blanket.
BERNA:	I heard the outside door.
HECTOR:	I did too.
BERNA:	She didn't seem such an easy one to frighten off. You managed it though.
HECTOR:	It was you. Did you think she was beautiful?
BERNA:	Her hands. I wondered about her health. I couldn't work it out.

Silence.

HECTOR:	What'll happen now, Berna? I don't know what's going to happen.
BERNA:	We'll test others.
HECTOR:	No, I'm not going through this again. I've got another four or five years in me, you another ten at least.
BERNA:	We could go on for another five, ten or twenty years. And we could also go gaga and do something stupid. Like handing over the collection to some nuns or a charity. But we can also use the time we have left to doing what we should be doing.
HECTOR:	What if we were to use the time we have left to returning each thing to where we found it, or set fire to everything, or throw it into the sea, and we live the time we have left as though the collection had never existed, and we look after each other instead? The time we have left. We could live like other couples, the time we have left.
BERNA:	You don't mean that. When you look at other couples, you see what I see. The same horror. You're horrified by the thought of what we would have become without the collection.
HECTOR:	Why did we not have children? Can you explain that to me?
BERNA:	So as not to leave the collection to someone who in all likelihood wouldn't deserve it.
HECTOR:	So much sacrifice … why? Who for?
BERNA:	Why? Who for? I've seen your face every time you go into the collection, the storm it unleashes inside you. On the other side of that door there's a meaning that the world doesn't have. Without the collection, we wouldn't understand anything. Without the collection, what shelter would we have?
HECTOR:	I should go and leave you with your damned collection.

Silence.

	I've read about others in the same situation.
BERNA:	What situation?
HECTOR:	Growing old without children.
BERNA:	The ones you've read about, what did they do? Those old people without children.

HECTOR: None of them found the solution.

Silence.

We're old. We have no children. People wonder what will happen to our collection. It's logical.

BERNA: Who wonders?

HECTOR: Everyone. You can tell by the way they look at us.

BERNA: Who are you talking about? Who have you seen recently?

HECTOR: What will happen to the collection when we're gone?

BERNA: There's still time.

HECTOR: We could die tonight. We should have done it years ago, when it wasn't urgent. Now that it is, we can't think clearly.

BERNA: One of us will die second. What about letting them decide?

HECTOR: We've always decided everything together. Whatever happens to the collection, we decide together. Set fire to it or throw it in the sea. But I can't do it alone, Berna. I need your help for this.

BERNA: You love it every bit as much as I do. You'd lay down your life for it.

HECTOR: Because of it, we've said unforgiveable things to each other. We've done unforgettable things to each other.

BERNA: It's brought us together like nothing else could.

HECTOR: It came between us so much that it kept us together.

Silence.

I didn't mind you sleeping with someone to get something. I'm not jealous of them. But I am jealous of the collection. We had so much love, how did we squander that on objects? It's perverse, this love for things, diabolical. How do we let things rule our lives? We could have loved each other so much. Do you remember that afternoon on the beach with the red sand?

BERNA: You don't let me forget.

HECTOR: Help me to remember.

Silence.

BERNA: Looking at the sea in silence, on a beach with red sand.

Silence. Perhaps, if they can, HECTOR and BERNA sit or lie down as they did then, on the sand.

Looking at the sea in silence, until I ask you "What are we doing here?"

Silence.

What are we doing here?

HECTOR: It's a beautiful place. Do you not think it's beautiful?

BERNA: It is beautiful. But what are we doing here?

HECTOR: We're in a beautiful place, enjoying it together. We're lucky, we're together.

BERNA: Let's go. Enough now.

HECTOR: Let's stay a little longer.

BERNA: Enough now.

HECTOR: You're very pretty.

BERNA: I've never been pretty. And you've never been handsome. Neither of us has ever been good-looking. We're an attractive couple though.

HECTOR: When you look at me, what do you see?

BERNA: I look at you and I remember I'm old, like you remember you're old when you look at me. We help each other to remember. If you've forgotten your last fight, I can tell you. It's important that someone knows who we are.

Silence.

HECTOR: My last fight … I don't remember.

BERNA: You went down three times, but we looked at each other, you got up, and you knocked him down.

Silence. HECTOR punches the air. Again and again. His body recalls or imagines moments from that fight.

HECTOR: If I ever go into the collection again, I'll do it alone. You never see anything as it really is when you're with someone you love.

He produces the sheet of paper on which SUSANA wrote the words he dictated to her. He gives it to BERNA, who reads it aloud.

BERNA: "On this day, I declare this to be my last will and testament: in the event of my death, with no heir designate, I request that my wife should destroy the collection, as I will do in the event of hers. It is to be destroyed in a manner in keeping with the safety of all concerned."

HECTOR hands her the pen.

HECTOR: You need to sign it. Please.

He holds the pen out to her.

Berna, please. What would the collection mean if there was no one to see it?

He holds out the pen insistently. Through the same door she first came in by, SUSANA enters. Her clothes are soaked. HECTOR puts away the pen and document.

BERNA: Have you been out walking in the rain? Carlos should have gone with you.

HECTOR: Carlos has gone to get some medicine.

BERNA: Do you want to rest? Have something to eat or drink? Have a hot bath at least and get into some dry clothes. We can postpone the visit to tomorrow.

HECTOR:　Sunrise tomorrow is at half past seven.

BERNA:　We can wait another day. And if we can wait one more day, we can wait two.

SUSANA lies down, face upwards, under the hole. Time passes. Until CARLOS comes in through the same door, carrying the briefcase she gave him. He stands at his usual distance. SUSANA sits up.

BERNA:　We missed you, Carlos. The visit hasn't begun yet. Did you get what Mrs Gelman asked for?

Silence.

CARLOS:　Half way there it began to rain. So hard I had to pull over. I fell asleep and dreamed the rain was washing the collection into the sea.

BERNA:　I've always wondered what the collection means to you.

CARLOS:　When I woke up the rain had gone and I drove on until I was outside the house of someone I don't know and who wasn't expecting me.

BERNA:　Carlos has been driving for hours, Hector. Lots of space to think.

CARLOS:　There was a light on inside. I sat in the car for a while, watching to see if anyone went in or out. No one. I knocked the door at midnight. I heard barking and slow shuffling footsteps, like someone limping, and eventually an old man opened the door. He wasn't expecting anyone until the next morning and I wasn't the one he was expecting, but he accepted my explanation and invited me into a room. He got out a bottle and we had a drink. Then he left me with the dog while he went to fetch a metal box. He took an envelope out of the box and from it a letter. I recognised the handwriting as soon as I saw it. "It's from someone my wife was in love with," he said. "But it was written to me, not her," and he asked me to read it out loud. He closed his eyes and listened. As I was reading, I began to imagine it in the collection. I don't mean the paper and the ink, I mean a voice reading it out loud. He listened to every word and every silence with his eyes closed. And when I finished reading he said: "Get those words away from here. I don't want anything for them. Anywhere but here."

He hands the briefcase to SUSANA, who opens it and finds the car keys, the money in the envelope and the tightly sealed bag, from which she takes out the letter. She reads it in silence. Pause. She reads it out loud.

SUSANA:　"Guimaraes, 5th of August, 2001. Dear Sir: You and I were not born to meet. Yet, we are not strangers. We are united by feelings – and what unites more than a shared feeling? Until tonight, for a time that now seems but an instant to me, your wife and the writer of this letter were as one. Nevertheless, the time has come for us to separate. I do not deny that when I imagine you now next to her, I feel a depth of rancour towards you, although I do not know you. How hard it is to separate passion and thought! How hard it is for me to understand – after so many sleepless nights – that, united by love for the same person, I should try to love you too! How hard it has been to realise that, although my heart is bleeding, I should desire her to be happy without me! And it is about that, her happiness, that I wish to address you here. It was not impossible that you would read this letter. Had you not, however, I would have found some other way to say to you what I must say. What I have to say to you is this: if, as I hope, you make her happy, you can count me as the best of friends. Make her happy and I will help you come what may. I'm sure this is the way it will be: you will bring her happiness and you will have no better friend than me. I don't need to know you to have a high opinion about you. I have no regard for people generally, and I expect the worst rather than the best, but my trust in you runs deep. My trust in you is rooted in my knowledge of the woman who is your wife. She would never be with someone she didn't admire, and anyone she does admire will not just be ordinary. I think you will make her happy and I will protect you, because in that way I will be protecting her happiness. But if one day someone should tell me they have seen any trace of unhappiness in her eyes, you will find in me the worst of enemies. Needless violence causes nothing but shame, and you need not expect any harm from me. But the greatest harm comes from the person we least expect it from. I am not talking about today or tomorrow, I am talking about what for me will become the task of a lifetime. At every single moment I will know how your wife feels. She could never conceal her sadness from me. The only thing left for me to desire, and I desire it beyond all measure, is for her to be happy, and you with her. Everything depends on you, everything is in your hands. Do what is right and never neglect her. And you will not neglect her if she matters to you as much as she matters to me. The three of us, her, you and me, we will either all be happy or we will all be miserable. I am fighting on my own behalf too, because I cannot be happy if she is unhappy. This is all I have to say. I have chosen my words with care. There is no need to reply with other words. Her life will be the reply. As for mine, I've told you what I intend to do with it. Should you wish, she need not know about this letter. If you are as I hope you are, you can forget me. I have no wish ever to meet you. If you are worthy of her, you will never see me. But I am not a prophet. I can only feel respect or disdain towards other people. Do not give me reason to disdain you. Because today my heart is full of love for you." Signed "Berna Pereira."

Silence.

Hector, Berna, long before I received your invitation, I had noticed something in you that I could recognise. An affinity. I searched out the former owners of your pieces and I asked them all the same question: "Who are Berna and Hector Pereira?" Bilbao 7.11.74. San José 5.5.17. And Guimaraes 5.8.1! Where this letter should be read, in front of Guimaraes 5.8.1. However, there is a difficulty about these words – whether you call them a piece or a thing – entering the collection. They're mine now. Why would I cull them from my collection to give them to a different one?

Silence.

CARLOS: There was a reply. A reply to the letter.

Silence.

The old man said: "Get those words away from here. I don't want anything for them. Anywhere but here." And he stood up for me to go. I didn't move. The dog barked. I didn't move. I said "Did you answer it? How do you answer a letter like that?" Finally he said: "My wife answered. But she never sent it." And he took another envelope out of the metal box, and asked me to open it. Inside was a sheet of paper torn into seven pieces. There are no words, but bits of drawings in red ink. He said: "That was the last time she painted. After that summer she never painted again." I tried to put the pieces together but I couldn't work out what the drawing was of. Then when I managed to put the pieces together, I saw it was the most beautiful drawing that told a story. The old man said: "Get it away from here. I don't want anything for it. Anywhere but here."

He takes out another envelope. SUSANA holds out her hand to CARLOS. He holds on to the envelope.

Underneath Guimaraes 5.8.1, that's where these seven pieces should go, like the remains saved from a fire. However, there is a difficulty about them entering the collection. They're mine now. To start my collection with.

Long silence

BERNA: No photographs.
HECTOR: You can map it.
BERNA: We will not be your guides.
HECTOR: We cannot be. Each visit we make to the collection presents us with something new we don't understand. There is a secret that the collection masks, just as every image is a mask of its own secret.
BERNA: There are no signs to guide you, or any words of explanation about what the pieces mean.

HECTOR: We have freed the things from words. You will think "there is no order."

BERNA: You will think "there is no order." Until you understand that each piece has to be discovered after the one that precedes it and before the one that follows it. And the space between them, their positions relative to each other – some are closer than others, some are higher than others, some exactly opposite each other. At one time all the pieces were fixed on a single wall, and another time they were left resting on the floor.

HECTOR: The collection is always seeking its form.

BERNA: It was essential the architecture should be unobtrusive. The lighting is key to that. But the lighting will not guide you either.

HECTOR: Go in with no preconceptions. Let yourselves be led by the things. If you have any fixed assumptions, leave them here.

BERNA: There are things that, outside the collection, would be worthless, others whose only value is that they were snatched from someone else, and others that belonged to kings and queens. Some were created by artists. There are works we rescued from the hands of restorers – none of them have actually been restored. Others are damaged. There are tiny pieces and others so huge that the eye can't take them in. Some are enormous and in the collection seem tiny, and some insignificant, that the collection makes huge.

HECTOR: Some of them enshrine the spirit of their age and others go against the grain of any age. Some works are duplicated and there are copies. There are images that contain the whole scale of human experience and there are images that are inhuman. Many of the images are stained. Morally stained.

BERNA: The collection is not for the faint-hearted. Whoever inherits it will have to accept everything that's in it, no matter where it's come from or how it got there. The stain is inherited too.

HECTOR: The collection is necessary. Someone had to make it, no matter what the cost. Things separated across oceans and centuries were waiting to be brought together. Their destiny was the collection. So that today, or in a thousand years' time, when any being that is capable of feelings and thought comes to it, they will know what humanity was, or what humanity could have been.

BERNA: Sometimes one of us closes our eyes and the other one leads us by the hand. Sometimes we just go in to feel the passage of time.

HECTOR: Each thing is made of time, all the time that has built up inside it, and the collection is all the time that each thing brings to it. Times predates the things, and what you are witness to is how something comes into being, or stops being, like a lost past or a past saved for the future. Each of them is an image separated by oceans and centuries, and in each of them appear the same stirrings of the soul, as though places and times were united by subterranean channels. You are witness to the contemporaneity of every human being who has ever lived, to the way an image made thousands of years ago expresses the mystery of human pain in all its fullness, and that anything to be said has already been said from the beginning.

BERNA: Which is why, once you have completed your visit, if you do, you will see everything from the perspective of the collection itself. Yourselves too.

HECTOR: The collection discovers you. Because it contains everything you are and are not.

BERNA: You're free to end the visit at any moment, or to extend it for as long as you like.

HECTOR: We find the visitor always returns late.

BERNA: On your return, you will come to a place from where all the pieces can be viewed together.

HECTOR: The place has been compared to a lighthouse, or two mirrors face to face, or the inside of an eye.

BERNA: You have to go through there before coming to the final piece. The final piece is a time of silence.

HECTOR: Before returning to the world, silence. That's all.

BERNA: That's not all. While you're in there each of you will be part of the collection for the other, just as the other is part of the collection for you. That's all now.

BERNA and HECTOR indicate where SUSANA and CARLOS should enter. They both hesitate. Finally they move towards it, each of them carrying their envelope. Fade.

6

SUSANA and CARLOS visit the collection in silence until they reach the point where all the pieces, all the things, can be seen together.

SUSANA: How terrible this place would be empty.

Fade.

7

BERNA and HECTOR are still waiting in the cave or ring. SUSANA and CARLOS return. Silence.

SUSANA: What did you see? What did you see in me?

CARLOS: At the start you acted as though you understood what was happening to you. You pulled faces.

He imitates them.

	and then you stopped pretending.
SUSANA:	I felt joy and despair, I felt sick and very strong, I wanted to be on my own, and I was frightened to be. I yearned for a fire or a flood, and to take all the pieces, each and every one of them with my own hands, back to the place and time where they belong. I had very simple thoughts that gradually became strange. I felt like the things were people bewitched, that they contained people, and I understood why visitors to the collection, after they've seen it, they lie.
CARLOS:	And you whispered: "How terrible this place would be empty."
SUSANA:	I have to go. I have to go back to my daughter.
CARLOS:	Sunrise tomorrow is at half past seven.
SUSANA:	I have to go.

Silence. BERNA goes to where HECTOR keeps his secret collection, and lifts it.

| BERNA: | The beach with the red sand, do you think we can find it? The beach with the red sand. |
| HECTOR: | One day, when nobody's left, there'll be people who break in and take things without knowing what they are. Or maybe animals will have them. Birds. Or rain or fire. One day everything will have gone. And then the collection really will be a legend. |

HECTOR and BERNA look up at the eye and leave through the same door through which SUSANA first appeared, while she lies down beside CARLOS, both of them looking up at it. Final fade.

Appendix

International Reach

As of this publication, Mayorga's works have been performed in the following 43 countries: Argentina, Australia, Belgium, Brazil, Bulgaria, Canada, Chile, China, Colombia, Costa Rica, Croatia, Cuba, Denmark, Ecuador, El Salvador, France, Germany, Greece, Hungary, Ireland, Israel, Italy, Japan, Korea, Latvia, Mexico, the Netherlands, Norway, Paraguay, Peru, Poland, Portugal, Romania, Russia, Serbia, Spain, Switzerland, Turkey, Ukraine, Uruguay, United Kingdom, United States, and Venezuela.

His work has been translated into the following 32 languages: Arabic, Basque (Euskera), Bulgarian, Catalan, Chinese, Croatian, Czech, Danish, Dutch, English, Esperanto, Estonian, Finnish, French, Gallego, German, Greek, Hebrew, Hungarian, Italian, Japanese, Korean, Latvian, Norwegian, Polish, Portuguese, Romanian, Russian, Serbian, Slovene, Turkish, and Ukrainian.

Bibliography

Full-length plays

Siete hombres buenos, Más ceniza, El traductor de Blumemberg, El sueño de Ginebra, El jardín quemado, Angelus Novus, Cartas de amor a Stalin, El Gordo y el Flaco, Himmelweg, Animales nocturnos, Palabra de perro, Últimas palabras de Copito de Nieve, *Hamelin, El chico de la última fila, Fedra, La tortuga de Darwin, La paz perpetua, El elefante ha ocupado la catedral, La lengua en pedazos, El crítico, El cartógrafo, Los yugoslavos, El arte de la entrevista, Reikiavik, Famélica, Amistad, El Golem, El Mago, Intensamente azules, La intérprete, La colección, Silencio, Voltaire, María Luisa,* and *La gran cacería.*

Co-author with Juan Cavestany: *Alejandro y Ana, lo que España no pudo ver de la boda de la hija del presidente* and *Penumbra.* With Daniel Montero Galán, he wrote the illustrated books *El elefante ha ocupado la catedral, Intensamente azules,* and *581 mapas.* Finally, he wrote the libretto of the opera based on *La paz perpetua,* with music by José Río Pareja.

One-act plays under the title of Teatro para minutos

Concierto fatal de la viuda Kolakowski, El hombre de oro, La mala imagen, Legión, El Guardián, La piel, Amarillo, El Crack, La mujer de mi vida, BRGS, La mano izquierda, La biblioteca del diablo, Una carta de Sarajevo, Encuentro en Salamanca, El buen vecino, Candidatos, Inocencia, Justicia, Manifiesto Comunista, Sentido de calle, El espíritu de Cernuda, Tres anillos, Mujeres en la cornisa, Método Le Brun para la felicidad, Departamento de Justicia, JK, La mujer de los ojos tristes, Las películas del invierno, Voltaire, 581 mapas, Quiero ser enjambre, Pastel de Lagrange, EAJ1, La puerta, Ramírez, Augusto y Margaret, Entre los árboles, Fracción, Las cuentas de Carmencita, La gran cacería, Político, La distancia, Noli me tangere y Herencia. (44)

Adaptations

Hécuba (Eurípides), *La dama boba* (Lope de Vega), *Fuente Ovejuna* (Lope de Vega), *El monstruo de los jardines* (Calderón de la Barca), *La vida es sueño* (Calderón de la Barca), *King Lear* (William Shakespeare), *Nathan the Wise* (Gotthold Ephraim Lessing), *Don Juan Tenorio* (José Zorrilla), *Woyzeck* (Georg Büchner), *The Grand Inquisitor* (Fyodor Dostoevsky), *An Enemy of the People* (Henrik Ibsen), *Platonov* (Anton Chekhov), *Before the Law* (Franz Kafka), *Divinas palabras* (Ramón María del Valle-Inclán), *The Visit of the Old Lady* (Friedrich Dürrenmatt), *El diablo cojuelo* (Luis Vélez de Guevara). (16)

Prizes

Talía Awards (Spain) Prize for Best Author for *El Golem* (2023); Princess of Asturias Prize for Literature (2022); Europe Prize for Theatrical Realities (2016); the National Prize for Dramatic Literature (2013); National Theater Prize (2007); the Max Awards (Spain) for Best Author (2006, 2008, and 2009), and for best adaptation (2008 and 2013); the Valle-Inclan Prize in 2009 for *Perpetual Peace*; the Enrique Llovet Prize in 2003 for *Way to Heaven*. His play *El chico de la última fila* (*Boy in the Back of the Room*) was adapted by François Ozon for the film *Dans la maison*, which won the Concha de Oro prize for Best Film and the Jury's Prize for best screenplay at the San Sebastian Film Festival in 2012. He has also received the following prizes: National Letters "Theresa of Ávila" Prize (2016), Ceres Prize for Best Theatrical Author (2013), La Barraca Prize (2013), Chamaco Prize from the Cuban Center at the International Institute of Theater for Best International Playwright (2017), Ojo Crítico Prize from National Radio for the 1999–2000 Season, "El Duende" Prize for the Most Original Creator 1988–2008, and he was the Honored Author at the Contemporary Authors of Spanish Theater Festival in 2009.

Works Cited

Agamben, Giorgio. *Homo Sacer: Sovereign Power and Bare Life*. Stanford, CA: Stanford University Press, 1995.

Bachmetjevas, Viktoras. "Imaginary Construction and Lessons in Living Forward." *History of European Ideas*, 47 (2021): 470–83.

Benjamin, Walter. "The Programme of the Coming Philosophy" [1917–1918]. In *Selected Writings, 1913–1926*, Vol. 1, pp. 100–10, edited by Howard Eiland and Michael W. Jennings, Cambridge, MA/London: Harvard University Press, 1996.

Berger, John. *Ways of Seeing*. Harmondsworth: Penguin Books, 1972.

———. "Understanding a Photograph." *Selected Essays and Articles: The Look of Things*. New York: Viking, 1974.

Borges, Jorge Luis. "On Exactitude in Science." https://kwarc.info/teaching/TDM/Borges.pdf. Accessed 16 August 2023. Originally published in *Los anales de Buenos Aires* [The Annals of Buenos Aires], no. 3, 1946, under the pseudonym Suarez Miranda. Collected in *El Hacedor* [Dreamtigers]. Buenos Aires: Emecé, 1960.

Celaya, Gabriel. "Poetry is a Weapon Loaded with the Future." Originally published in *Cantos Iberos* [Iberian Chants]. Madrid: Verbo, 1955.

Hare, David. *Writing Left-Handed*. London: Faber & Faber, 1991.

Havel, Vaclav. *The Art of the Impossible: Politics as Morality in Practice*. New York: Fromm International, 1998.

Heaney, Seamus. *Finders Keepers: Selected Prose 1971–2001*. London: Faber & Faber, 2003.

Korzybski, Alfred. *Science and Sanity: An Introduction to Non-Aristotelian Systems and General Semantics*. New York: Institute of General Semantics, 1995.

Mayorga, Juan. *Elipses: Ensayos 1990–2016*. Segovia: Ediciones La uÑa RoTa, 2016.

———. "Mi teatro histórico." In *Elipses*, pp. 317–19.

———. "La representación teatral del Holocausto." In *Elipses*, pp. 165–72.

———. *Silencio/Razón del teatro*. Segovia: Ediciones La uÑa RoTa, 2019.

———. "Razón del teatro." In *Silencio/Razón del teatro*, pp. 51–81.

———. "Teatro y cartografía." *Boletín Hispánico Helvético: Historia, teoría(s), prácticas culturales*, Spring, 9 (2012): 85–88.

———. *Teatro 1989–2014*. Madrid: La Uña Rota, 2014.

———. *El golem*. Madrid: La Uña Rota, 2022.

———. "Quiero ser enjambre/I Want to Swarm." www.youtube.com/watch?v=72Ljf-PbjT8. Accessed 16 August 2023.

———. "Todos estamos llamados a ser filósofos." Filsofía & Co., 24 April 2019, https://filco.es/juan-mayorga-todos-llamados-a-ser-filosofos/.

Ojeda, Alberto. "Juan Mayorga: Para mí, nación, bandera y frontera significan fracaso." *elespañol*, Madrid, Spain, 4 November 2016, www.elespanol.com/el-cultural/escenarios/20161104/juan-mayorga-nacion-bandera-frontera-significan-fracaso/168233892_0.html.

Roberts, Richard. *Fischer/Spassky: The New York Times Report on the Chess Match of the Century*. New York: Bantam Books, 1972.

Spivak, Gayatri Chakravorty, *Death of a Discipline*. New York: Columbia University Press, 2003.

Tagliacozzo, Tamara. *Experience and Infinite Task: Knowledge, Language and Messianism in the Philosophy of Walter Benjamin*. Lanham MD: Rowman and Littlefield, 2017.

Vidales, Raquel. "El dramaturgo Juan Mayorga gana el Premio Princesa de Asturias de las Letras 2022," *El País*, Madrid, Spain, 2 June 2022, elpais.com/cultura/2022–06-01/el-dramaturgo-juan-mayorga-gana-con-el-premio-princesa-de-asturias-de-las-letras-2022.html.